CALGARY PUBLIC LIBRARY

MAR   2013

SCIENCE.
BAD.

JONATHAN HICKMAN
WRITER

NICK PITARRA
ARTIST

JORDIE BELLAIRE
COLORS

RUS WOOTON
LETTERS

IMAGE COMICS, INC.
Robert Kirkman - chief operating officer
Erik Larsen - chief financial officer
Todd McFarlane - president
Marc Silvestri - chief executive officer
Jim Valentino - vice-president

Eric Stephenson - publisher
Todd Martinez - sales & licensing coordinator
Jennifer de Guzman - pr & marketing director
Branwyn Bigglestone - accounts manager
Emily Miller - accounting assistant
Jamie Parreno - marketing assistant
Jenna Savage - administrative assistant
Sarah deLaine - events coordinator
Kevin Yuen - digital rights coordinator
Jonathan Chan - production manager
Drew Gill - art director
Monica Garcia - production artist
Vincent Kukua - production artist
Jana Cook - production artist
www.imagecomics.com

THE MANHATTAN PROJECTS, VOLUME 1
Second Printing / January 2013
ISBN: 978-1-60706-608-8

Published by Image Comics, Inc. Office of publication: 2001 Center St., 6th Floor, Berkeley, CA 94704. Copyright © 2013 Jonathan Hickman & Nick Pitarra. Originally published in single magazine form as THE MANHATTAN PROJECTS #1-5. All rights reserved. THE MANHATTAN PROJECTS (including all prominent characters featured herein), its logo and all character likenesses are trademarks of Jonathan Hickman & Nick Pitarra, unless otherwise noted. Image Comics® and its logos are registered trademarks of Image Comics, Inc. No part of this publication may be reproduced or transmitted, in any form or by any means (except for short excerpts for review purposes) without the express written permission of Jonathan Hickman, Nick Pitarra, or Image Comics, Inc. All names, characters, events and locales in this publication are entirely fictional. Any resemblance to actual persons (living or dead), events or places, without satiric intent, is coincidental. Printed in the U.S.A. For information regarding the CPSIA on this printed material call: 203-595-3636 and provide reference # RICH – 467678 International Rights/Foreign Licensing: foreignlicensing @imagecomics.com

MP

THE MANHATTAN PROJECTS

I AM NOT MY
BROTHER

"I WAS SURROUNDED BY THOSE WILLING TO SACRIFICE ALL OF MANKIND IF DOING SO ACHIEVED THEIR GOALS. EVIL DEEDS BY EVIL MEN THAT ONLY I COULD PREVENT.

MOURN THEN THE PASSING OF THE WORLD. FOR WHEN THE TIME CAME, I COULD FIND NO GOOD IN MYSELF, ONLY MISCHIEF."

CLAVIS AUREA
THE RECORDED FEYNMAN | **VOL. 4**

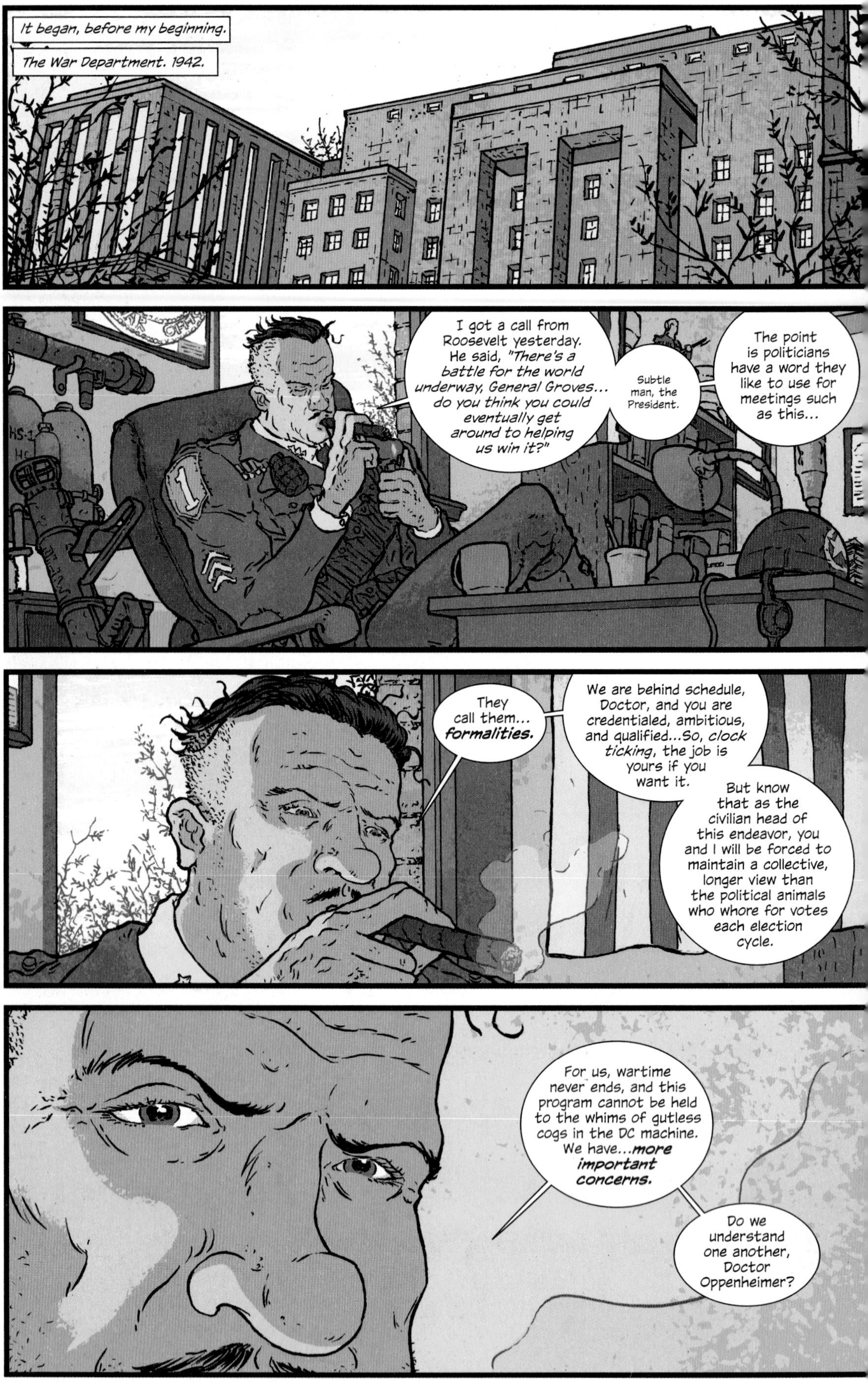
It began, before my beginning.
The War Department. 1942.
I got a call from Roosevelt yesterday. He said, "There's a battle for the world underway, General Groves... do you think you could eventually get around to helping us win it?"
Subtle man, the President.
The point is politicians have a word they like to use for meetings such as this...
They call them... formalities.
We are behind schedule, Doctor, and you are credentialed, ambitious, and qualified...So, clock ticking, the job is yours if you want it.
But know that as the civilian head of this endeavor, you and I will be forced to maintain a collective, longer view than the political animals who whore for votes each election cycle.
For us, wartime never ends, and this program cannot be held to the whims of gutless cogs in the DC machine. We have...more important concerns.
Do we understand one another, Doctor Oppenheimer?

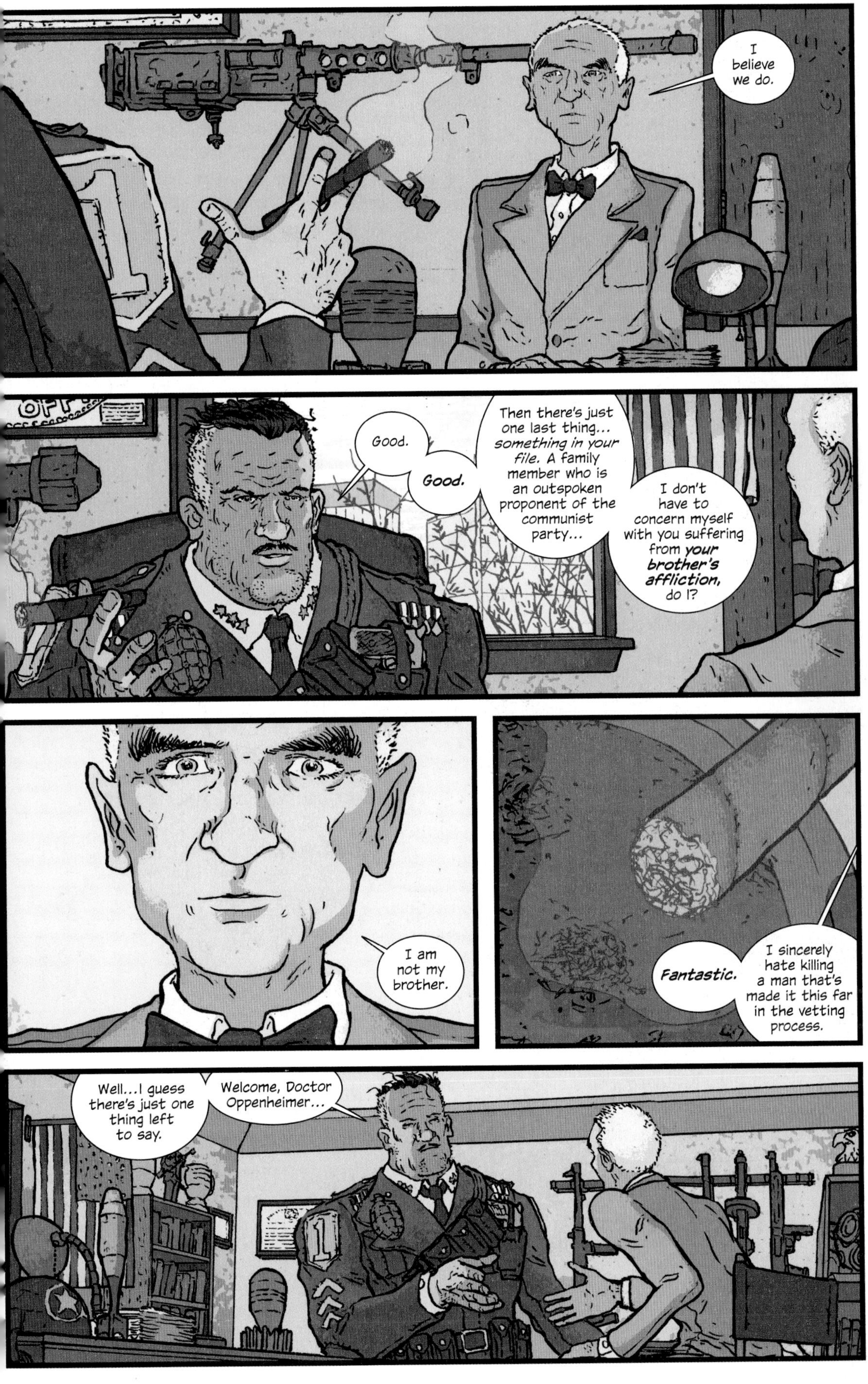

I believe we do.
Good.
Good.
Then there's just one last thing... *something in your file.* A family member who is an outspoken proponent of the communist party...
I don't have to concern myself with you suffering from ***your brother's affliction,*** do I?
I am not my brother.
Fantastic.
I sincerely hate killing a man that's made it this far in the vetting process.
Well...I guess there's just one thing left to say.
Welcome, Doctor Oppenheimer...

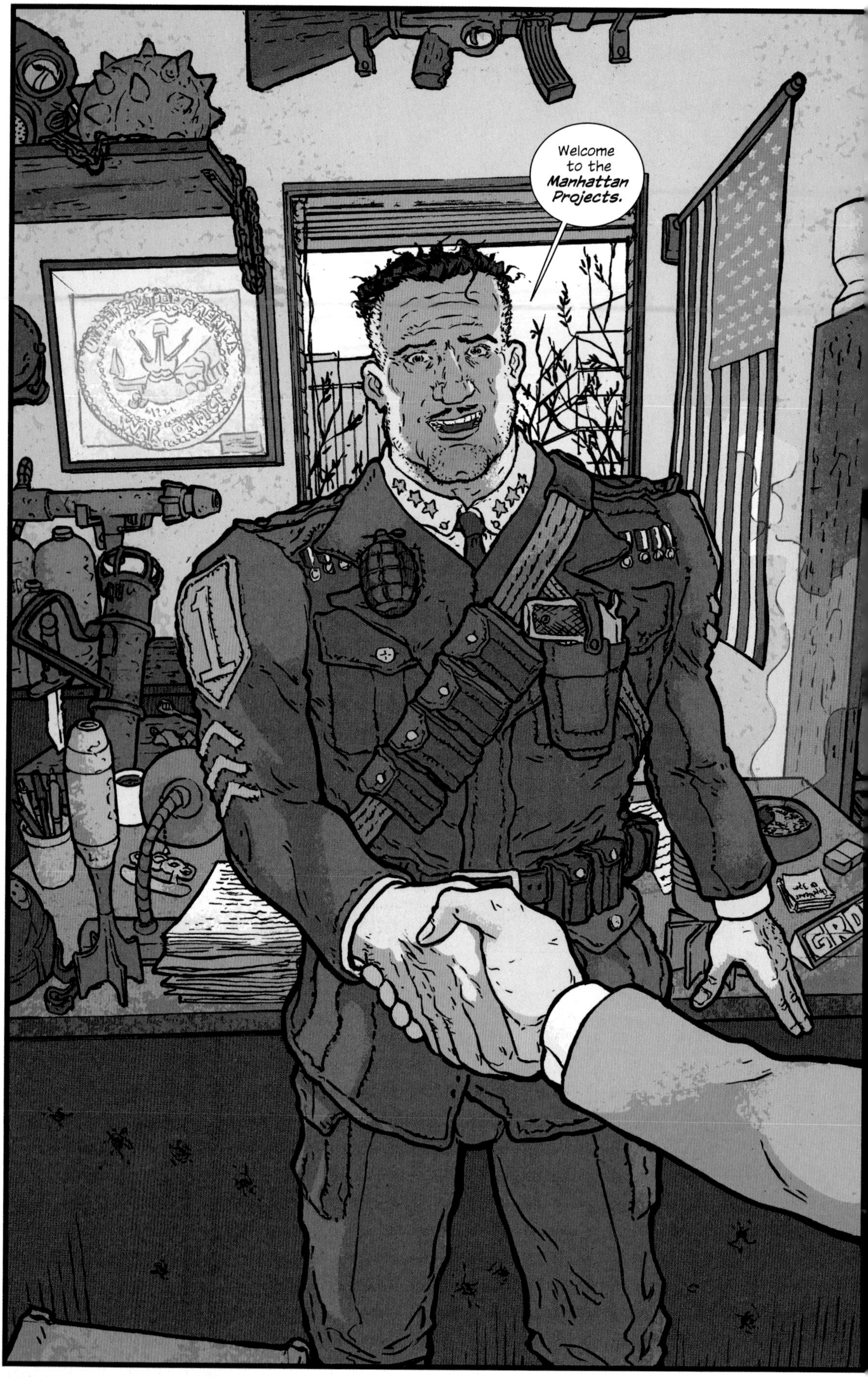
Welcome to the *Manhattan Projects.*

"ON MY FIRST DAY, I WAS GIVEN A GOVERNMENT-ISSUED DISASTER PACKET.

IT INCLUDED: A SOLAR-POWERED RADIO BEACON, ANTIBIOTICS, A CYANIDE CAPSULE, AN ETERNAL FLAME, A COLLAPSABLE KNIFE, AN INFINITY PEN, AND A JOURNAL."

CLAVIS AUREA
THE RECORDED FEYNMAN

VOL. 1

01

INFINITE
OPPENHEIMERS

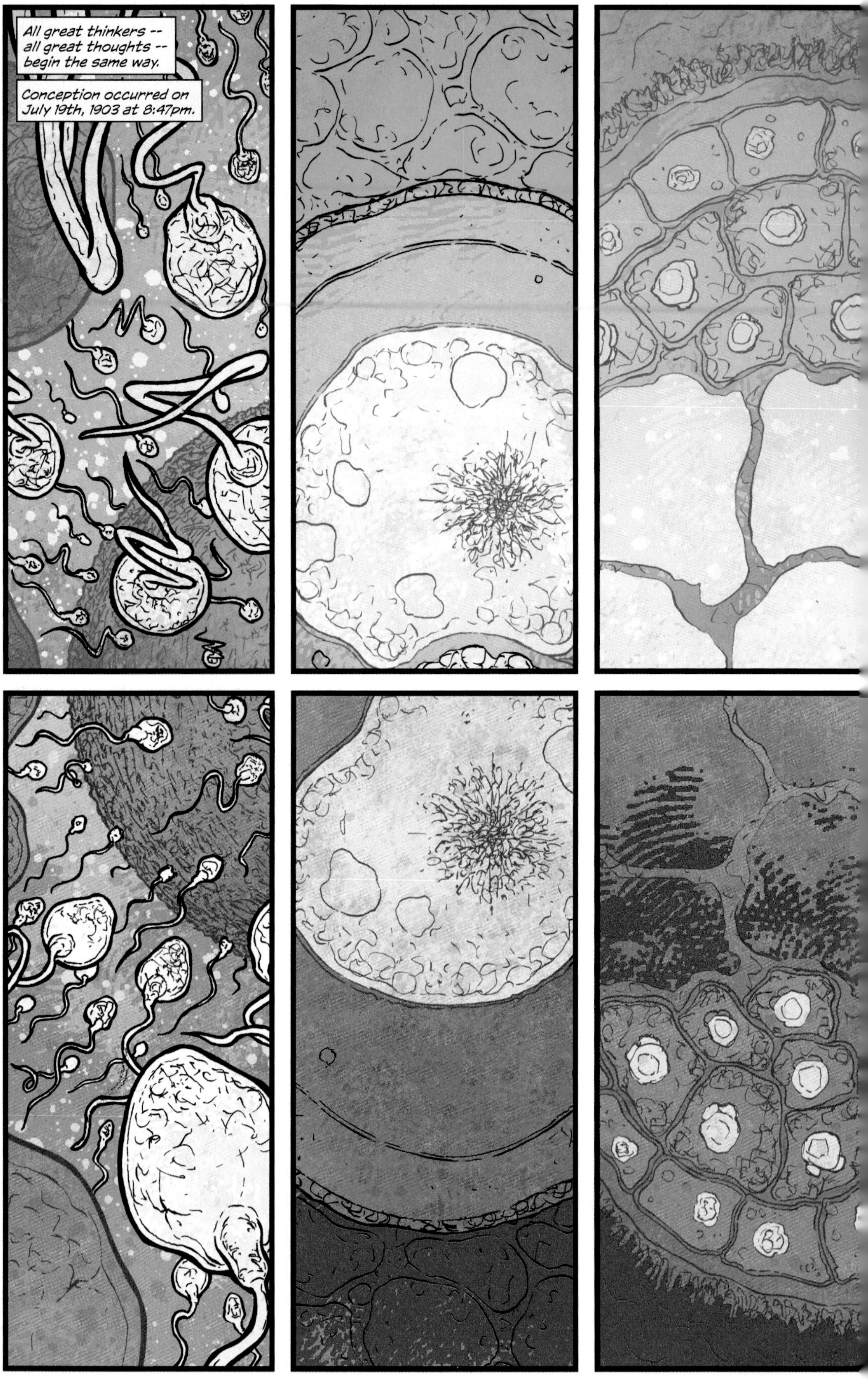
All great thinkers -- all great thoughts -- begin the same way.
Conception occurred on July 19th, 1903 at 8:47pm.

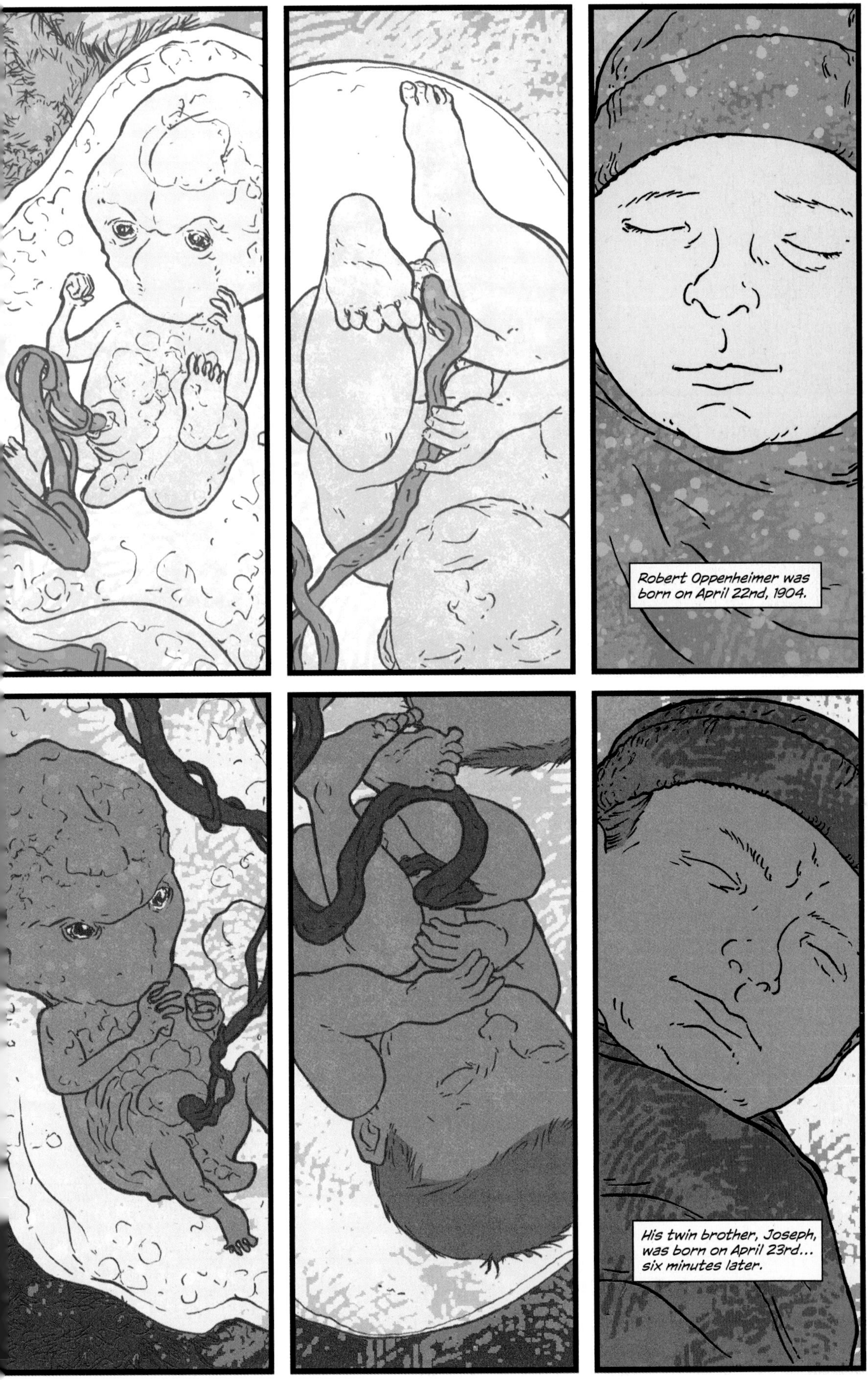
Robert Oppenheimer was born on April 22nd, 1904.
His twin brother, Joseph, was born on April 23rd... six minutes later.

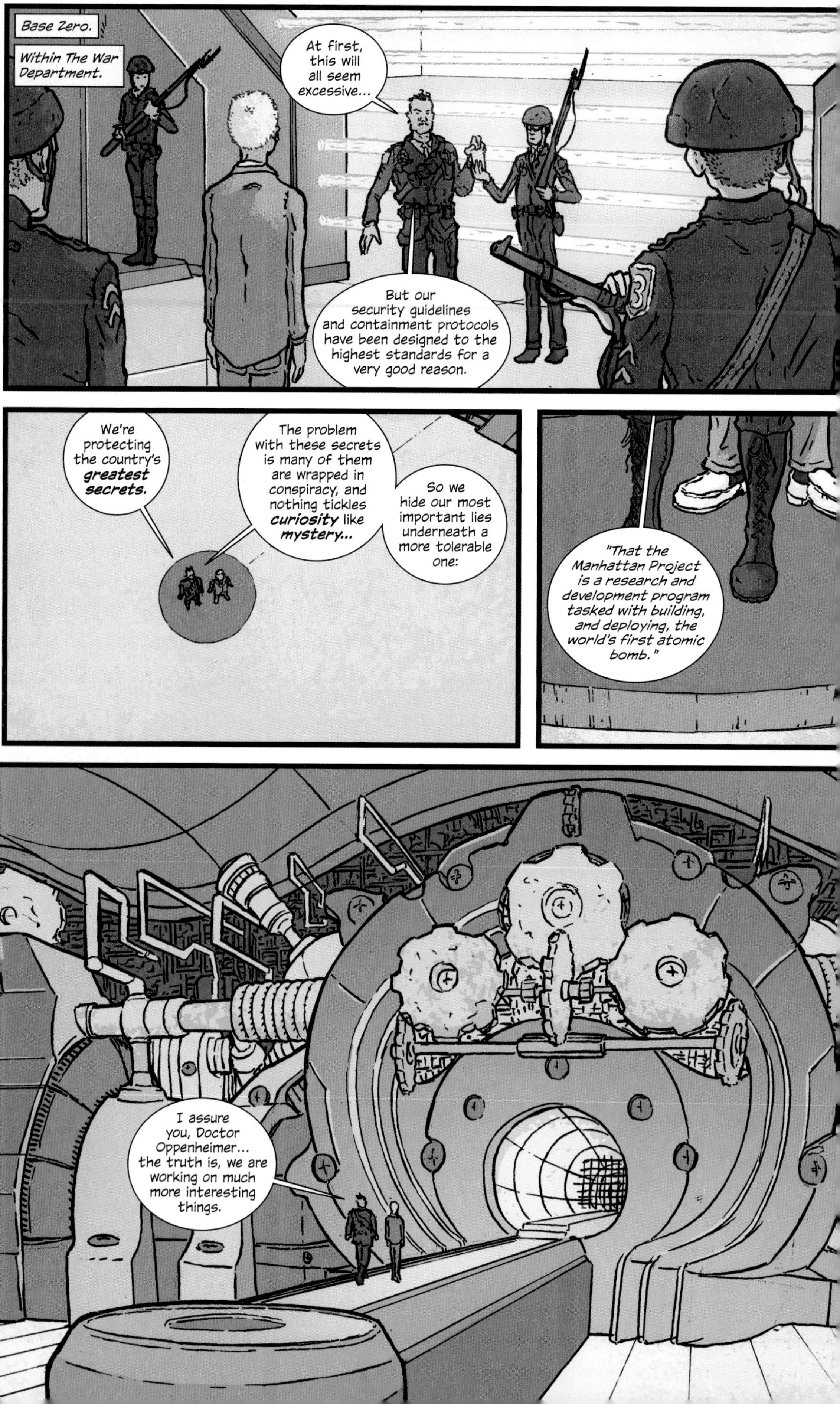
Base Zero.
Within The War Department.
At first, this will all seem excessive...
But our security guidelines and containment protocols have been designed to the highest standards for a very good reason.
We're protecting the country's **greatest secrets.**
The problem with these secrets is many of them are wrapped in conspiracy, and nothing tickles **curiosity** like **mystery...**
So we hide our most important lies underneath a more tolerable one:
"That the Manhattan Project is a research and development program tasked with building, and deploying, the world's first atomic bomb."
I assure you, Doctor Oppenheimer... the truth is, we are working on much more interesting things.

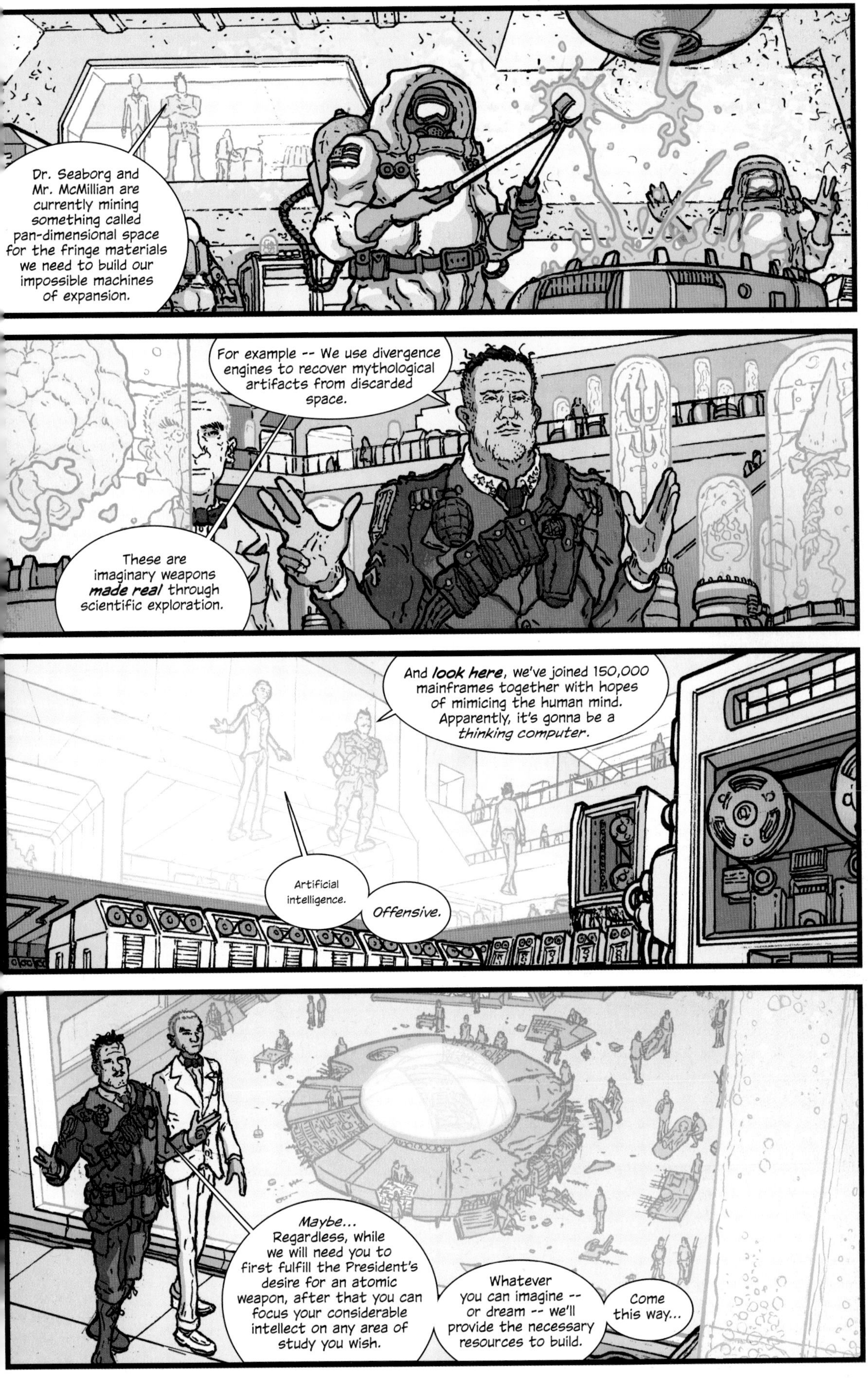
Dr. Seaborg and Mr. McMillian are currently mining something called pan-dimensional space for the fringe materials we need to build our impossible machines of expansion.
For example -- We use divergence engines to recover mythological artifacts from discarded space.
These are imaginary weapons made real through scientific exploration.
And look here, we've joined 150,000 mainframes together with hopes of mimicing the human mind. Apparently, it's gonna be a thinking computer.
Artificial intelligence.
Offensive.
Maybe... Regardless, while we will need you to first fulfill the President's desire for an atomic weapon, after that you can focus your considerable intellect on any area of study you wish.
Whatever you can imagine -- or dream -- we'll provide the necessary resources to build.
Come this way...

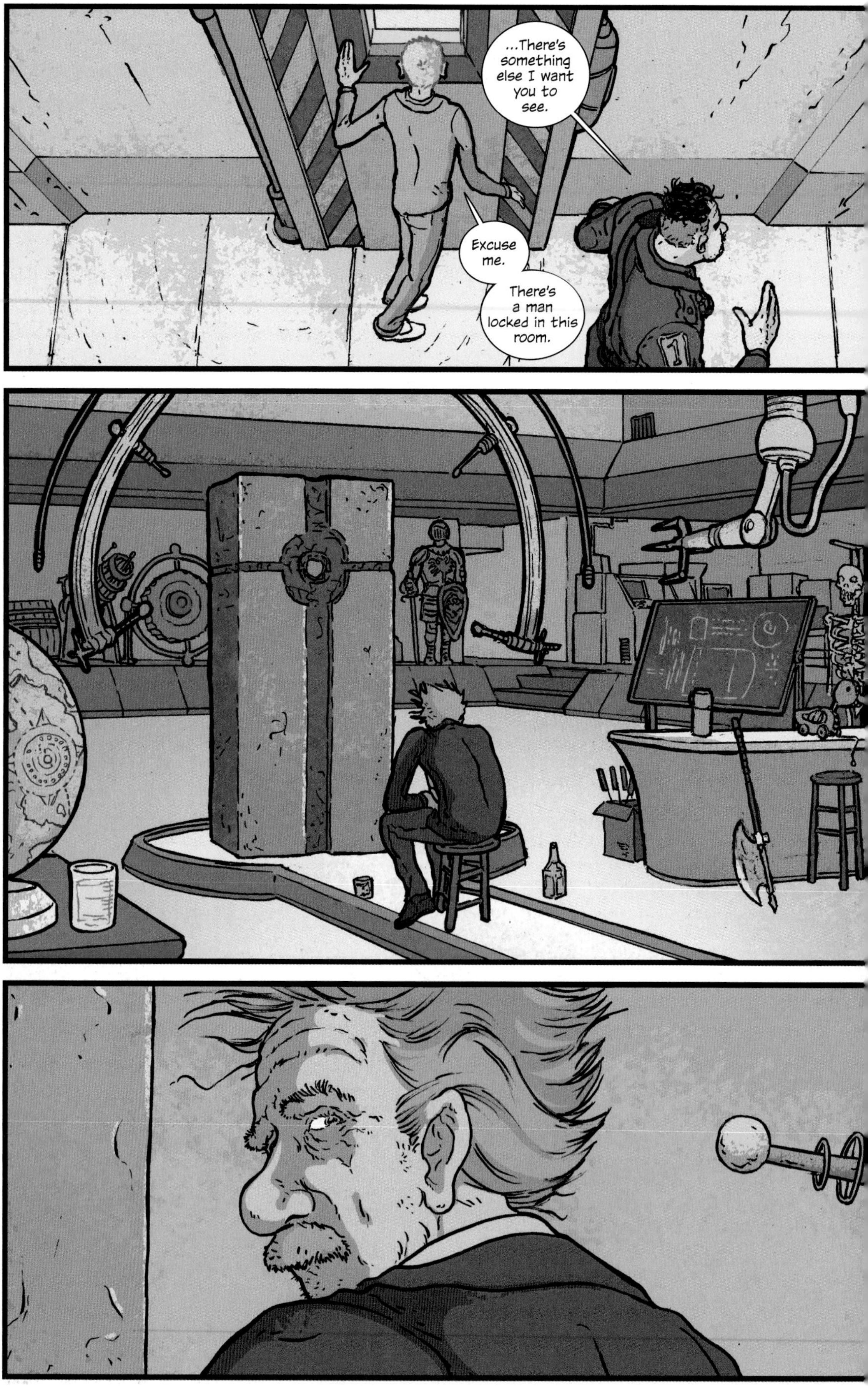
...There's something else I want you to see.
Excuse me.
There's a man locked in this room.

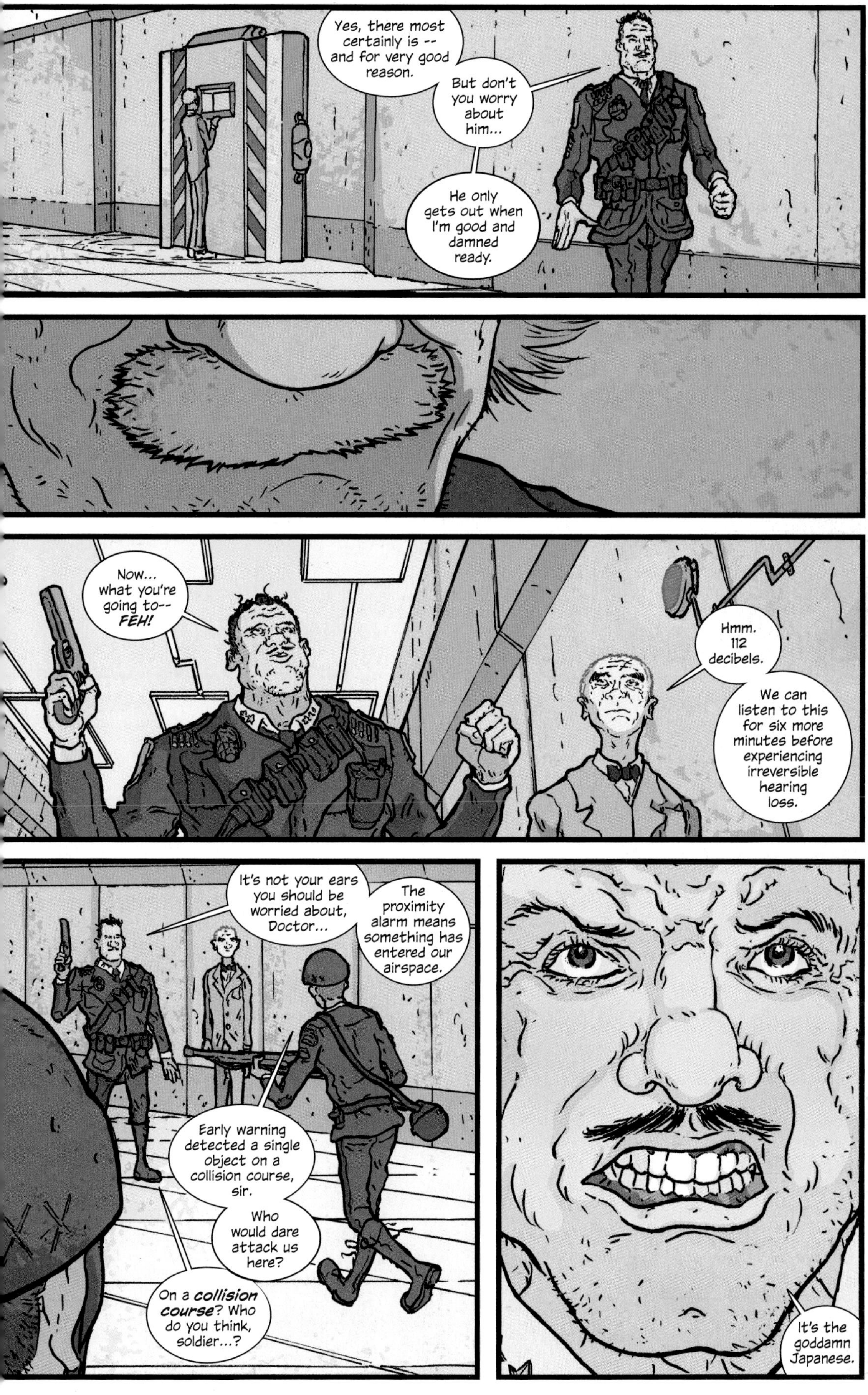
Yes, there most certainly is -- and for very good reason.
But don't you worry about him...
He only gets out when I'm good and damned ready.
Now... what you're going to-- **FEH!**
Hmm. 112 decibels.
We can listen to this for six more minutes before experiencing irreversible hearing loss.
It's not your ears you should be worried about, Doctor...
The proximity alarm means something has entered our airspace.
Early warning detected a single object on a collision course, sir.
Who would dare attack us here?
On a ***collision course***? Who do you think, soldier...?
It's the goddamn Japanese.

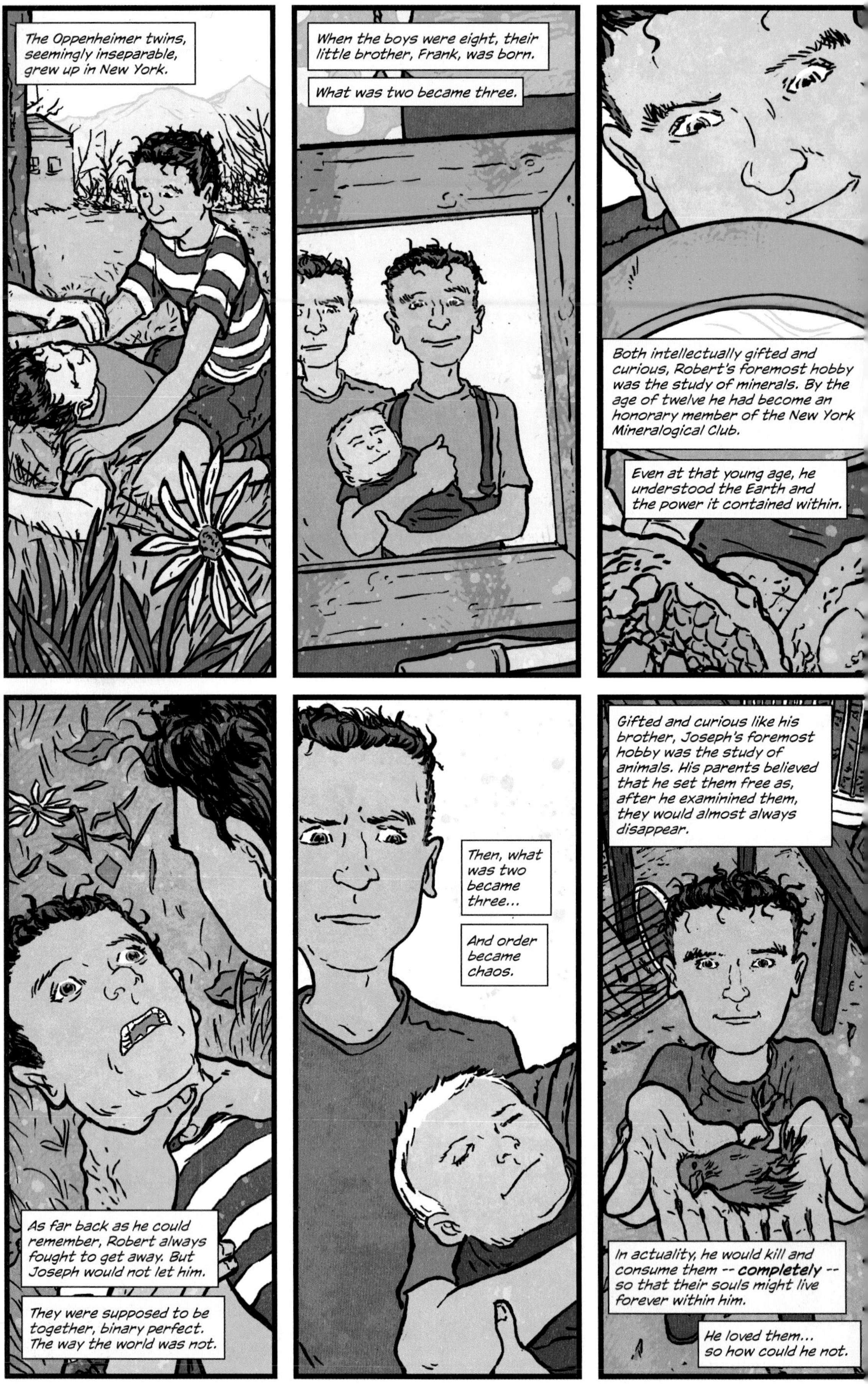
The Oppenheimer twins, seemingly inseparable, grew up in New York.
When the boys were eight, their little brother, Frank, was born.
What was two became three.
Both intellectually gifted and curious, Robert's foremost hobby was the study of minerals. By the age of twelve he had become an honorary member of the New York Mineralogical Club.
Even at that young age, he understood the Earth and the power it contained within.
As far back as he could remember, Robert always fought to get away. But Joseph would not let him.
They were supposed to be together, binary perfect. The way the world was not.
Then, what was two became three...
And order became chaos.
Gifted and curious like his brother, Joseph's foremost hobby was the study of animals. His parents believed that he set them free as, after he examinined them, they would almost always disappear.
In actuality, he would kill and consume them -- **completely** -- so that their souls might live forever within him.
He loved them... so how could he not.

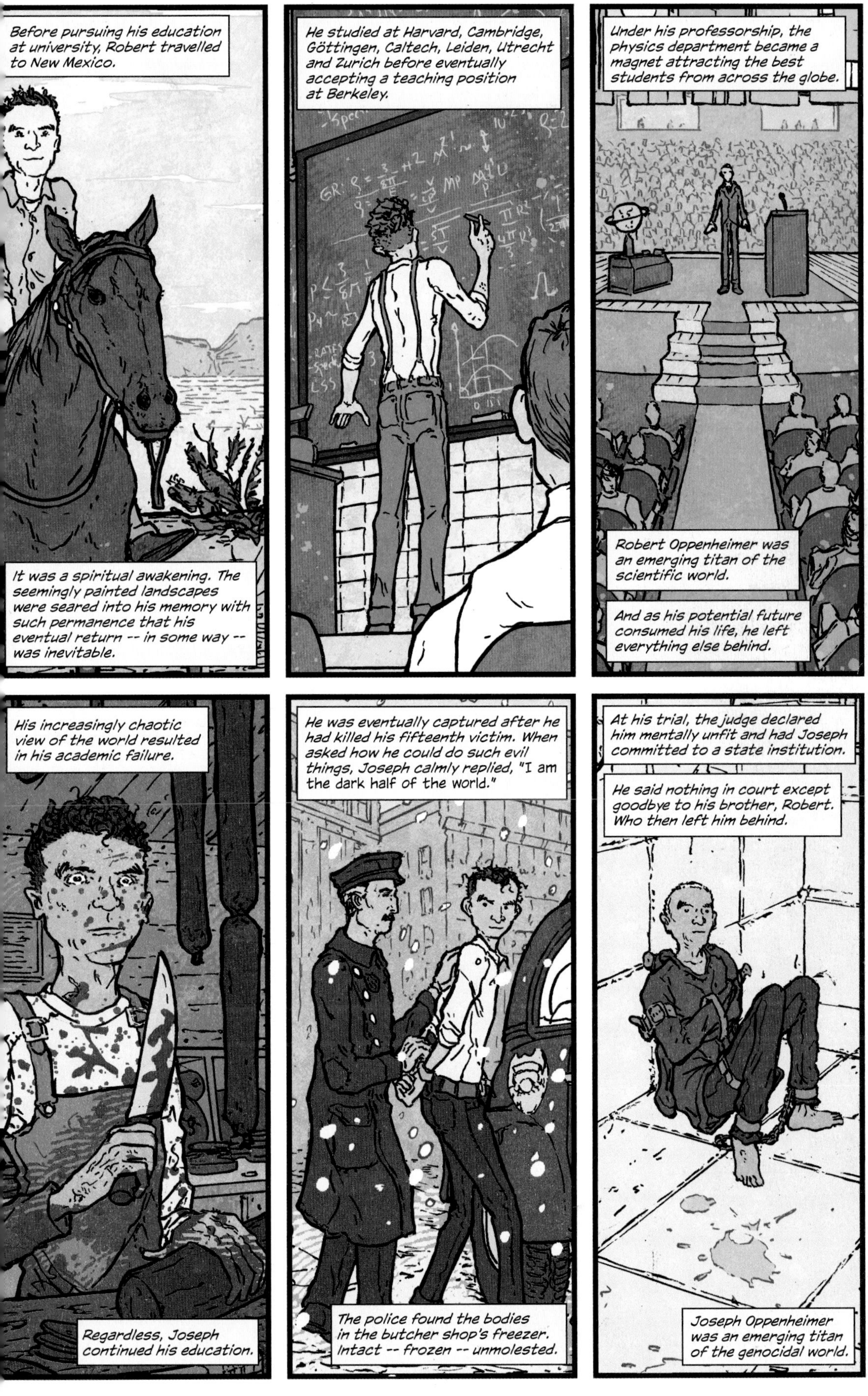
Before pursuing his education at university, Robert travelled to New Mexico.
It was a spiritual awakening. The seemingly painted landscapes were seared into his memory with such permanence that his eventual return -- in some way -- was inevitable.
He studied at Harvard, Cambridge, Göttingen, Caltech, Leiden, Utrecht and Zurich before eventually accepting a teaching position at Berkeley.
Under his professorship, the physics department became a magnet attracting the best students from across the globe.
Robert Oppenheimer was an emerging titan of the scientific world.
And as his potential future consumed his life, he left everything else behind.
His increasingly chaotic view of the world resulted in his academic failure.
Regardless, Joseph continued his education.
He was eventually captured after he had killed his fifteenth victim. When asked how he could do such evil things, Joseph calmly replied, "I am the dark half of the world."
The police found the bodies in the butcher shop's freezer. Intact -- frozen -- unmolested.
At his trial, the judge declared him mentally unfit and had Joseph committed to a state institution.
He said nothing in court except goodbye to his brother, Robert. Who then left him behind.
Joseph Oppenheimer was an emerging titan of the genocidal world.

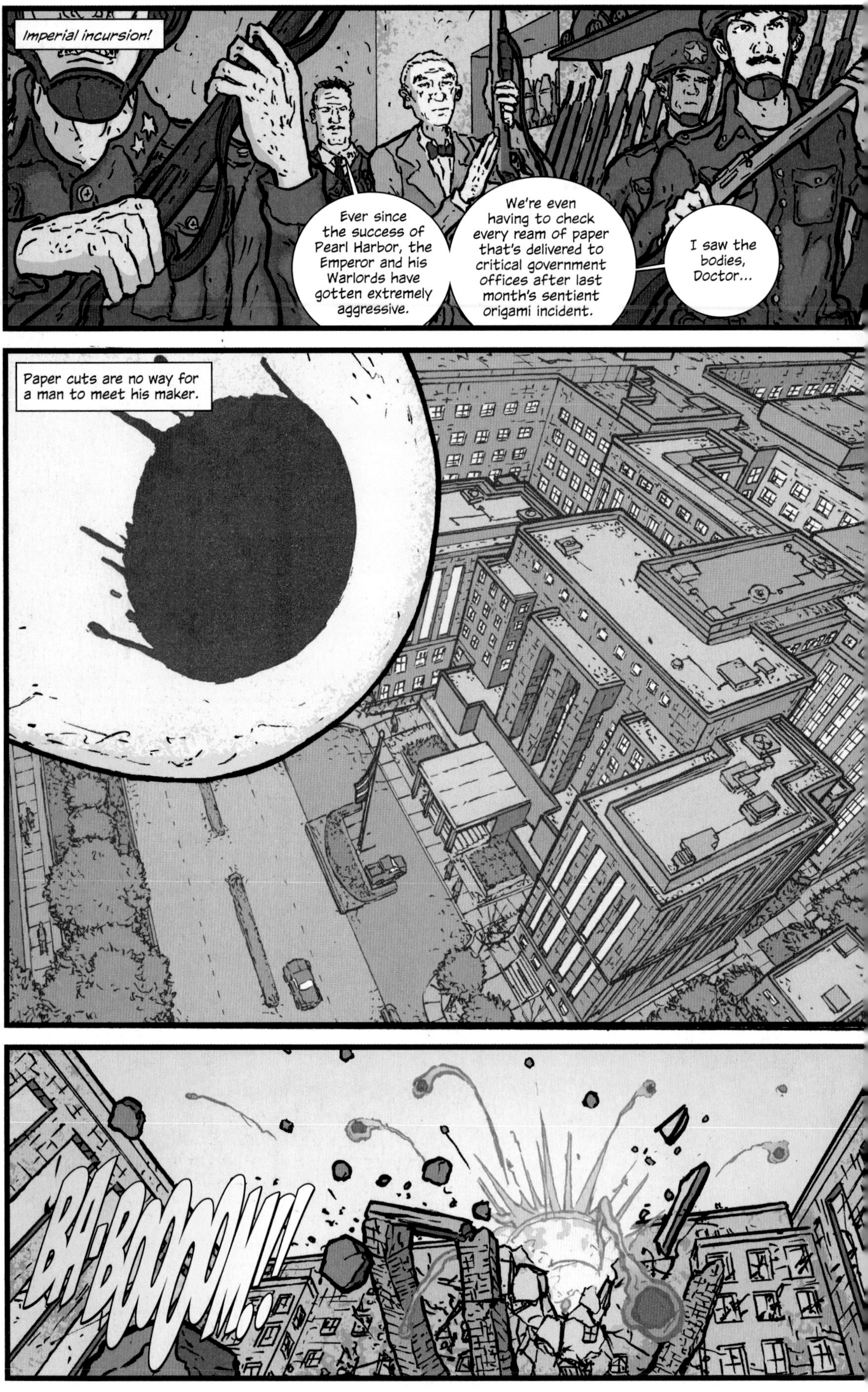
Imperial incursion!
Ever since the success of Pearl Harbor, the Emperor and his Warlords have gotten extremely aggressive.
We're even having to check every ream of paper that's delivered to critical government offices after last month's sentient origami incident.
I saw the bodies, Doctor...
Paper cuts are no way for a man to meet his maker.
BABOOOOM!!!

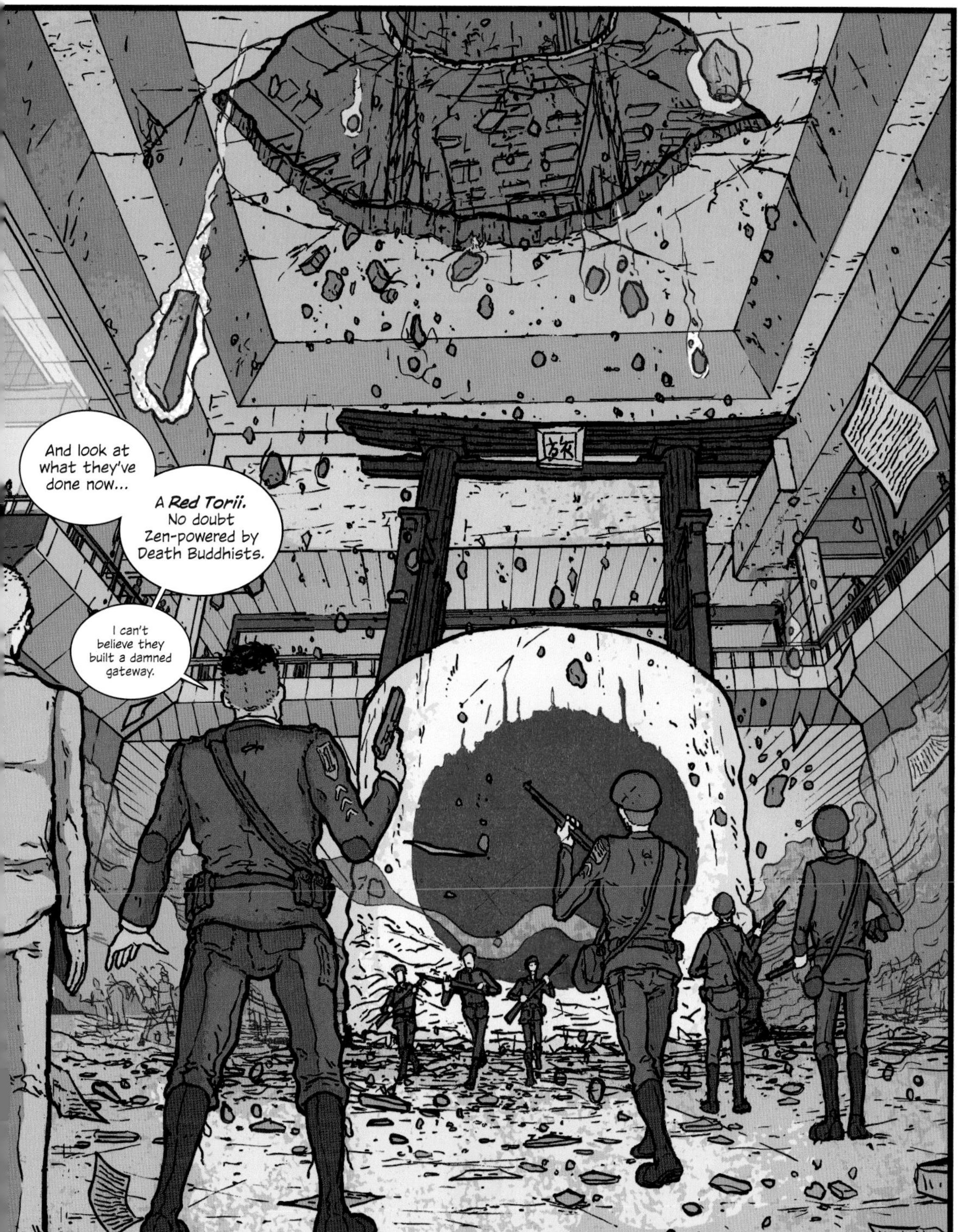
And look at what they've done now...
A **Red Torii.** No doubt Zen-powered by Death Buddhists.
I can't believe they built a damned gateway.

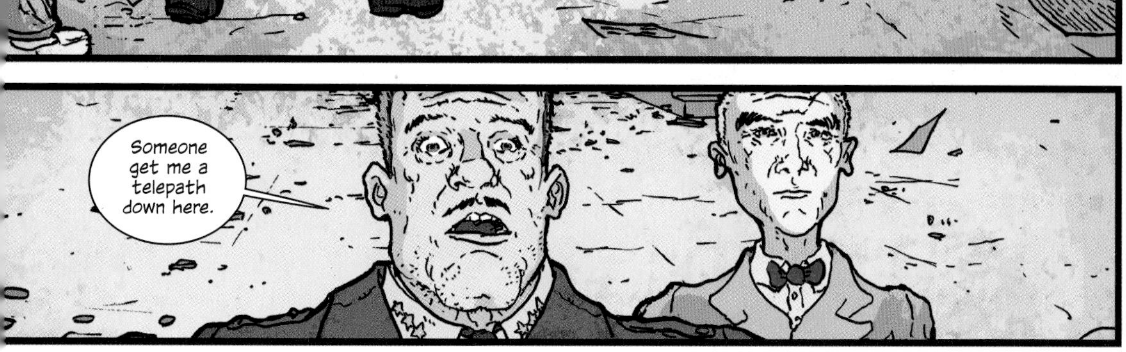
Someone get me a telepath down here.

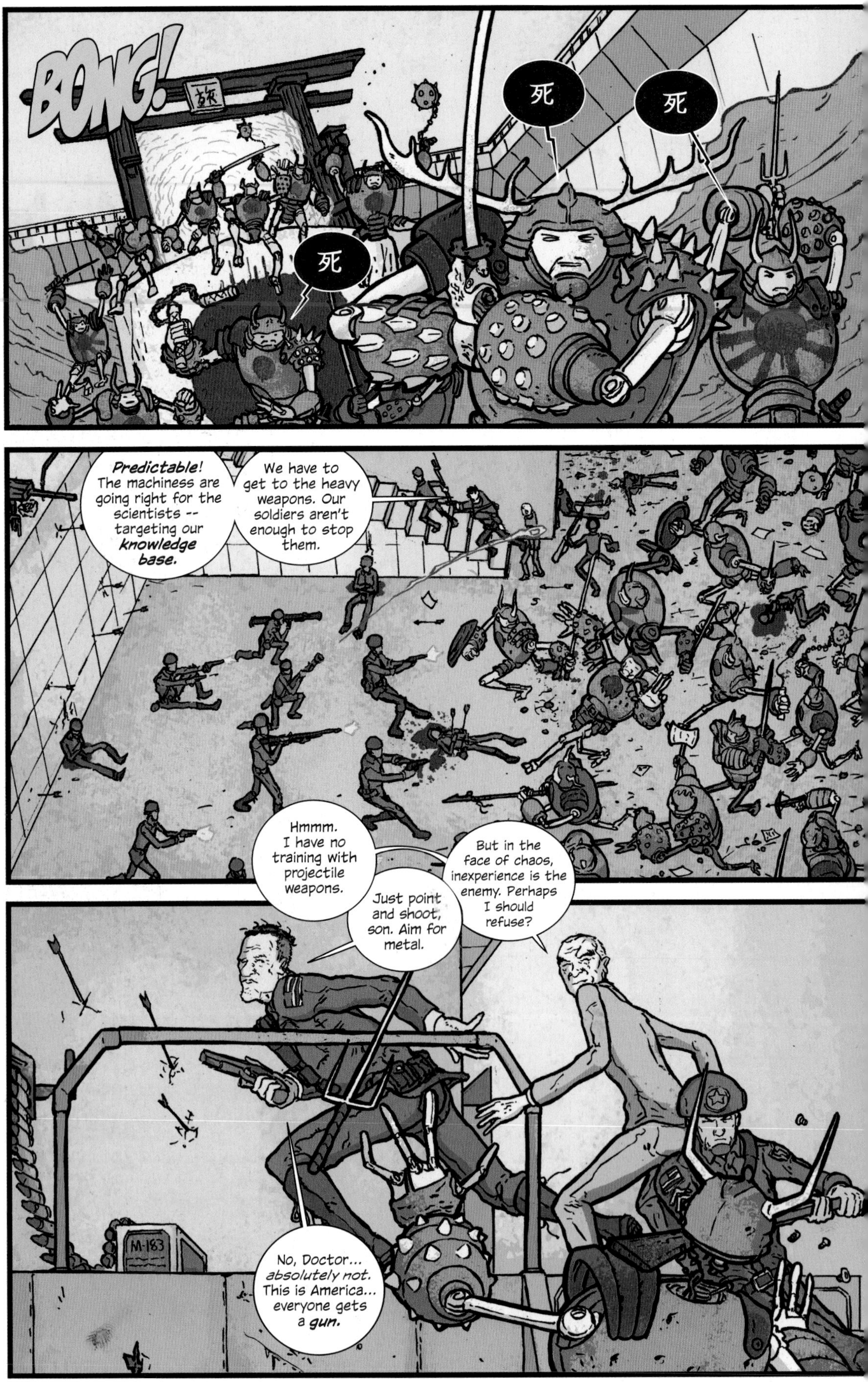
BONG!
死
死
死
Predictable! The machiness are going right for the scientists -- targeting our knowledge base.
We have to get to the heavy weapons. Our soldiers aren't enough to stop them.
Hmmm. I have no training with projectile weapons.
But in the face of chaos, inexperience is the enemy. Perhaps I should refuse?
Just point and shoot, son. Aim for metal.
M-183
No, Doctor... absolutely not. This is America... everyone gets a gun.

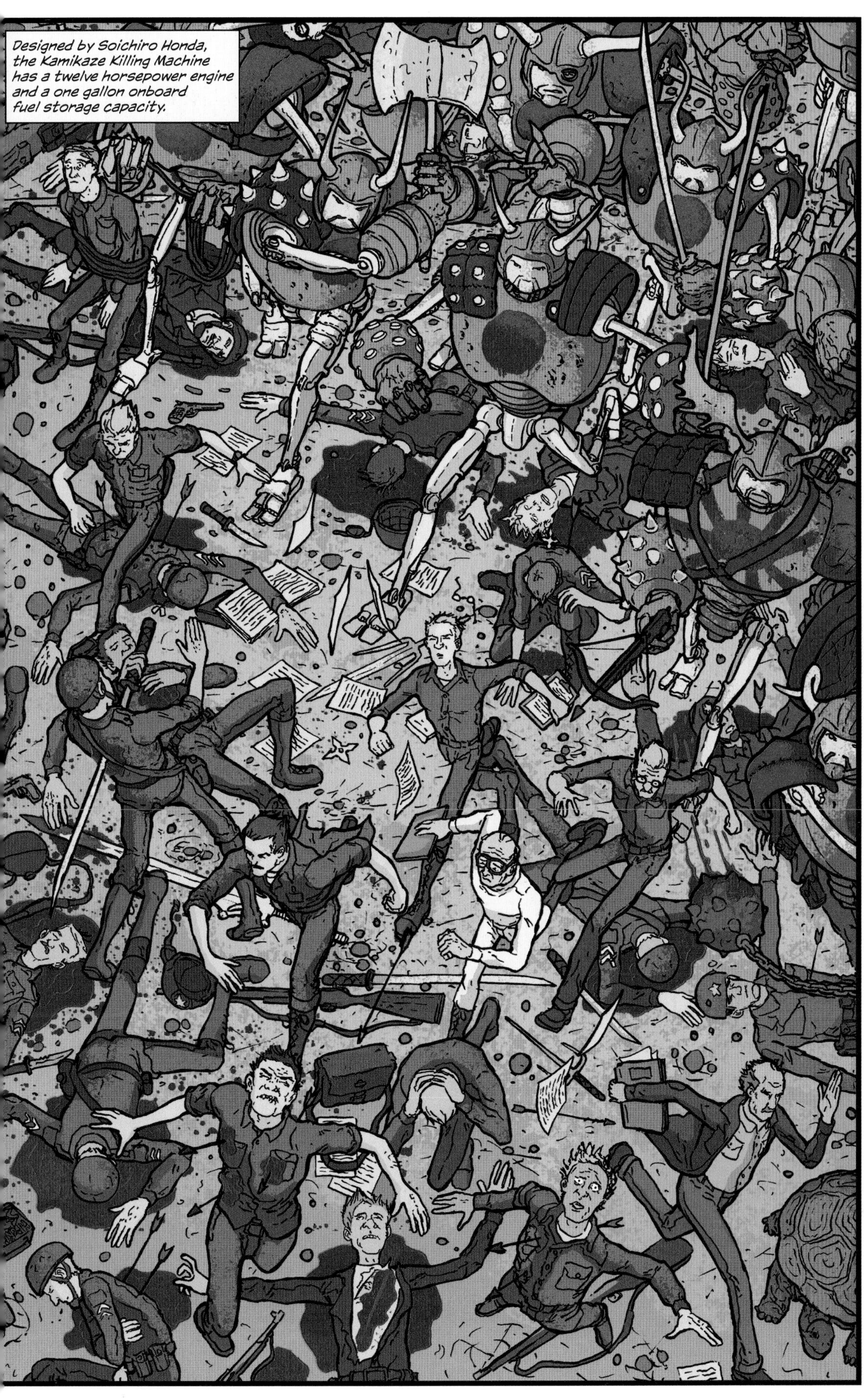
Designed by Soichiro Honda, the Kamikaze Killing Machine has a twelve horsepower engine and a one gallon onboard fuel storage capacity.

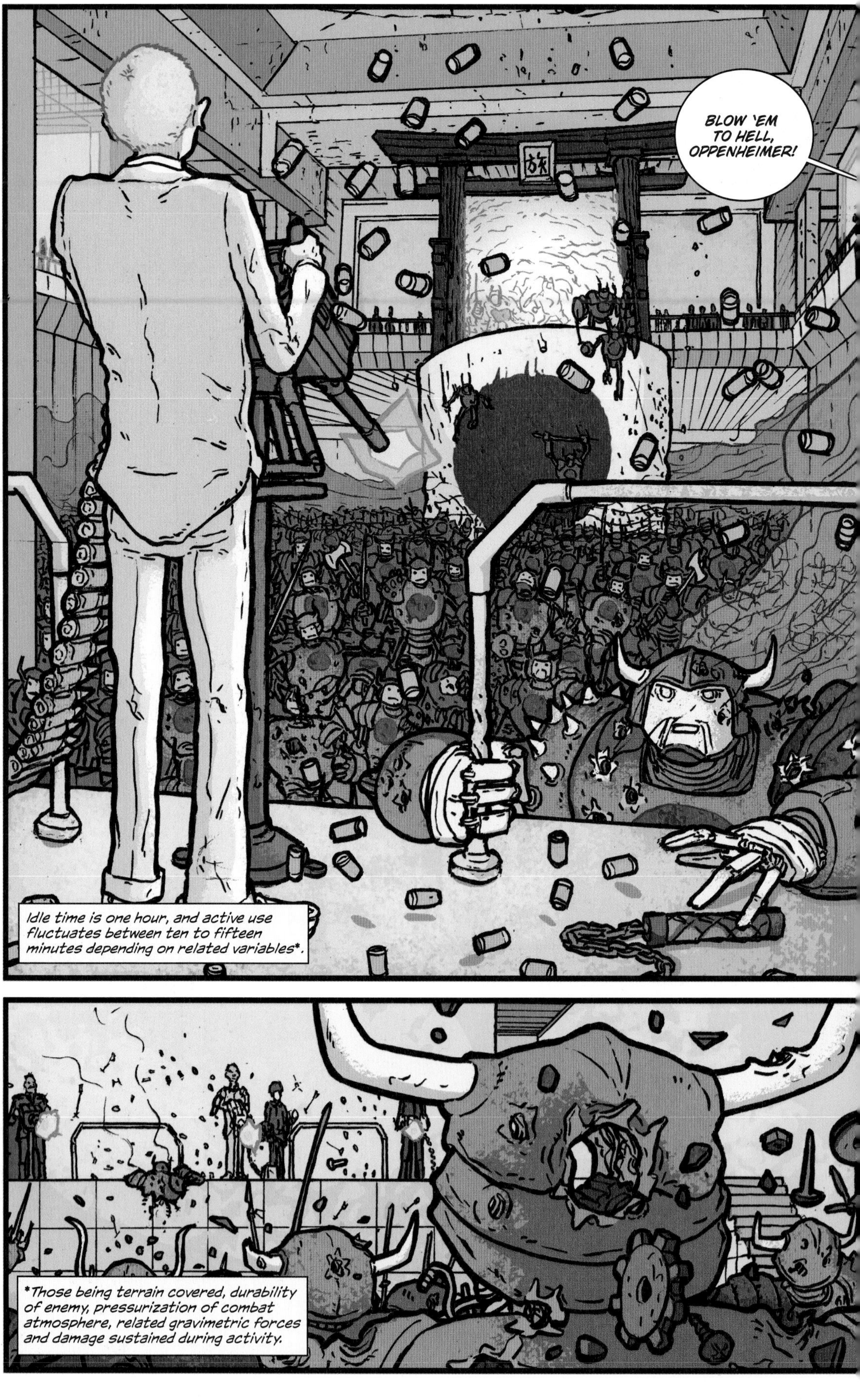
BLOW 'EM TO HELL, OPPENHEIMER!
Idle time is one hour, and active use fluctuates between ten to fifteen minutes depending on related variables*.
*Those being terrain covered, durability of enemy, pressurization of combat atmosphere, related gravimetric forces and damage sustained during activity.

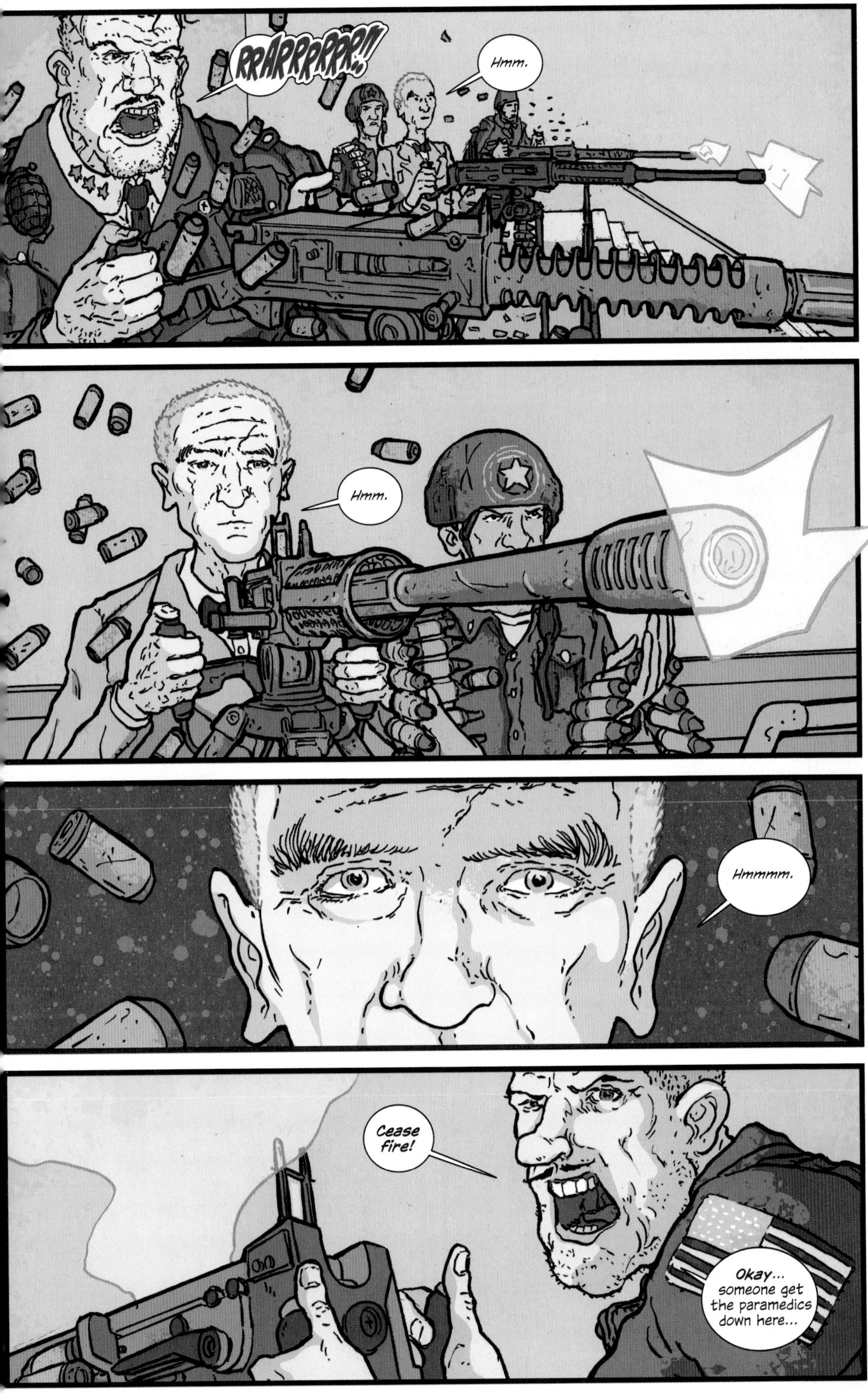
RRARRRRPR!!
Hmm.
Hmm.
Hmmmm.
Cease fire!
Okay... someone get the paramedics down here...

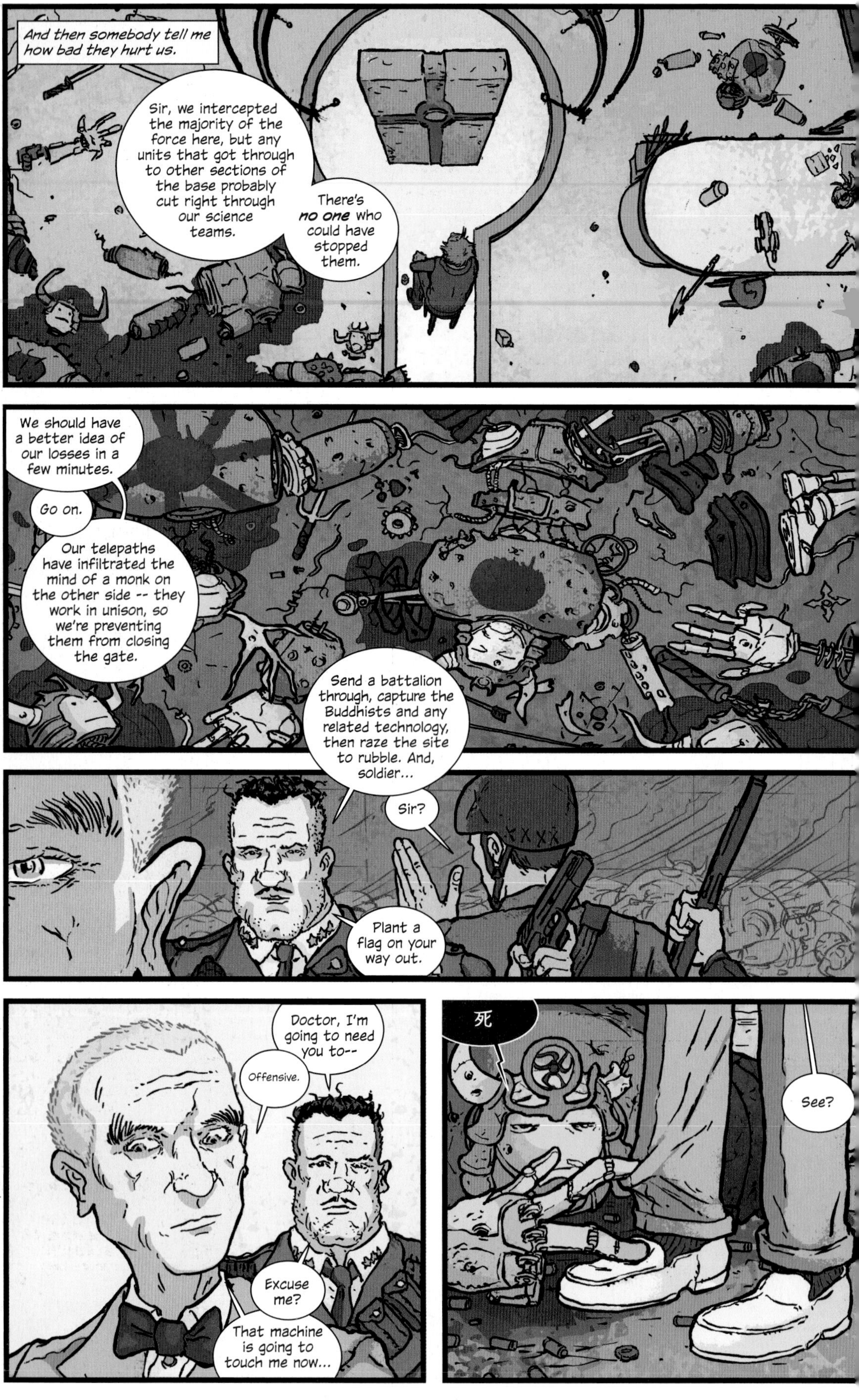
And then somebody tell me how bad they hurt us.
Sir, we intercepted the majority of the force here, but any units that got through to other sections of the base probably cut right through our science teams.
There's no one who could have stopped them.
We should have a better idea of our losses in a few minutes.
Go on.
Our telepaths have infiltrated the mind of a monk on the other side -- they work in unison, so we're preventing them from closing the gate.
Send a battalion through, capture the Buddhists and any related technology, then raze the site to rubble. And, soldier...
Sir?
Plant a flag on your way out.
Doctor, I'm going to need you to--
Offensive.
Excuse me?
That machine is going to touch me now...
死
See?

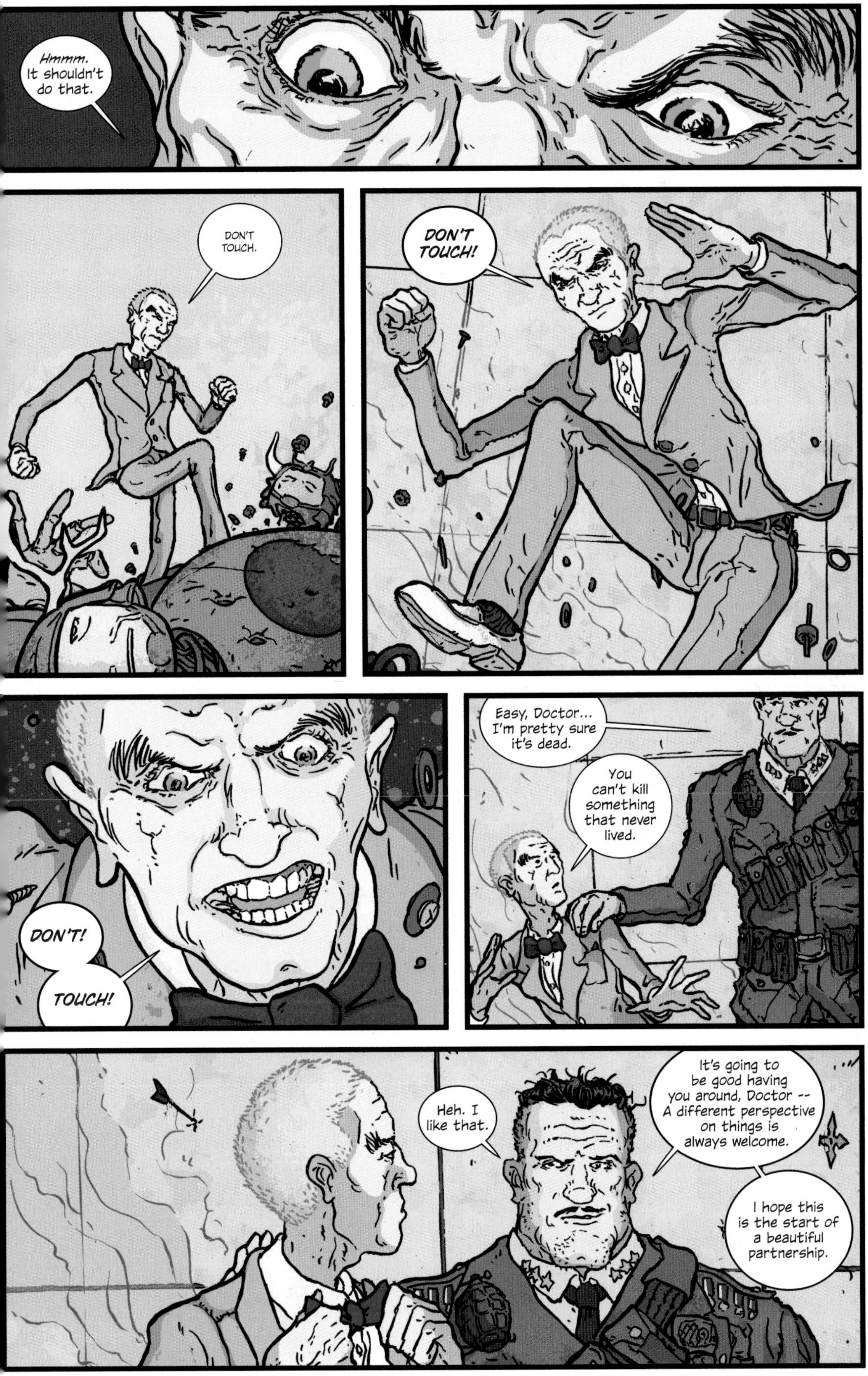

Hmmm.
It shouldn't do that.
DON'T TOUCH.
DON'T TOUCH!
DON'T!
TOUCH!
Easy, Doctor... I'm pretty sure it's dead.
You can't kill something that never lived.
Heh. I like that.
It's going to be good having you around, Doctor -- A different perspective on things is always welcome.
I hope this is the start of a beautiful partnership.

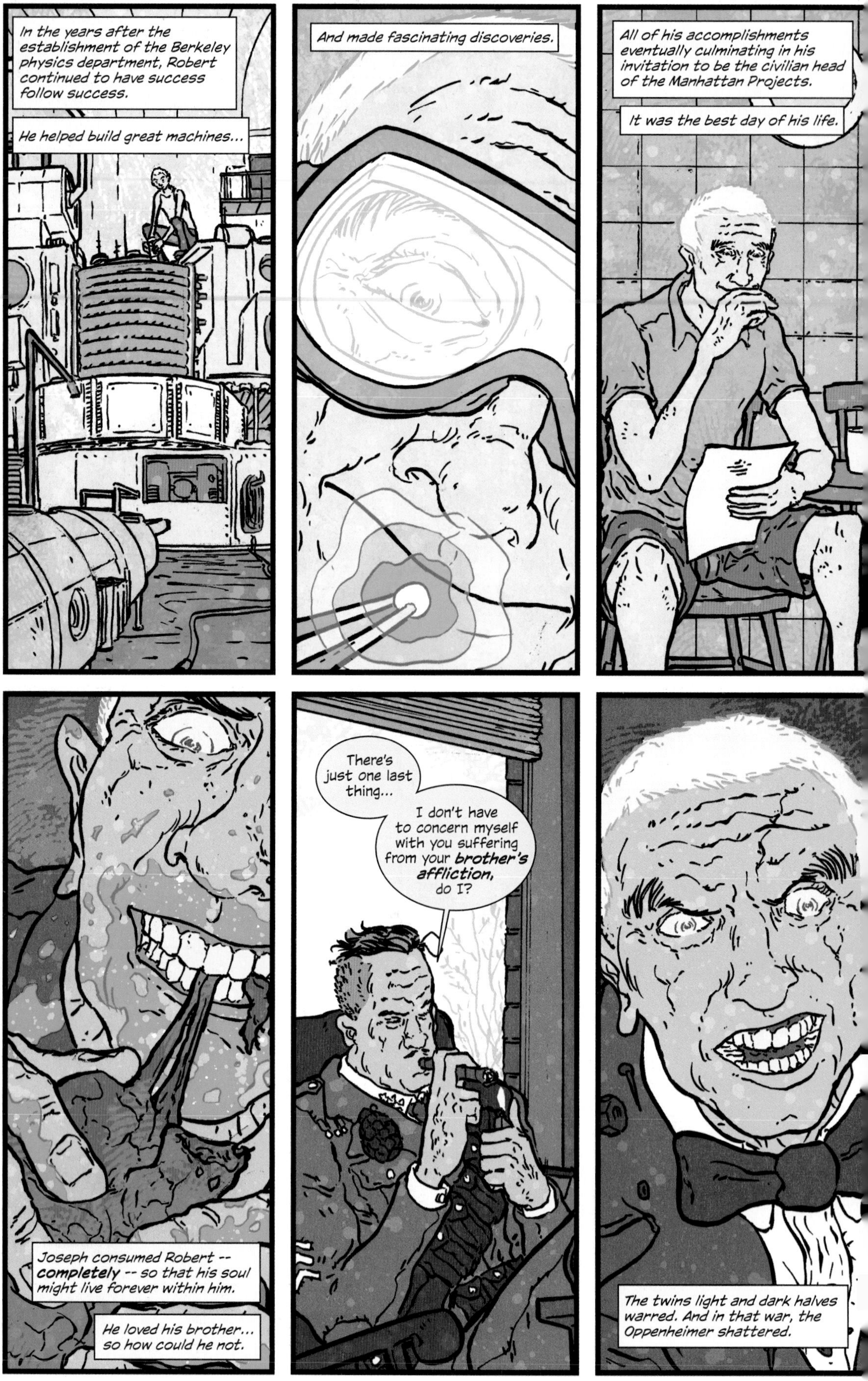
In the years after the establishment of the Berkeley physics department, Robert continued to have success follow success.
He helped build great machines...
And made fascinating discoveries.
All of his accomplishments eventually culminating in his invitation to be the civilian head of the Manhattan Projects.
It was the best day of his life.
Joseph consumed Robert -- **completely** -- so that his soul might live forever within him.
He loved his brother... so how could he not.
There's just one last thing...
I don't have to concern myself with you suffering from your **brother's affliction,** do I?
The twins light and dark halves warred. And in that war, the Oppenheimer shattered.

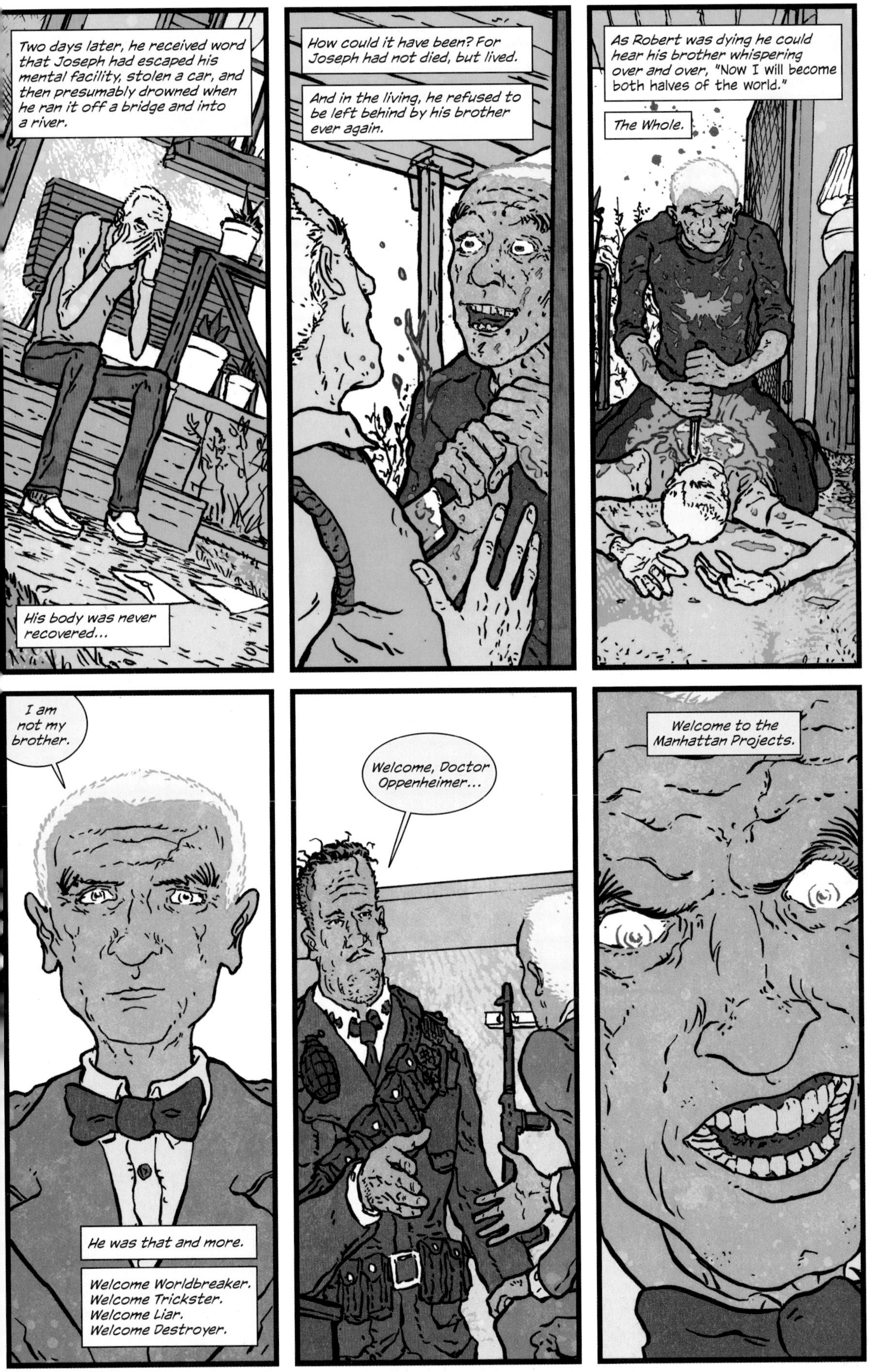

Two days later, he received word that Joseph had escaped his mental facility, stolen a car, and then presumably drowned when he ran it off a bridge and into a river.
His body was never recovered...
How could it have been? For Joseph had not died, but lived.
And in the living, he refused to be left behind by his brother ever again.
As Robert was dying he could hear his brother whispering over and over, "Now I will become both halves of the world."
The Whole.
I am not my brother.
He was that and more.
Welcome Worldbreaker.
Welcome Trickster.
Welcome Liar.
Welcome Destroyer.
Welcome, Doctor Oppenheimer...
Welcome to the Manhattan Projects.

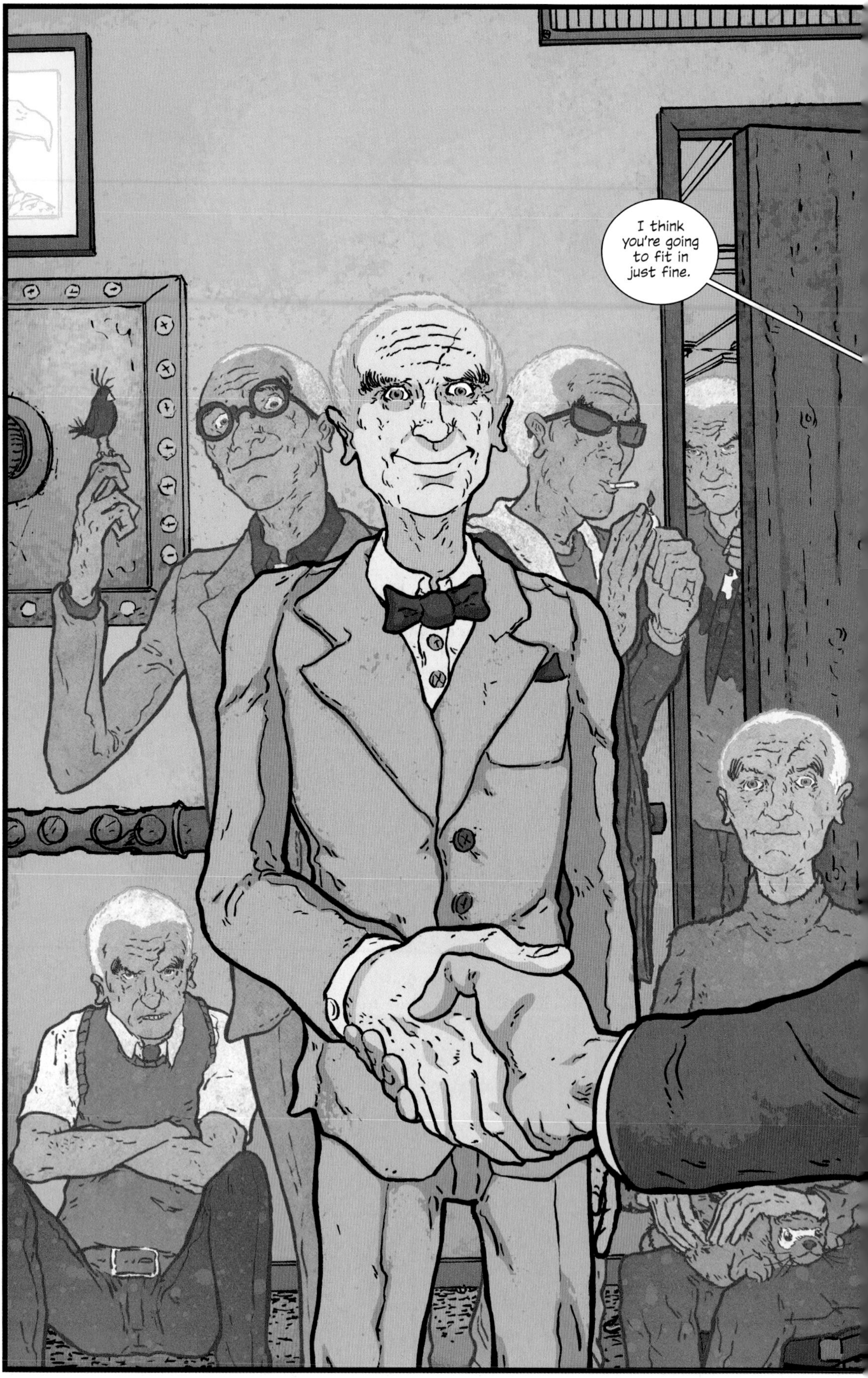
I think you're going to fit in just fine.

"IN THE BEGINNING, WHEN I FIRST JOINED THE PROJECTS – BEFORE HIS INTERNAL CIVIL WAR, BEFORE THE GREAT CULLING, BEFORE THE AMALGAMATED OPPENHEIMER COALESCED, THIRTY-TWO DISTINCT VERSIONS OF THE DOCTOR EXISTED.

FROM THERE, THE RATE OF FRACTURE INCREASED EXPONENTIALLY, AND BY 1968 THAT NUMBER WAS VIRTUALLY ENDLESS."

CLAVIS AUREA
THE RECORDED FEYNMAN

VOL. 1

I HOPE YOU LIKE NEW
EXPERIENCES

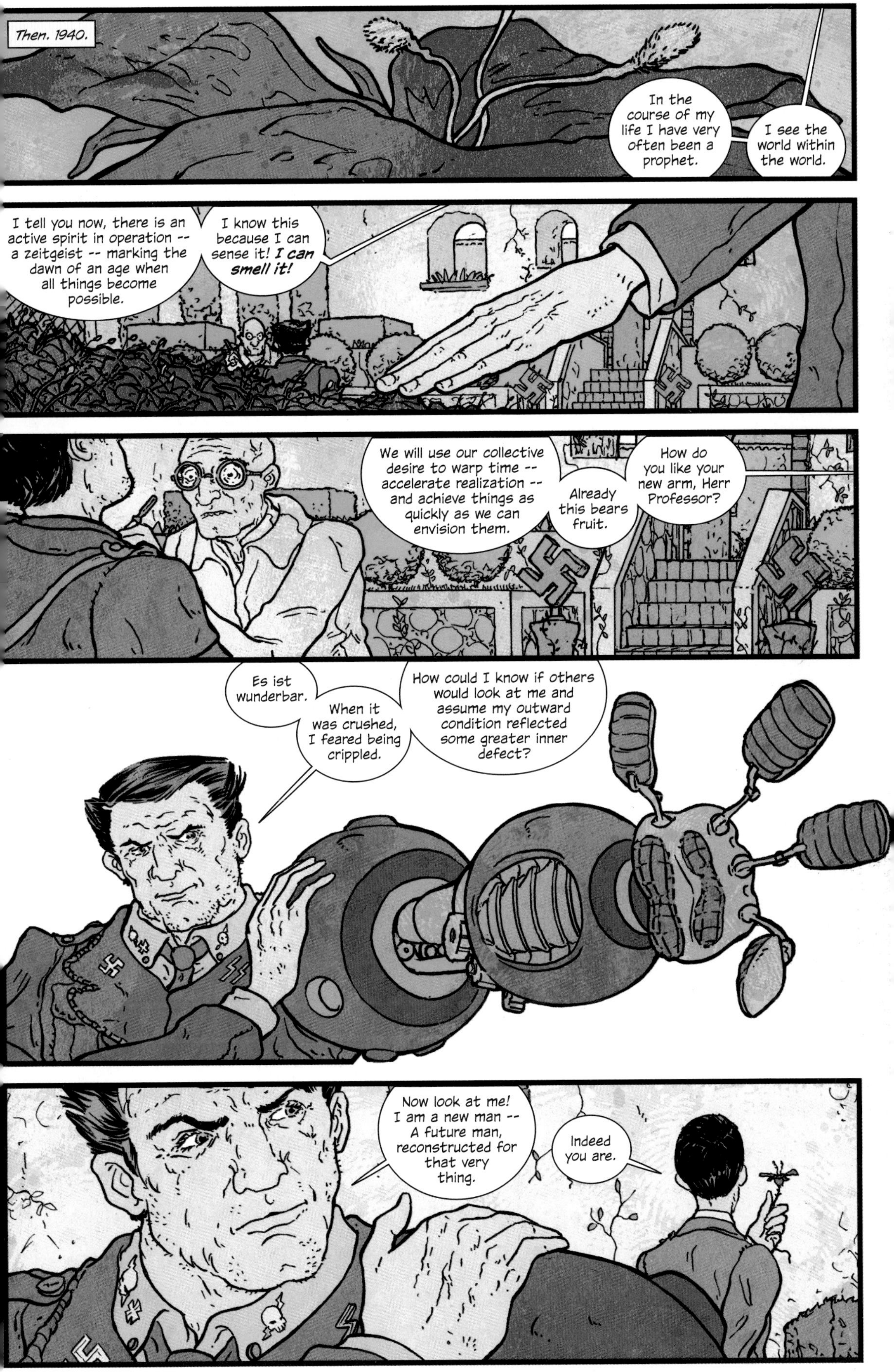
Then. 1940.
In the course of my life I have very often been a prophet.
I see the world within the world.
I tell you now, there is an active spirit in operation -- a zeitgeist -- marking the dawn of an age when all things become possible.
I know this because I can sense it! ***I can smell it!***
We will use our collective desire to warp time -- accelerate realization -- and achieve things as quickly as we can envision them.
Already this bears fruit.
How do you like your new arm, Herr Professor?
Es ist wunderbar.
When it was crushed, I feared being crippled.
How could I know if others would look at me and assume my outward condition reflected some greater inner defect?
Now look at me! I am a new man -- A future man, reconstructed for that very thing.
Indeed you are.

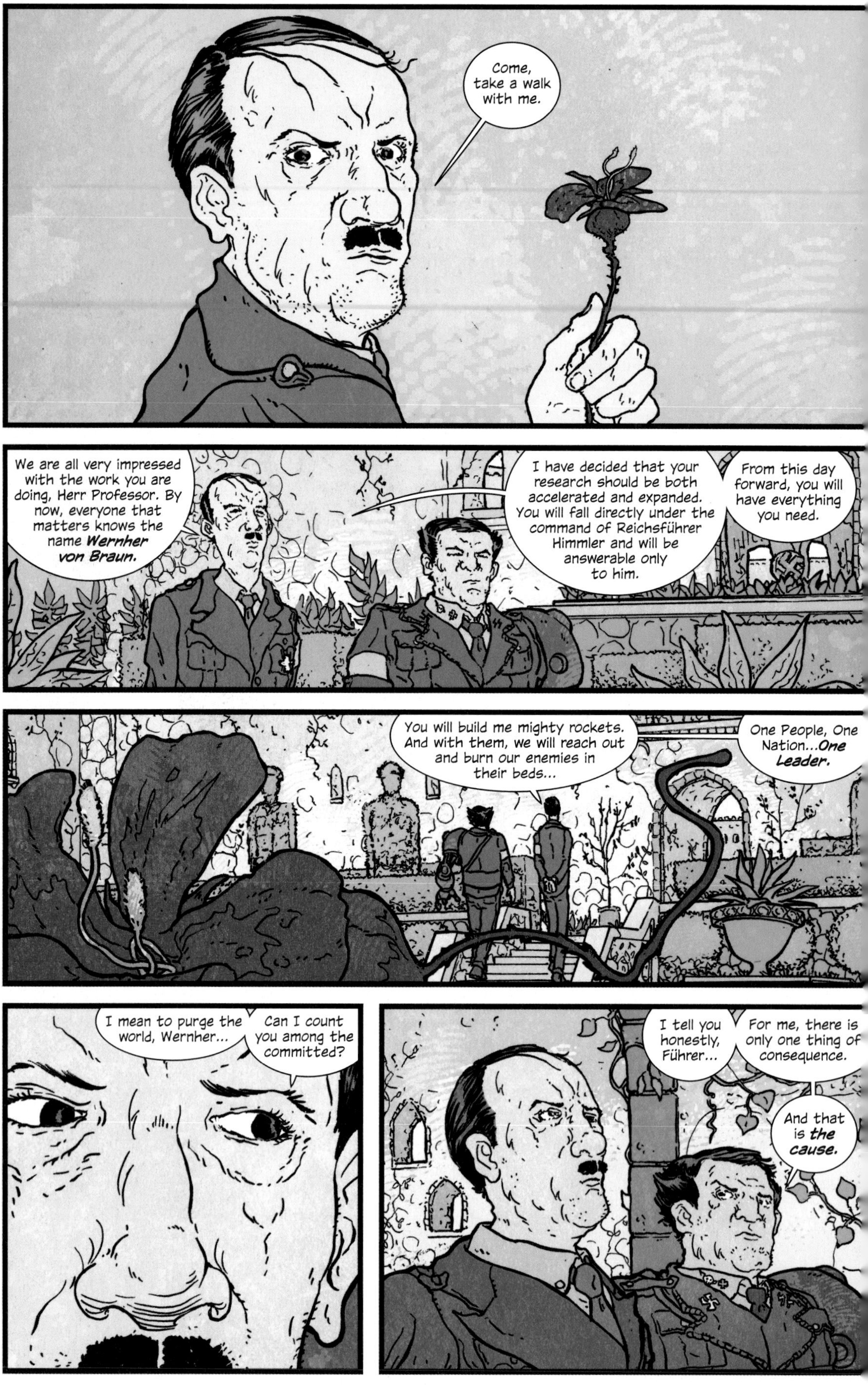

Come, take a walk with me.
We are all very impressed with the work you are doing, Herr Professor. By now, everyone that matters knows the name ***Wernher von Braun.***
I have decided that your research should be both accelerated and expanded. You will fall directly under the command of Reichsführer Himmler and will be answerable only to him.
From this day forward, you will have everything you need.
You will build me mighty rockets. And with them, we will reach out and burn our enemies in their beds...
One People, One Nation...***One Leader.***
I mean to purge the world, Wernher...
Can I count you among the committed?
I tell you honestly, Führer...
For me, there is only one thing of consequence.
And that is ***the cause.***

"NEVER FORGET, WE OWE THE FUTURE TO THE FASCISTS."

CLAVIS AUREA
THE RECORDED FEYNMAN

VOL. 1

02

ROCKET MAN

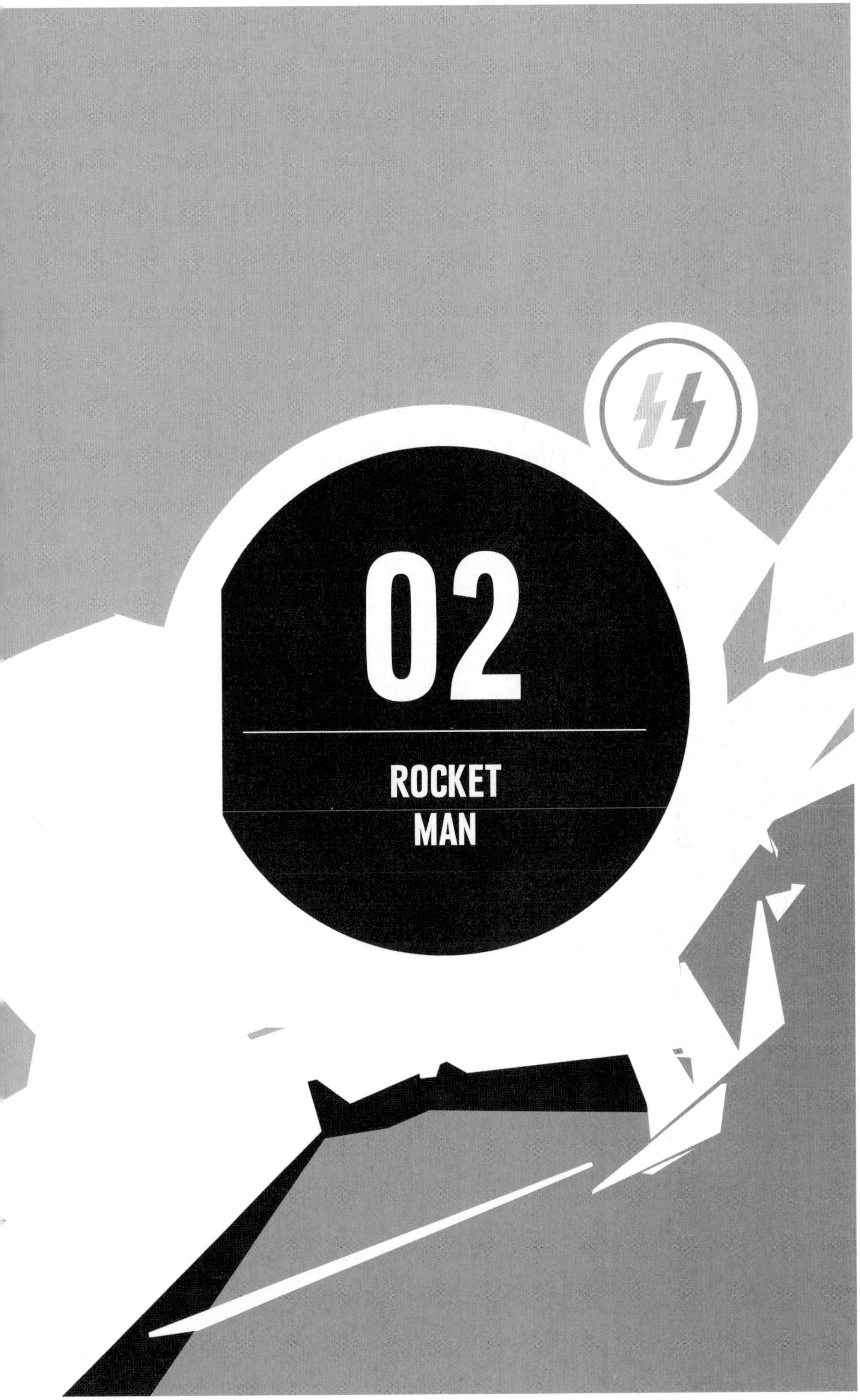

"I APOLOGIZE IF I'M EXCEEDINGLY FORMAL, BUT I FIND IT A NECESSARY COPING MECHANISM. YOU SEE, I SUFFER FROM AN EMBARRASSINGLY MUNDANE AFFLICTION THAT, WHEN UNADDRESSED, RESULTS IN A SHAMEFUL LACK OF MANNERS.

I AM CURSED WITH BURDEN OF ALWAYS BEING RIGHT."

CLAVIS AUREA
THE RECORDED FEYNMAN | **VOL. 1**

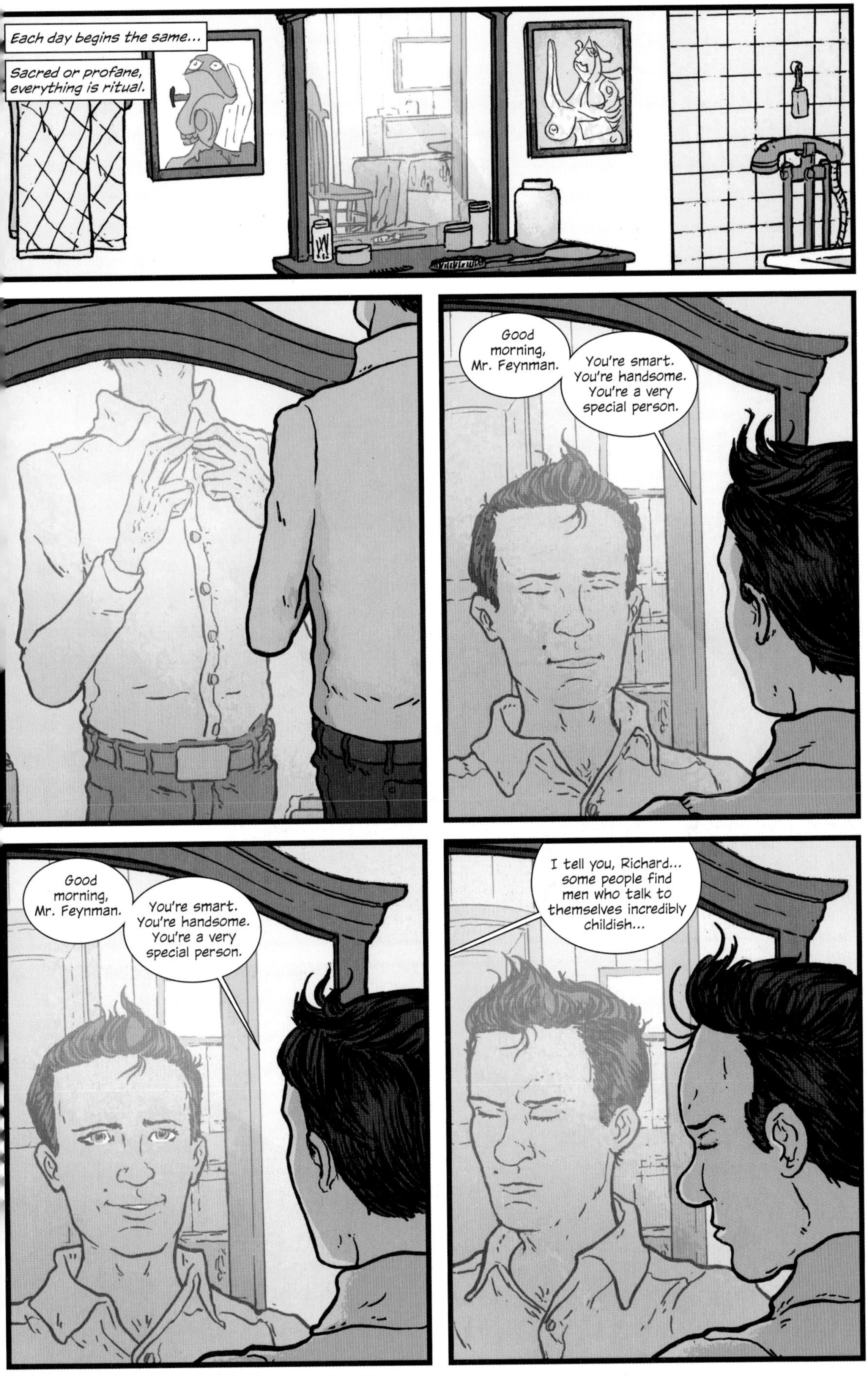
Each day begins the same...
Sacred or profane, everything is ritual.
Good morning, Mr. Feynman.
You're smart. You're handsome. You're a very special person.
Good morning, Mr. Feynman.
You're smart. You're handsome. You're a very special person.
I tell you, Richard... some people find men who talk to themselves incredibly childish...

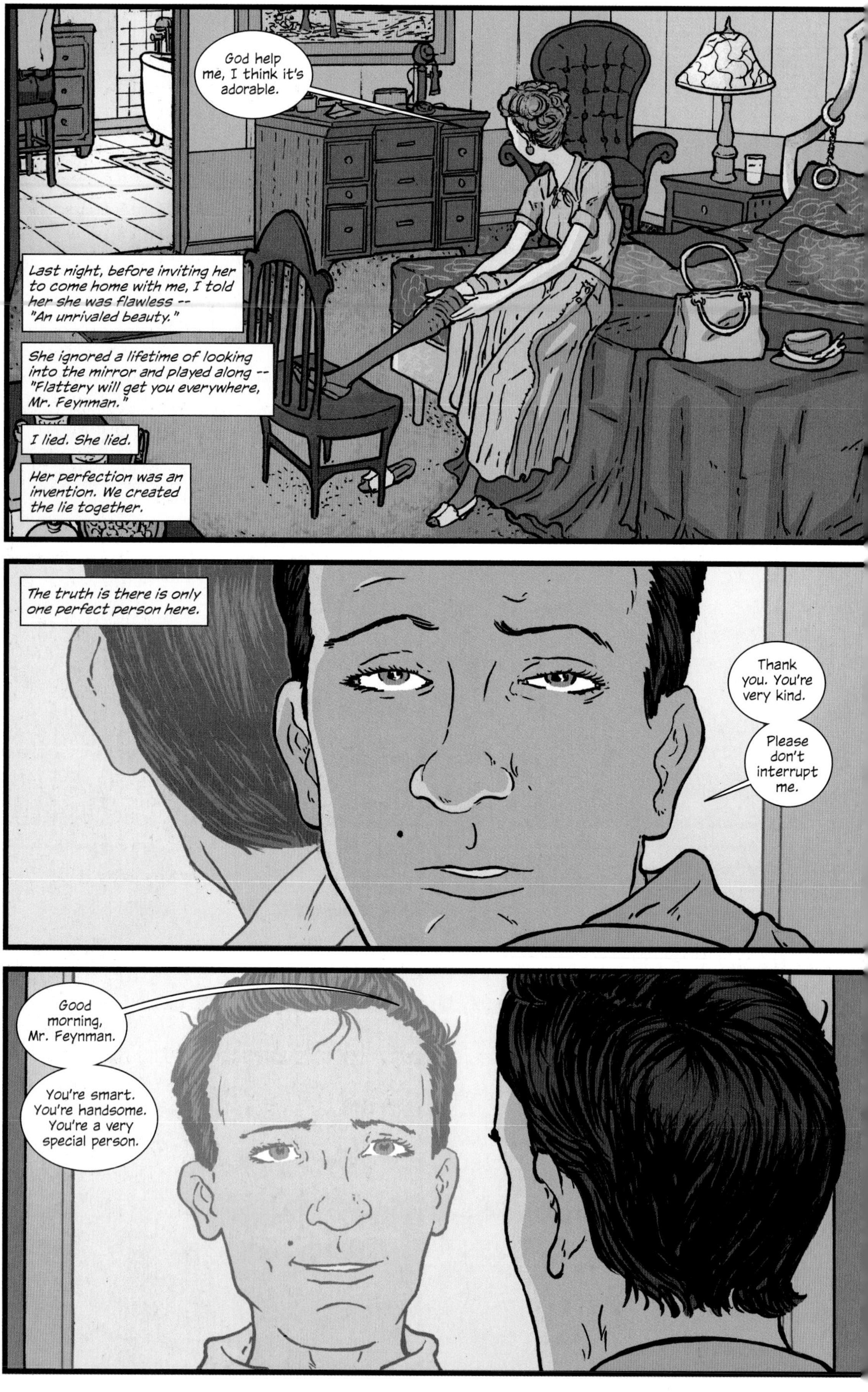
God help me, I think it's adorable.
Last night, before inviting her to come home with me, I told her she was flawless -- "An unrivaled beauty."
She ignored a lifetime of looking into the mirror and played along -- "Flattery will get you everywhere, Mr. Feynman."
I lied. She lied.
Her perfection was an invention. We created the lie together.
The truth is there is only one perfect person here.
Thank you. You're very kind.
Please don't interrupt me.
Good morning, Mr. Feynman.
You're smart. You're handsome. You're a very special person.

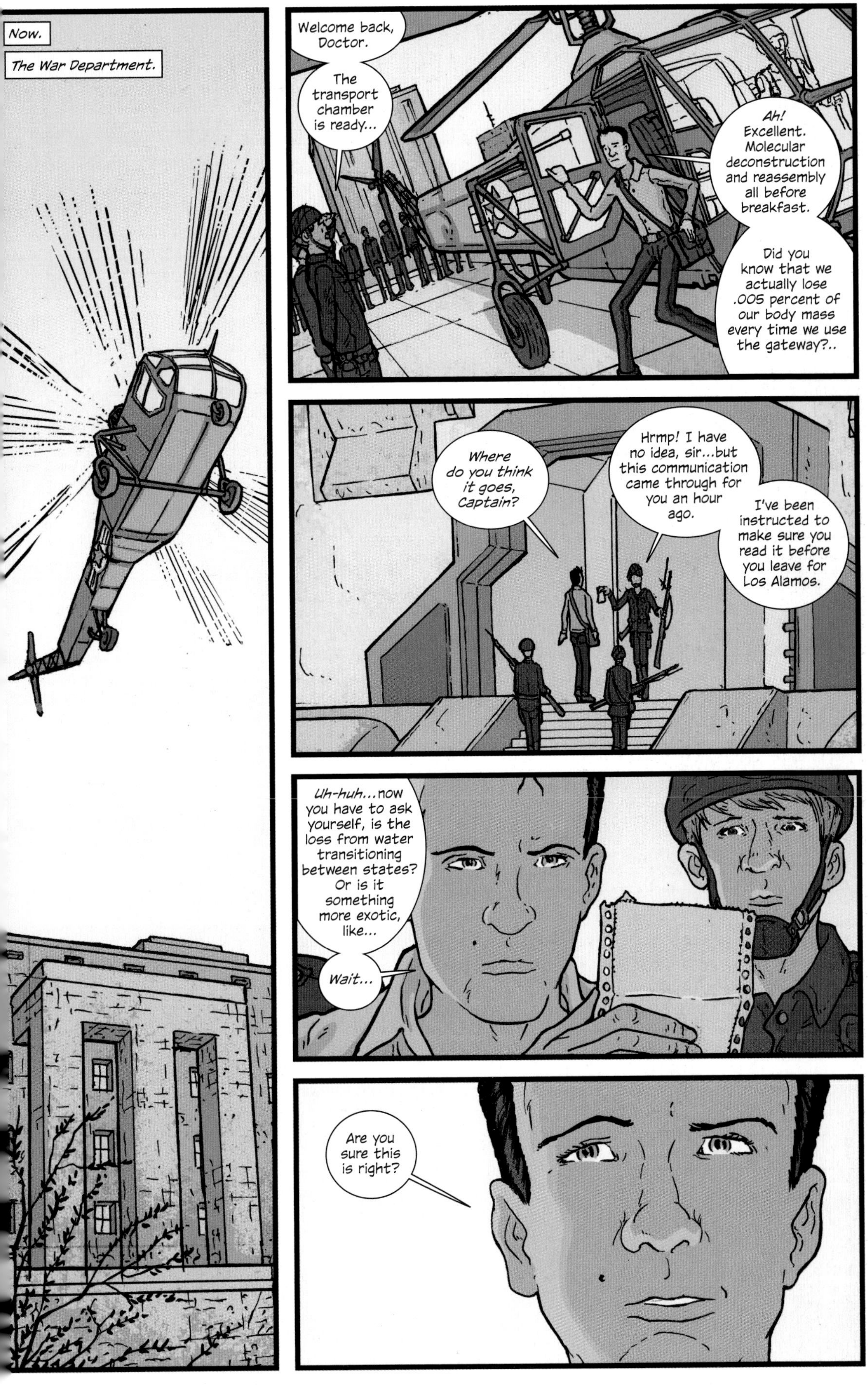
Now.
The War Department.
Welcome back, Doctor.
The transport chamber is ready...
Ah! Excellent. Molecular deconstruction and reassembly all before breakfast.
Did you know that we actually lose .005 percent of our body mass every time we use the gateway?..
Where do you think it goes, Captain?
Hrmp! I have no idea, sir...but this communication came through for you an hour ago.
I've been instructed to make sure you read it before you leave for Los Alamos.
Uh-huh...now you have to ask yourself, is the loss from water transitioning between states? Or is it something more exotic, like...
Wait...
Are you sure this is right?

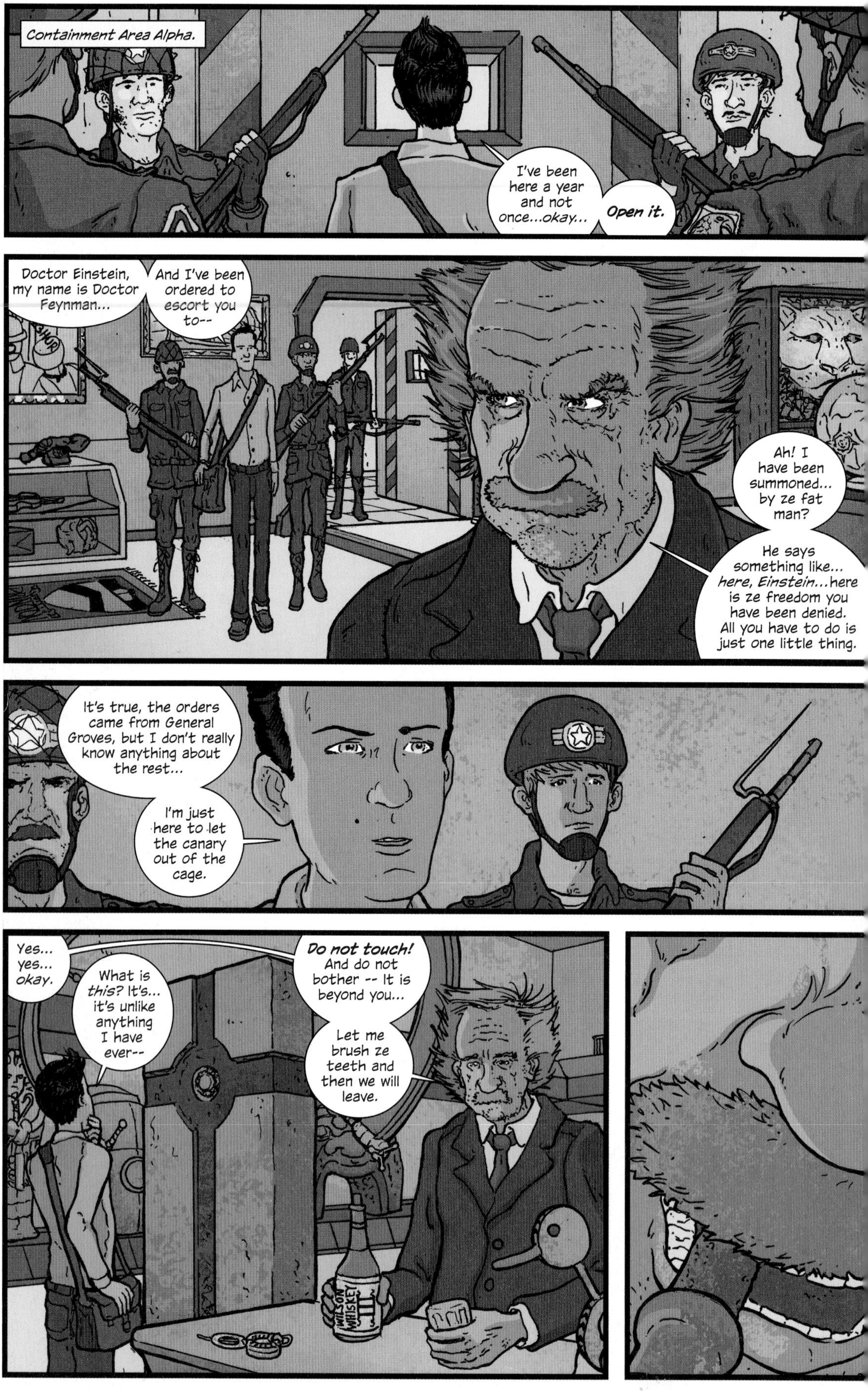

Containment Area Alpha.
I've been here a year and not once...okay...
Open it.
Doctor Einstein, my name is Doctor Feynman...
And I've been ordered to escort you to--
Ah! I have been summoned... by ze fat man?
He says something like... here, Einstein...here is ze freedom you have been denied. All you have to do is just one little thing.
It's true, the orders came from General Groves, but I don't really know anything about the rest...
I'm just here to let the canary out of the cage.
Yes... yes... okay.
What is this? It's... it's unlike anything I have ever--
Do not touch! And do not bother -- It is beyond you...
Let me brush ze teeth and then we will leave.
WILSON WHISKEY

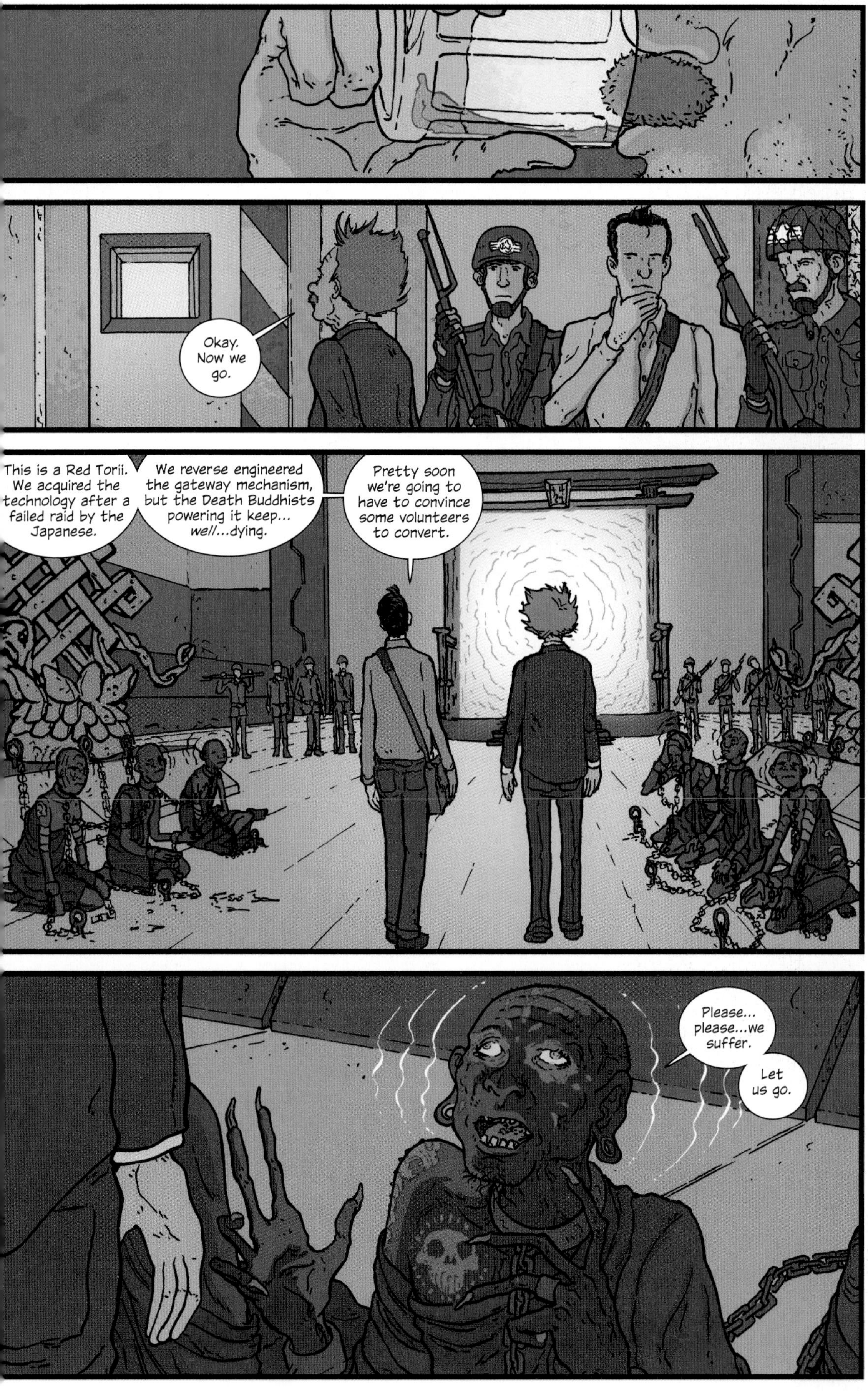

Okay. Now we go.
This is a Red Torii. We acquired the technology after a failed raid by the Japanese.
We reverse engineered the gateway mechanism, but the Death Buddhists powering it keep... *well*...dying.
Pretty soon we're going to have to convince some volunteers to convert.
Please... please...we suffer.
Let us go.

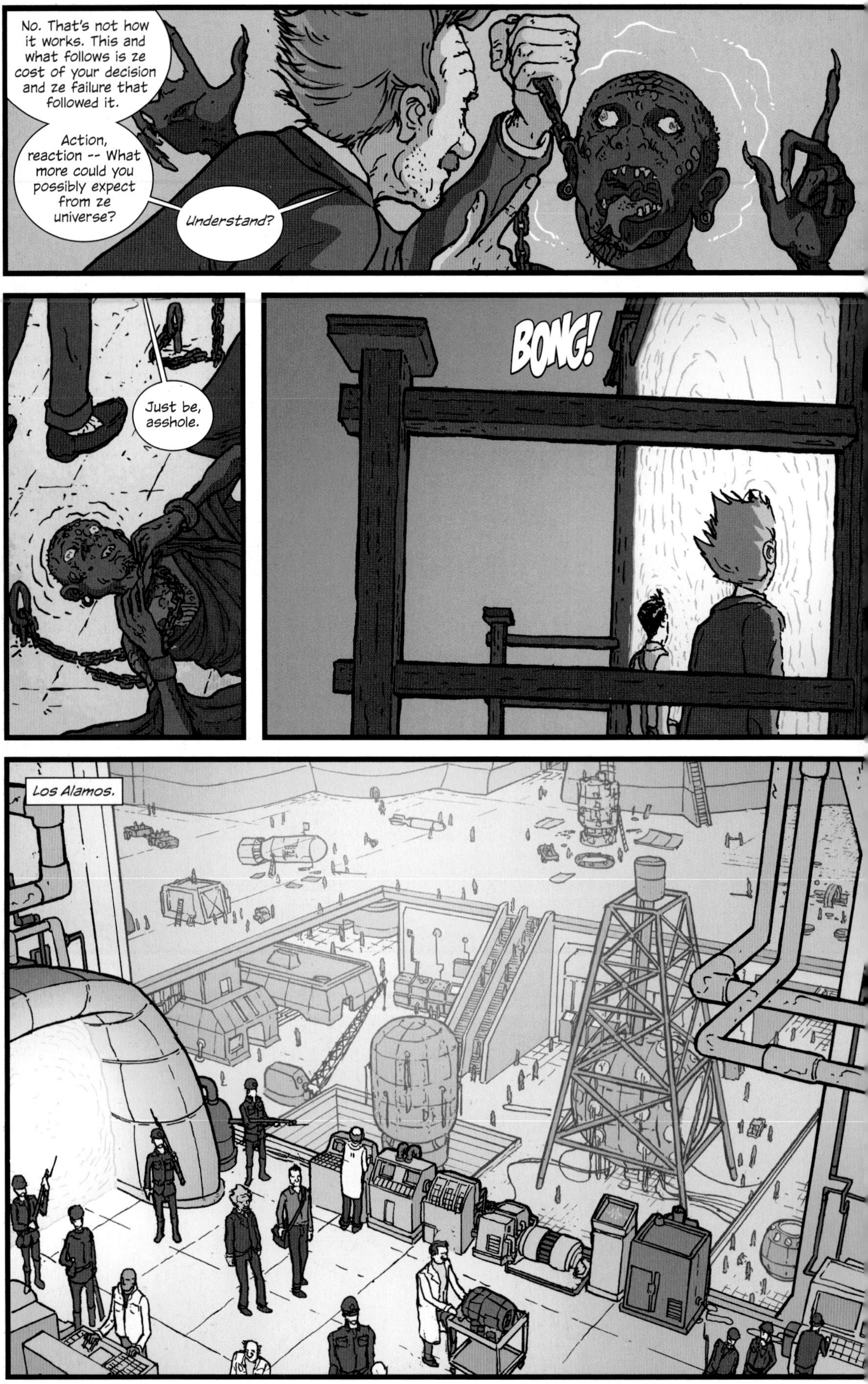
No. That's not how it works. This and what follows is ze cost of your decision and ze failure that followed it.
Action, reaction -- What more could you possibly expect from ze universe?
Understand?
Just be, asshole.
BONG!
Los Alamos.

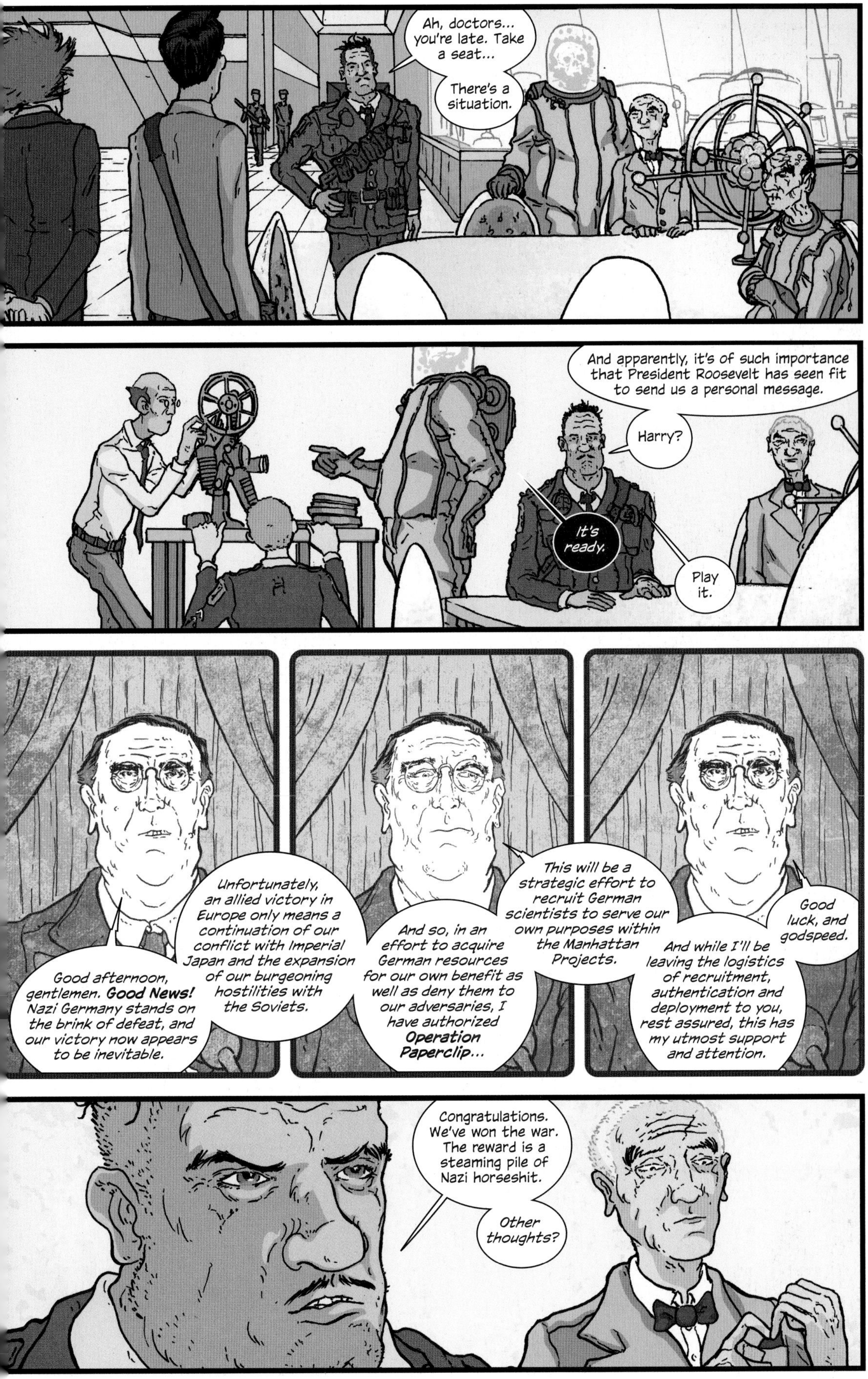
Ah, doctors... you're late. Take a seat...
There's a situation.
And apparently, it's of such importance that President Roosevelt has seen fit to send us a personal message.
Harry?
It's ready.
Play it.
Good afternoon, gentlemen. Good News! Nazi Germany stands on the brink of defeat, and our victory now appears to be inevitable.
Unfortunately, an allied victory in Europe only means a continuation of our conflict with Imperial Japan and the expansion of our burgeoning hostilities with the Soviets.
And so, in an effort to acquire German resources for our own benefit as well as deny them to our adversaries, I have authorized Operation Paperclip...
This will be a strategic effort to recruit German scientists to serve our own purposes within the Manhattan Projects.
And while I'll be leaving the logistics of recruitment, authentication and deployment to you, rest assured, this has my utmost support and attention.
Good luck, and godspeed.
Congratulations. We've won the war. The reward is a steaming pile of Nazi horseshit.
Other thoughts?

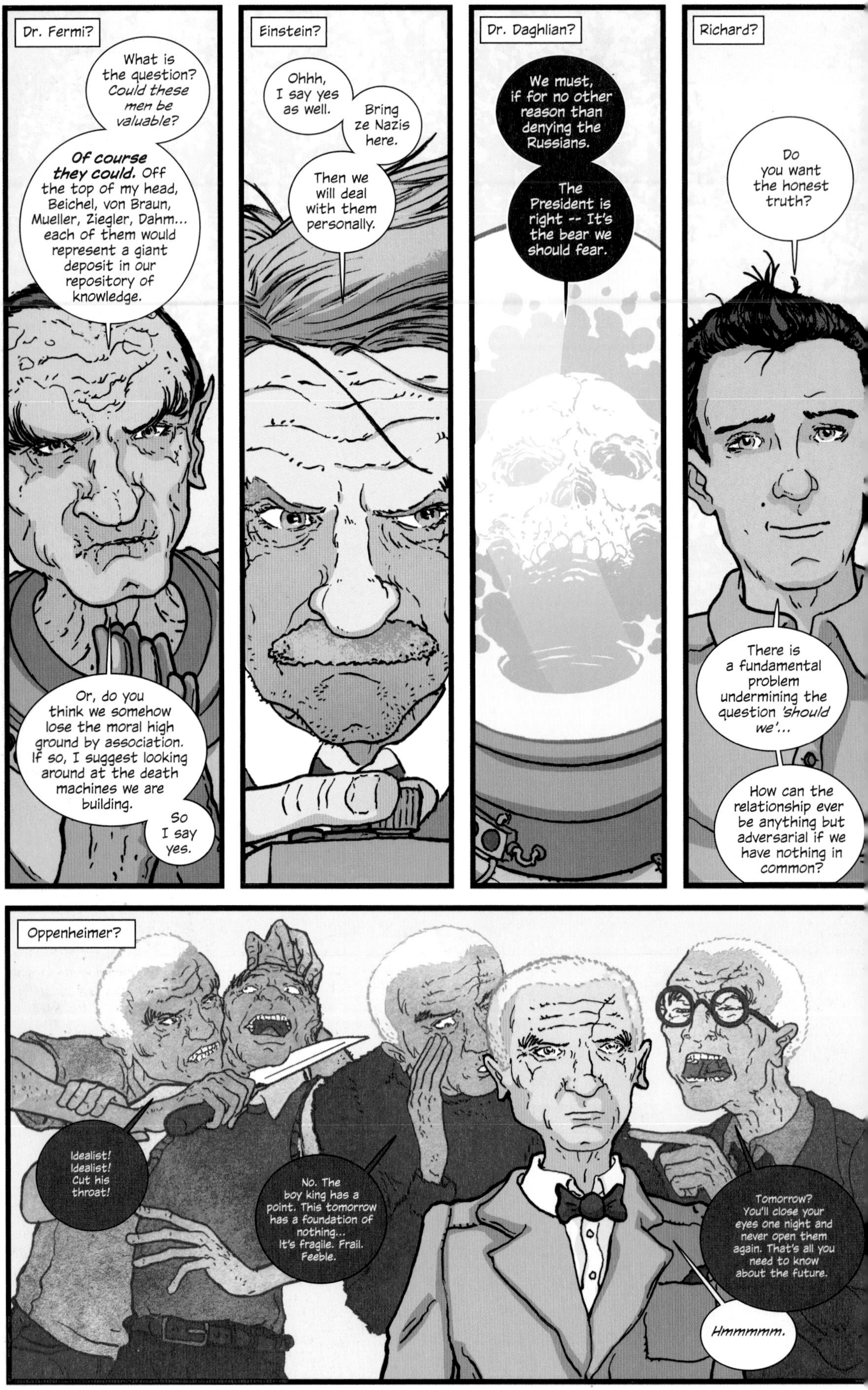
Dr. Fermi?
What is the question? *Could these men be valuable?*
Of course they could. Off the top of my head, Beichel, von Braun, Mueller, Ziegler, Dahm... each of them would represent a giant deposit in our repository of knowledge.
Or, do you think we somehow lose the moral high ground by association. If so, I suggest looking around at the death machines we are building.
So I say yes.
Einstein?
Ohhh, I say yes as well.
Bring ze Nazis here.
Then we will deal with them personally.
Dr. Daghlian?
We must, if for no other reason than denying the Russians.
The President is right -- It's the bear we should fear.
Richard?
Do you want the honest truth?
There is a fundamental problem undermining the question *'should we'*...
How can the relationship ever be anything but adversarial if we have nothing in common?
Oppenheimer?
Idealist! Idealist! Cut his throat!
No. The boy king has a point. This tomorrow has a foundation of nothing... It's fragile. Frail. Feeble.
Tomorrow? You'll close your eyes one night and never open them again. That's all you need to know about the future.
Hmmmmm.

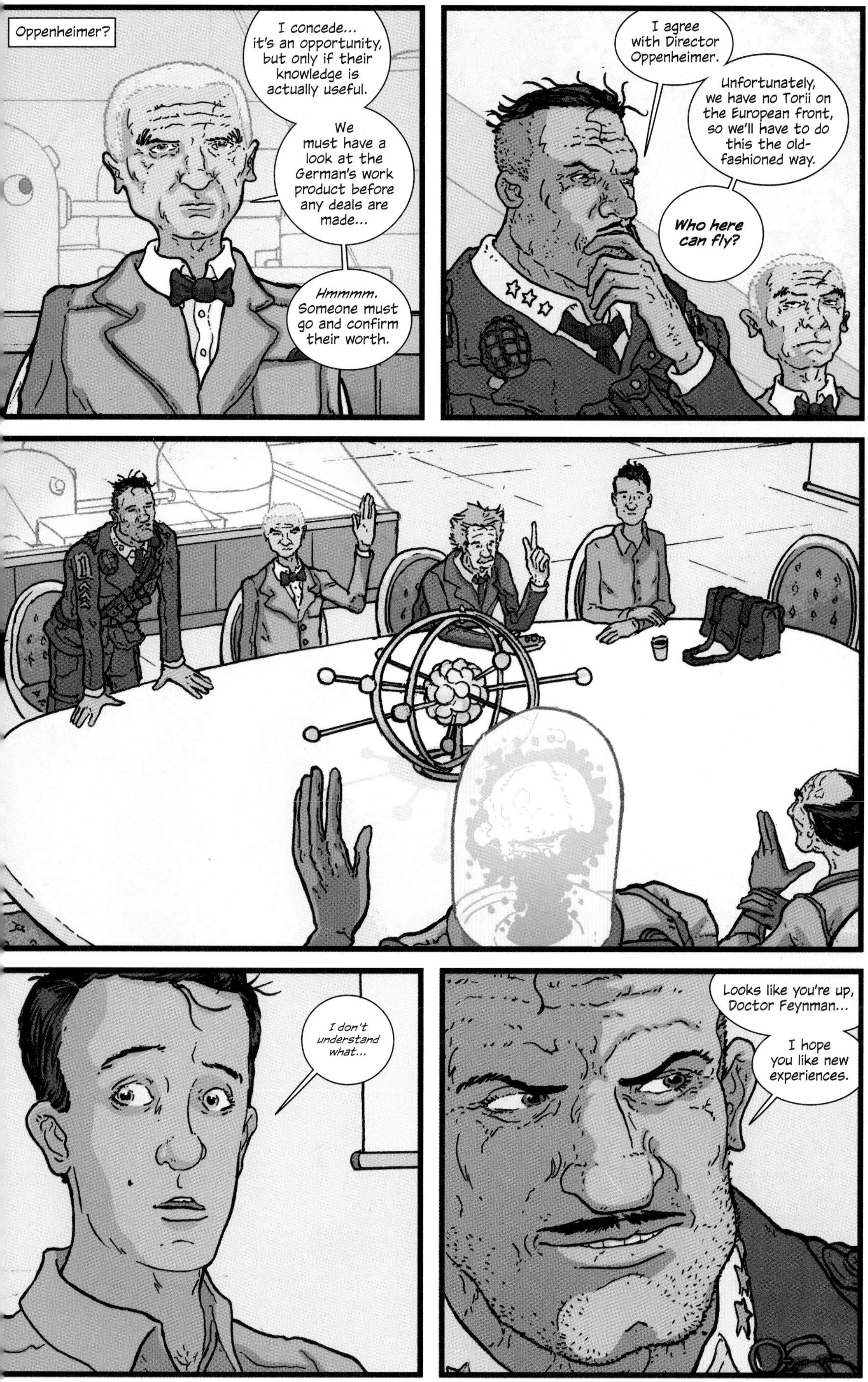
Oppenheimer?
I concede... it's an opportunity, but only if their knowledge is actually useful.
We must have a look at the German's work product before any deals are made...
Hmmmm. Someone must go and confirm their worth.
I agree with Director Oppenheimer.
Unfortunately, we have no Torii on the European front, so we'll have to do this the old-fashioned way.
Who here can fly?
I don't understand what...
Looks like you're up, Doctor Feynman...
I hope you like new experiences.

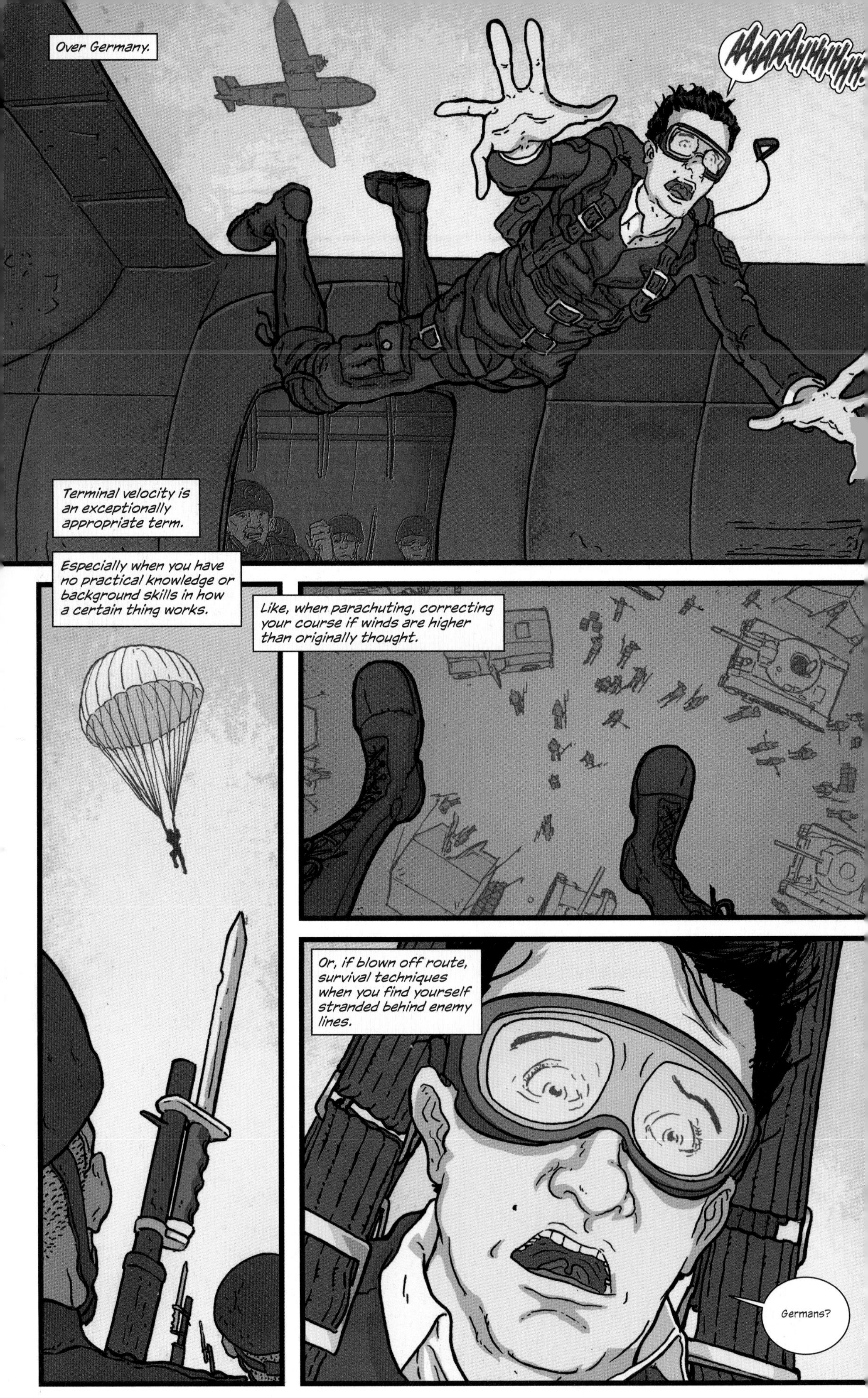
Over Germany.
AAAAAAHHHHH!
Terminal velocity is an exceptionally appropriate term.
Especially when you have no practical knowledge or background skills in how a certain thing works.
Like, when parachuting, correcting your course if winds are higher than originally thought.
Or, if blown off route, survival techniques when you find yourself stranded behind enemy lines.
Germans?

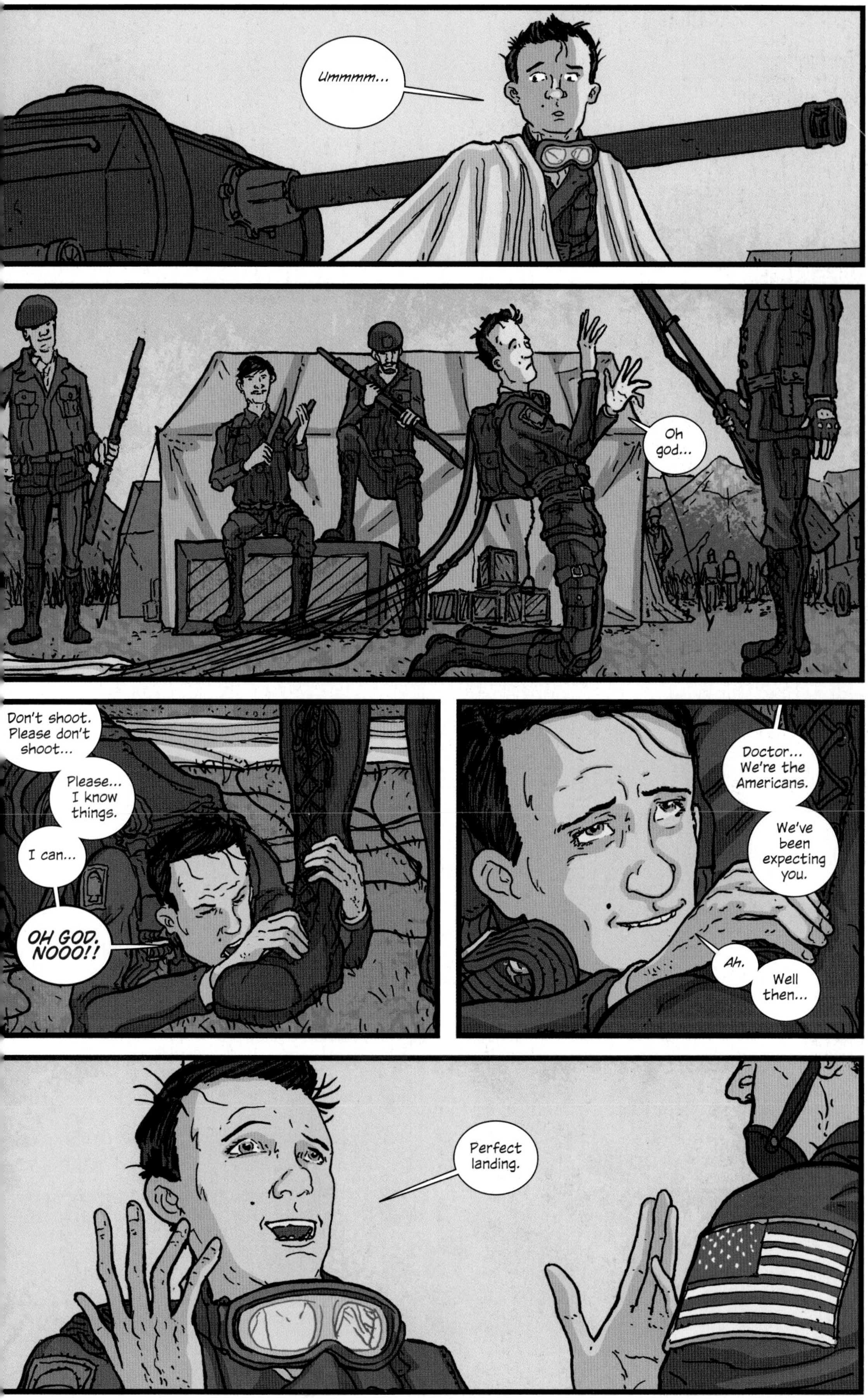
Ummmm...
Oh god...
Don't shoot. Please don't shoot...
Please... I know things.
I can...
OH GOD. NOOO!!
Doctor... We're the Americans.
We've been expecting you.
Ah.
Well then...
Perfect landing.

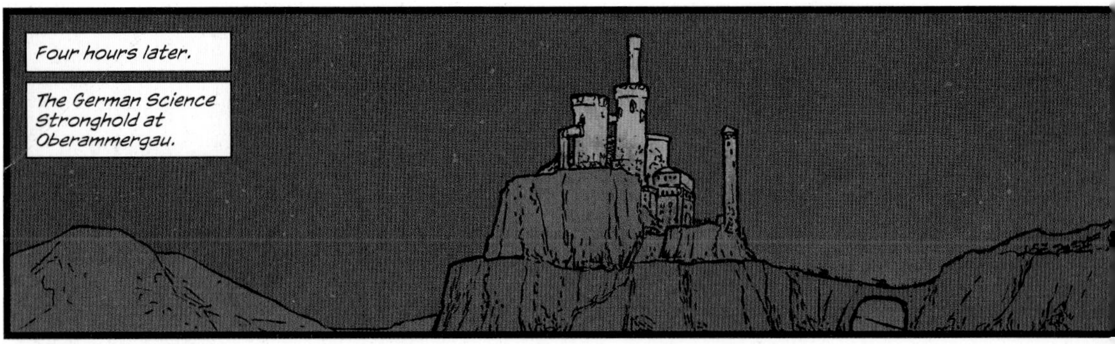
Four hours later.
The German Science Stronghold at Oberammergau.

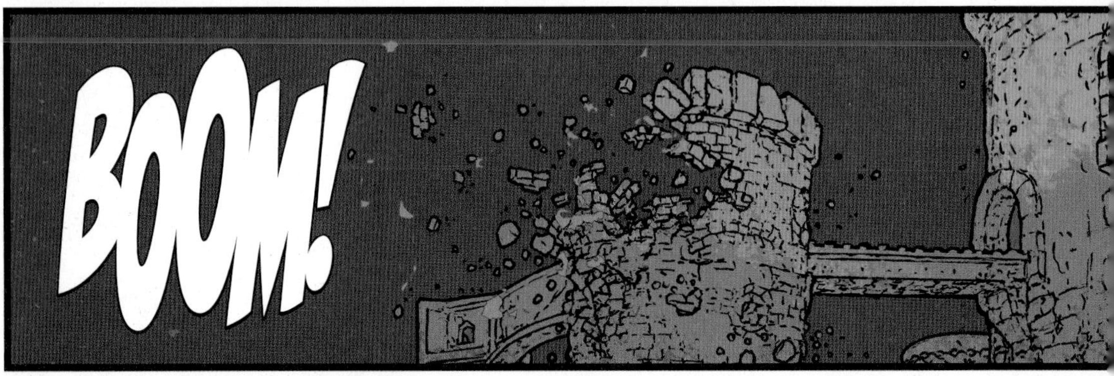
BOOM!

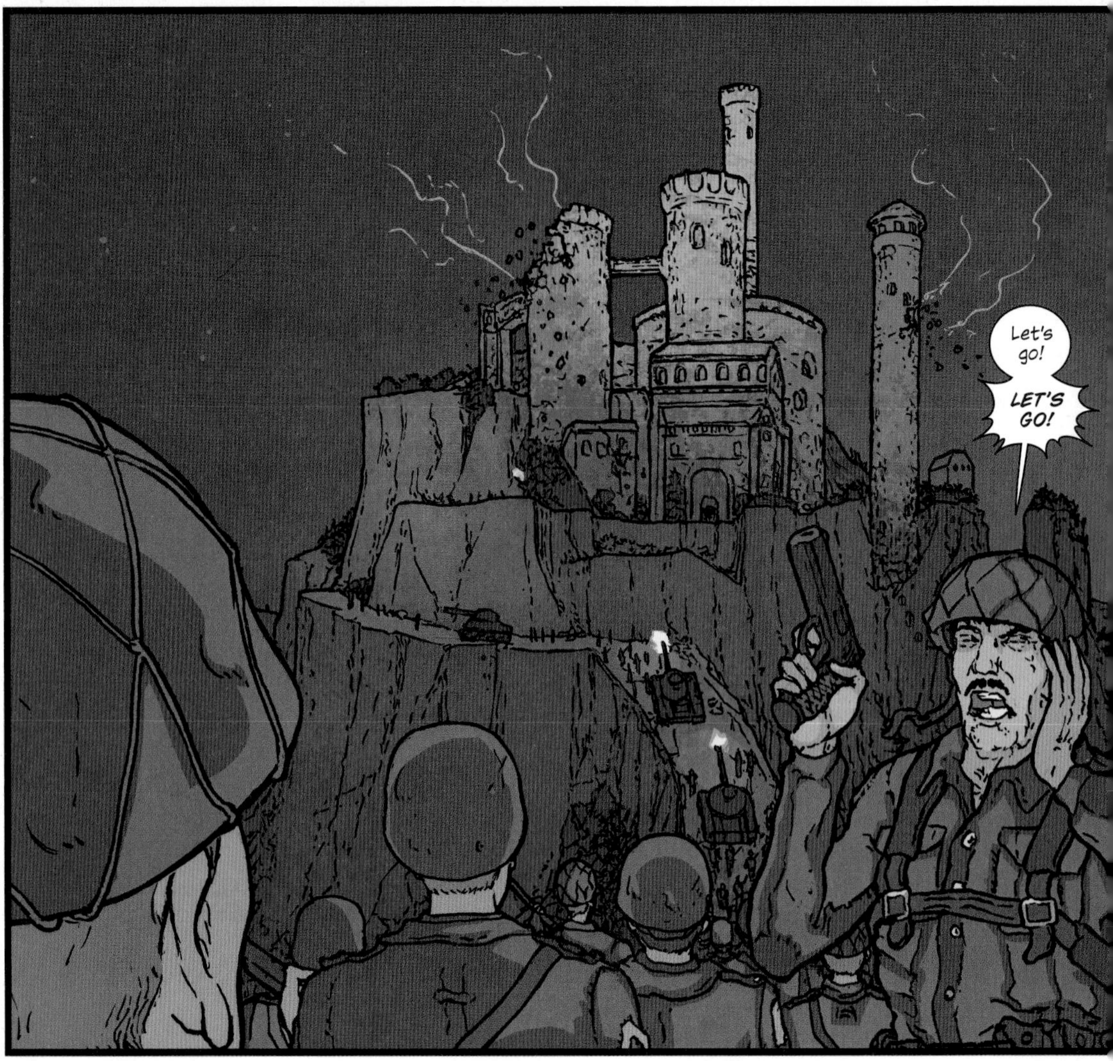
Let's go!
LET'S GO!

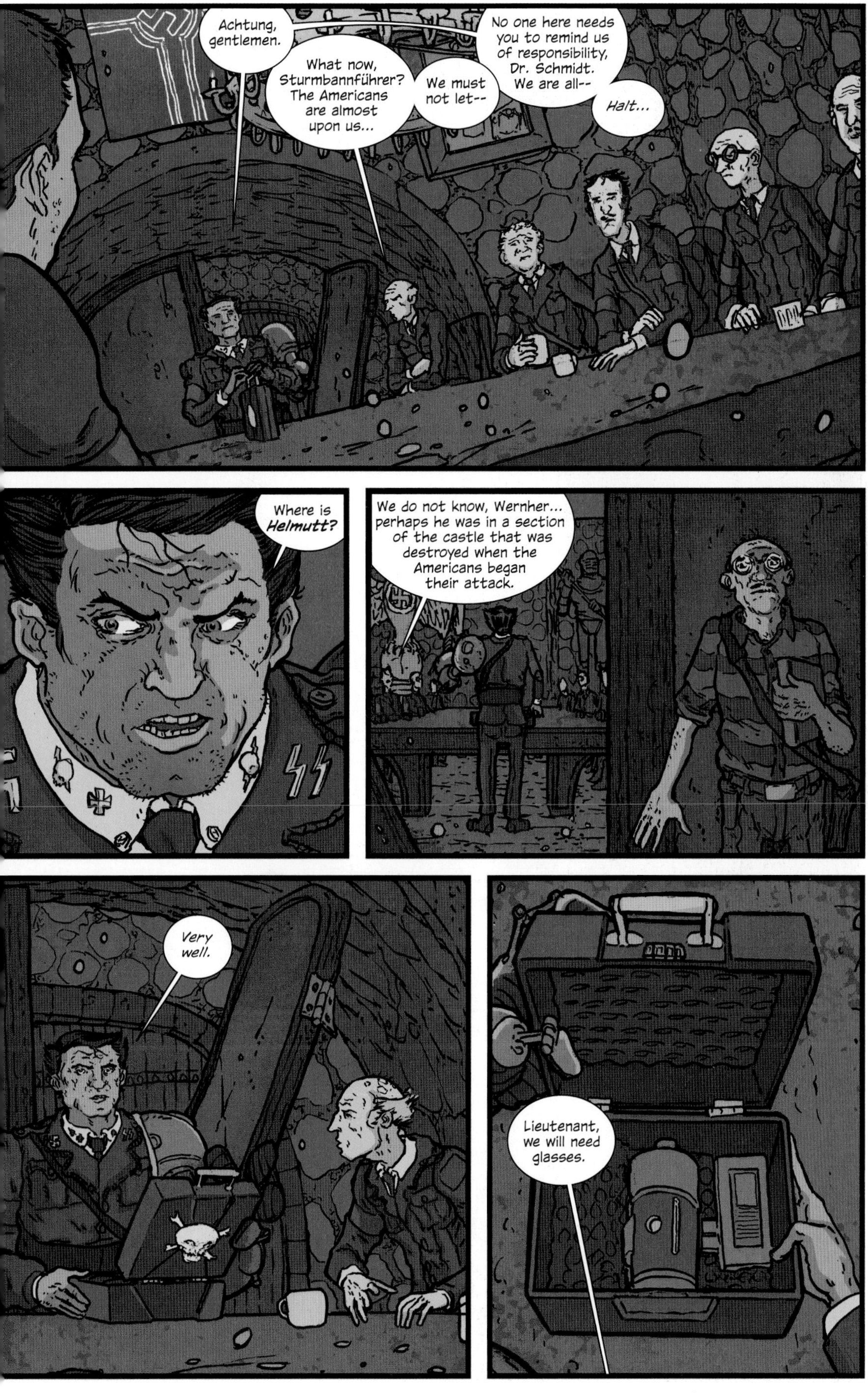

Achtung, gentlemen.
What now, Sturmbannführer? The Americans are almost upon us...
We must not let--
No one here needs you to remind us of responsibility, Dr. Schmidt. We are all--
Halt...
Where is ***Helmutt?***
We do not know, Wernher... perhaps he was in a section of the castle that was destroyed when the Americans began their attack.
Very well.
Lieutenant, we will need glasses.

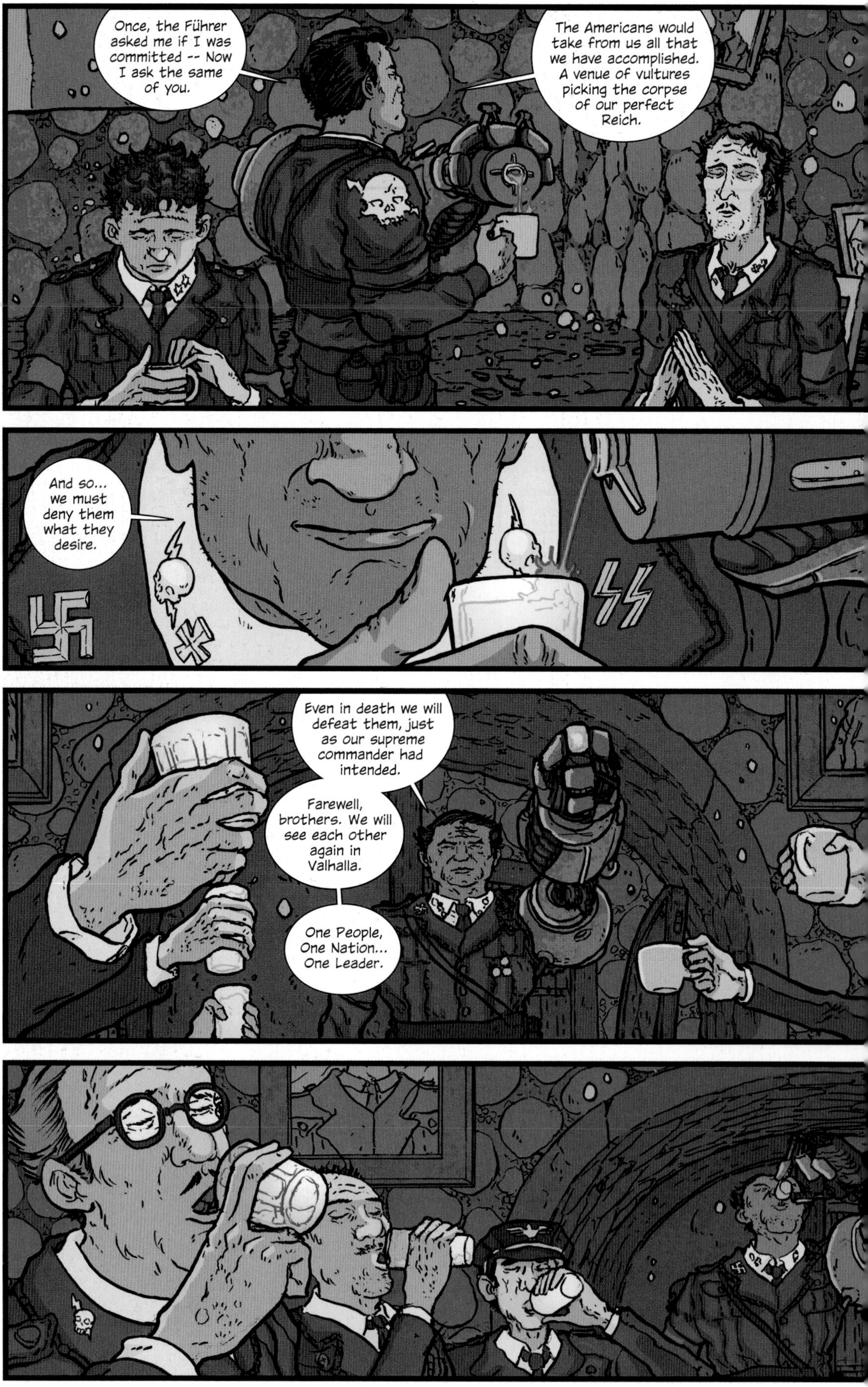

Once, the Führer asked me if I was committed -- Now I ask the same of you.
The Americans would take from us all that we have accomplished. A venue of vultures picking the corpse of our perfect Reich.
And so... we must deny them what they desire.
Even in death we will defeat them, just as our supreme commander had intended.
Farewell, brothers. We will see each other again in Valhalla.
One People, One Nation... One Leader.

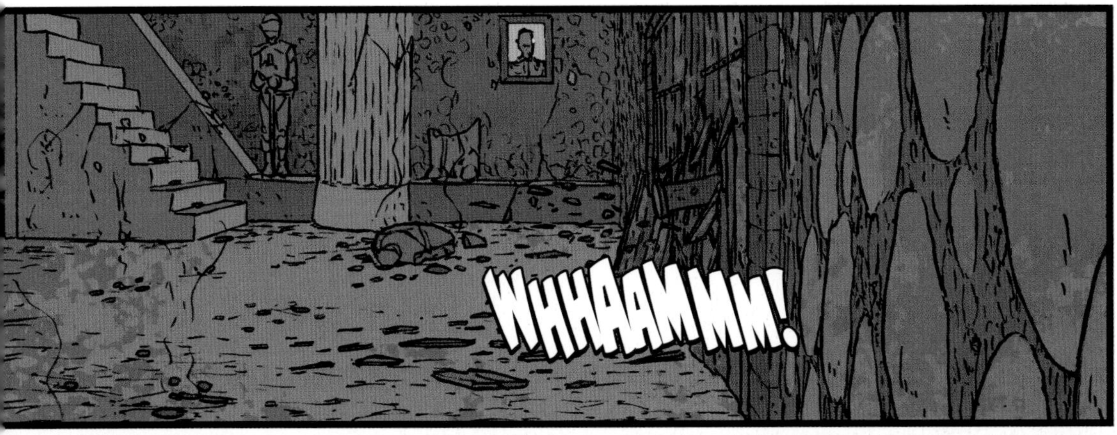
WHHAAMMMM!

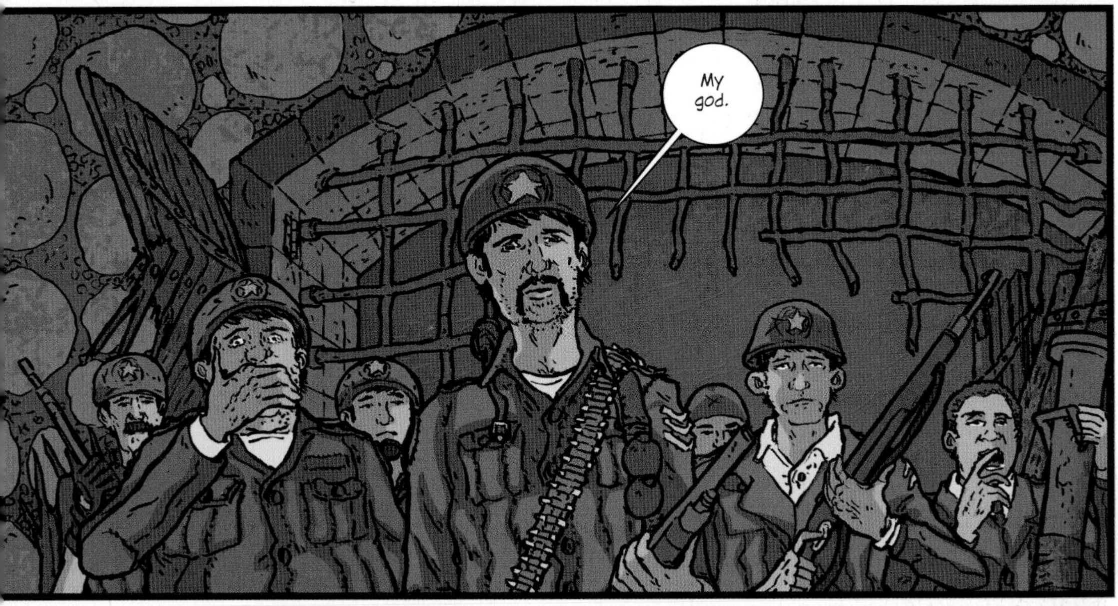
My god.

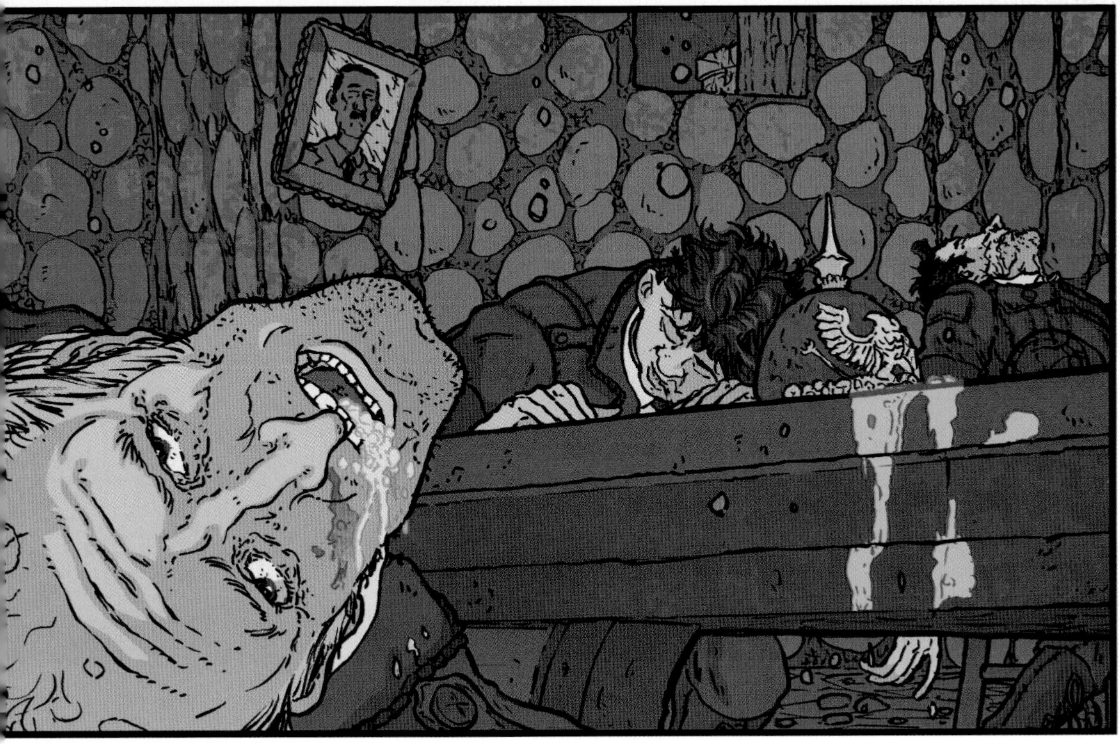

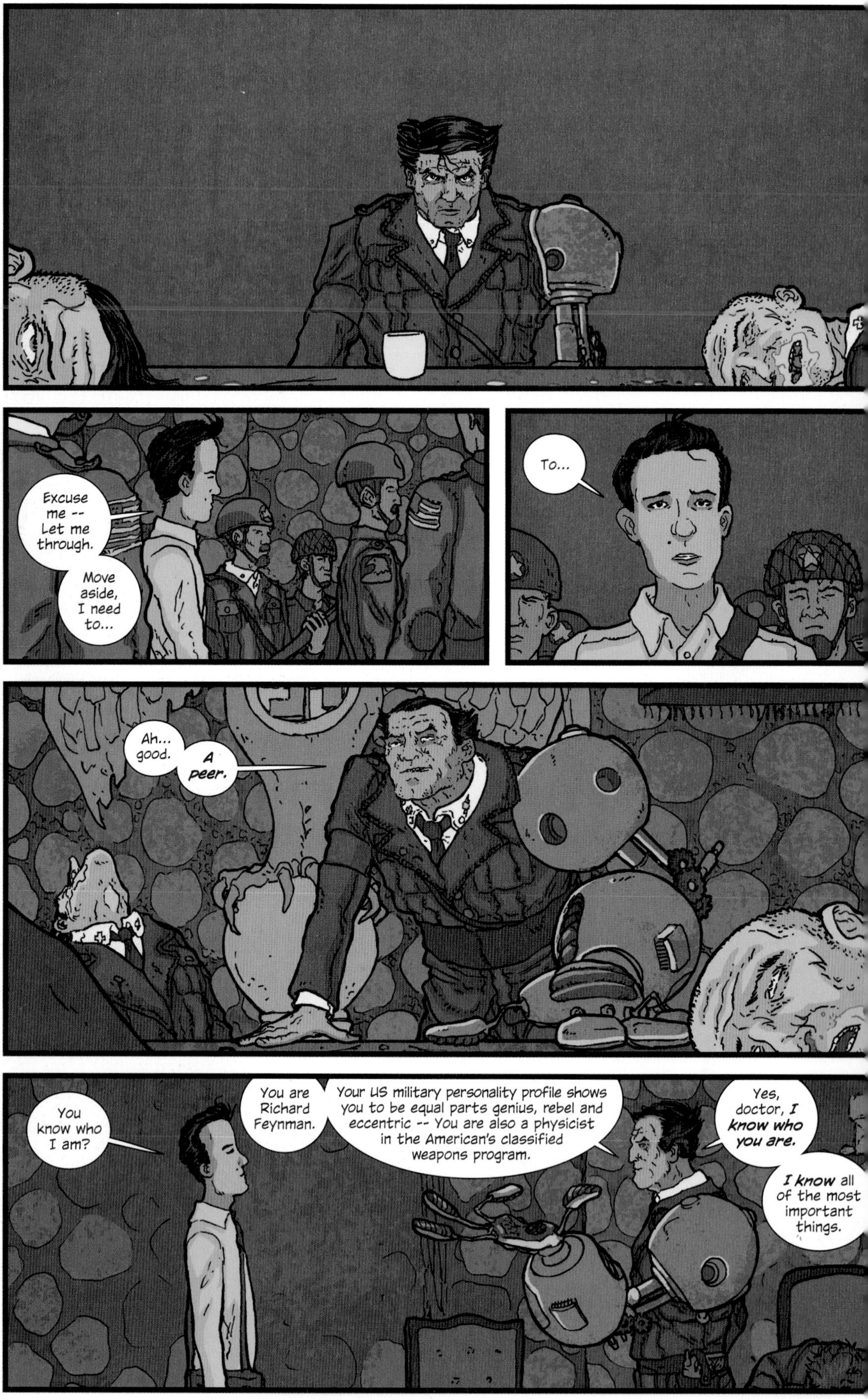

Excuse me -- Let me through.
Move aside, I need to...
To...
Ah... good.
A peer.
You know who I am?
You are Richard Feynman.
Your US military personality profile shows you to be equal parts genius, rebel and eccentric -- You are also a physicist in the American's classified weapons program.
Yes, doctor, I know who you are.
I know all of the most important things.

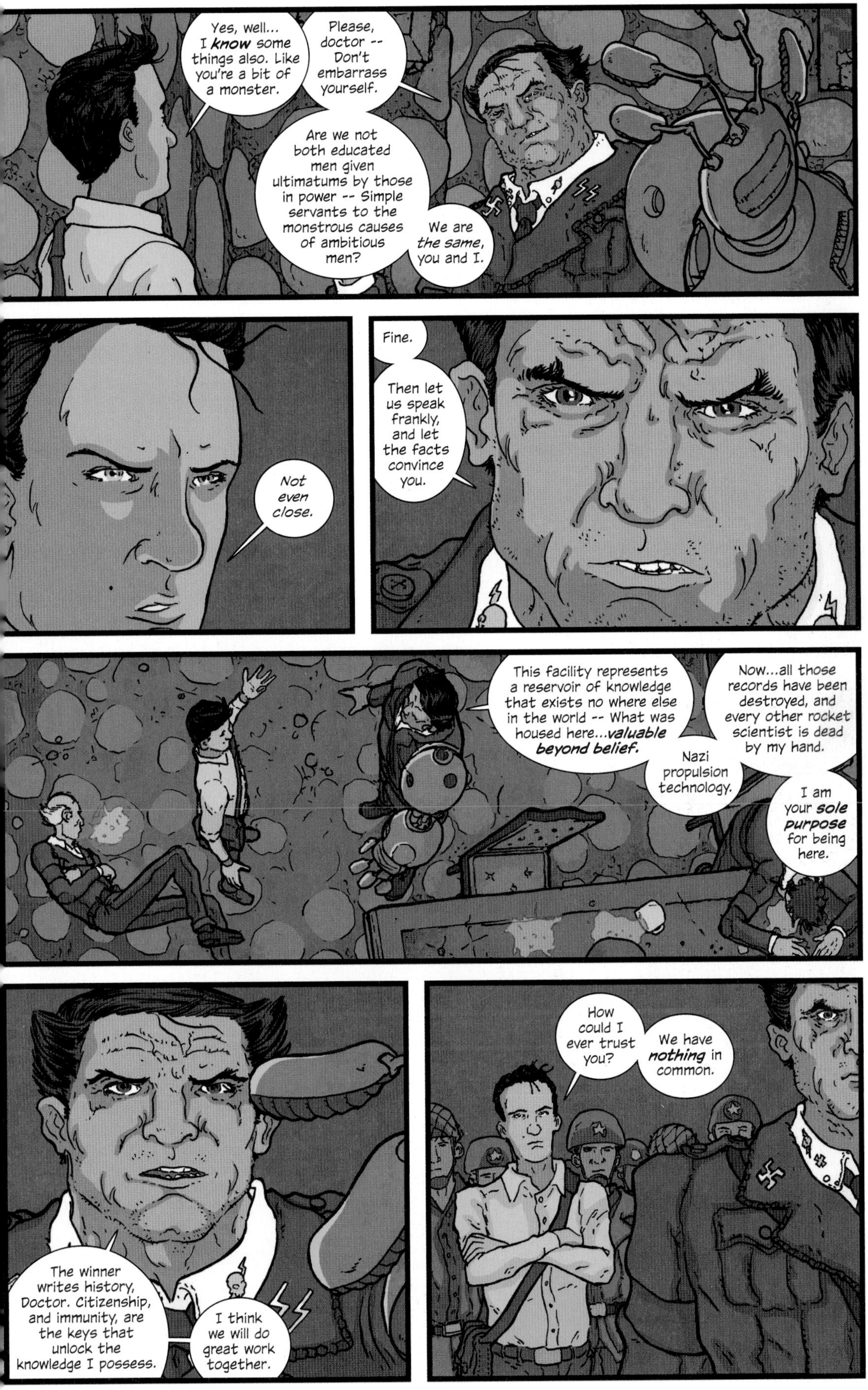
Yes, well... I *know* some things also. Like you're a bit of a monster.
Please, doctor -- Don't embarrass yourself.
Are we not both educated men given ultimatums by those in power -- Simple servants to the monstrous causes of ambitious men?
We are *the same,* you and I.
Not even close.
Fine.
Then let us speak frankly, and let the facts convince you.
This facility represents a reservoir of knowledge that exists no where else in the world -- What was housed here...***valuable beyond belief.***
Nazi propulsion technology.
Now...all those records have been destroyed, and every other rocket scientist is dead by my hand.
I am your ***sole purpose*** for being here.
The winner writes history, Doctor. Citizenship, and immunity, are the keys that unlock the knowledge I possess.
I think we will do great work together.
How could I ever trust you?
We have ***nothing*** in common.

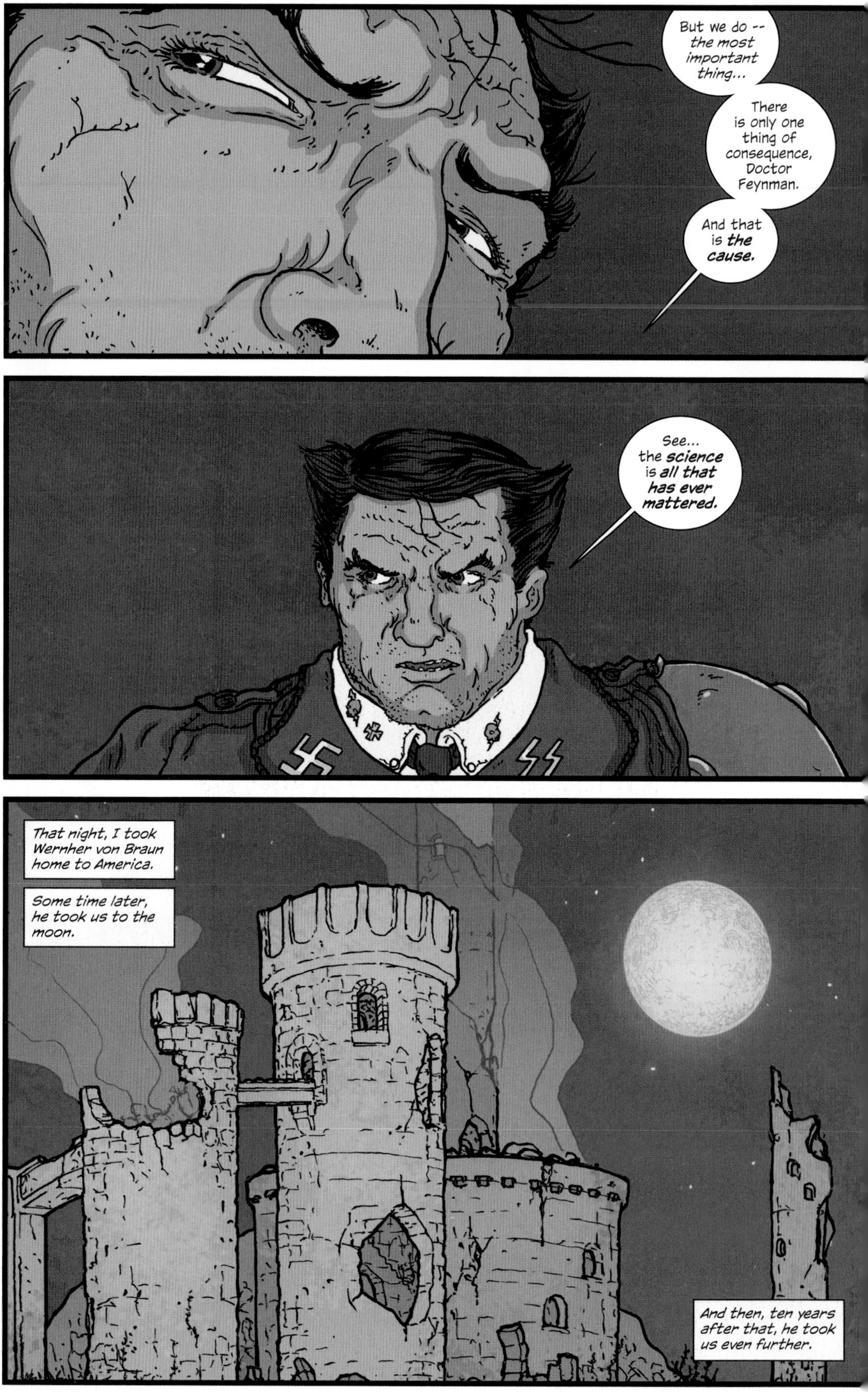
But we do -- *the most important thing...*
There is only one thing of consequence, Doctor Feynman.
And that is ***the cause.***
See... the ***science*** is ***all that has ever mattered.***
That night, I took Wernher von Braun home to America.
Some time later, he took us to the moon.
And then, ten years after that, he took us even further.

"THE EXPLORATORY, FOREVER-CLASS FRIGATE, UTDF VON BRAUN, LEFT THE SOLAR SYSTEM IN THE YEAR 1997.

IT NEVER RETURNED."

CLAVIS AUREA
THE RECORDED FEYNMAN | **VOL. 3**

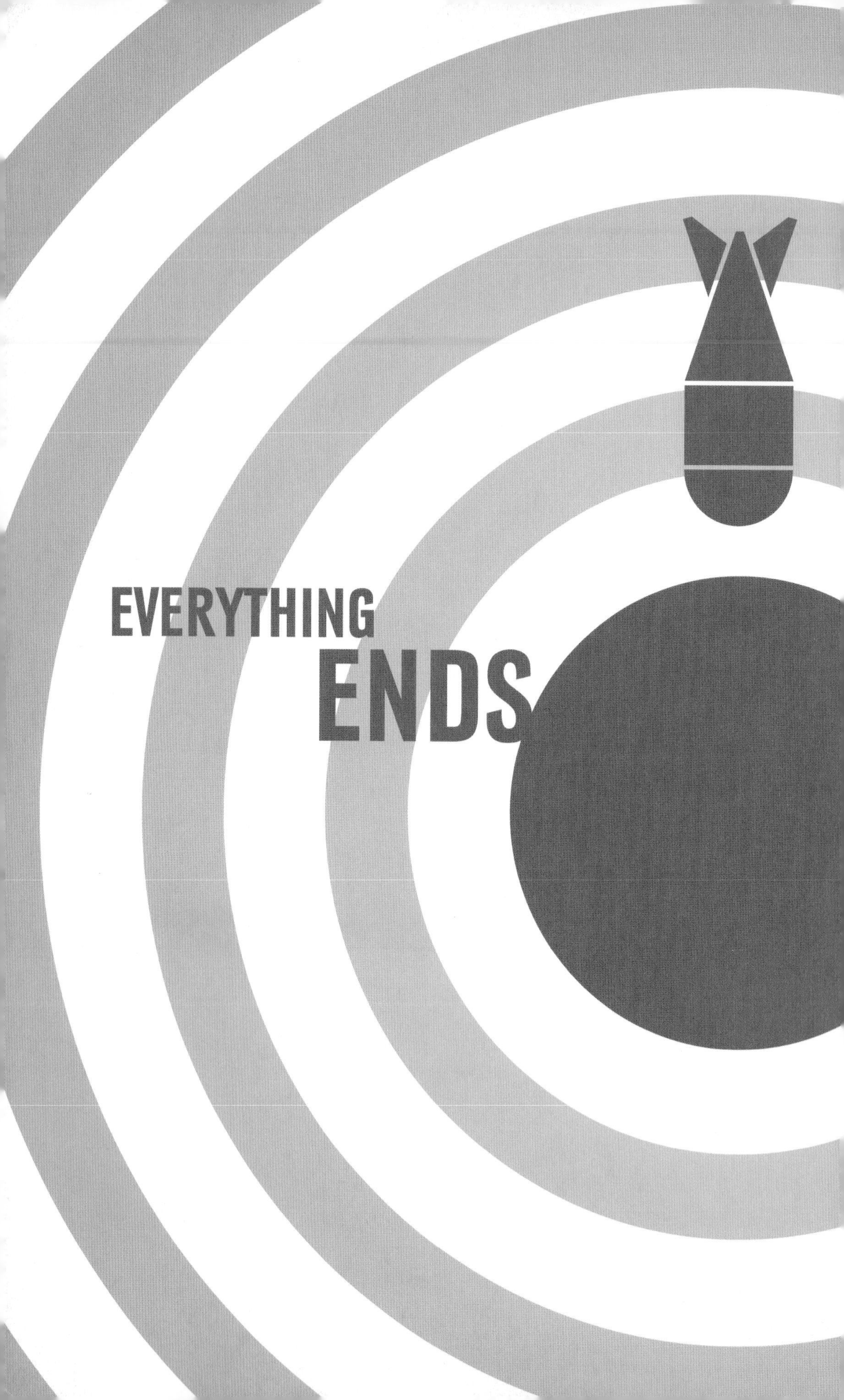
EVERYTHING
ENDS

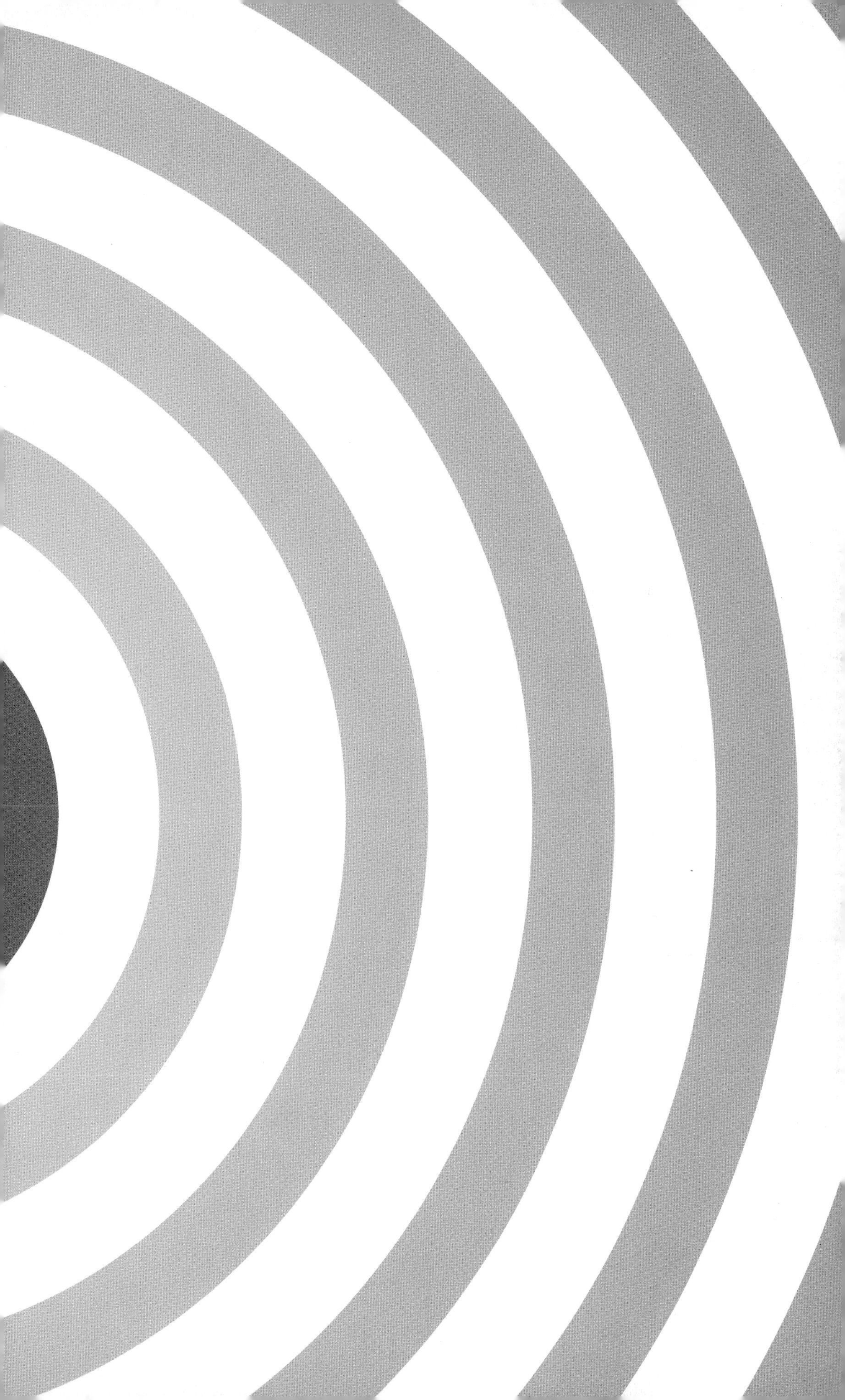

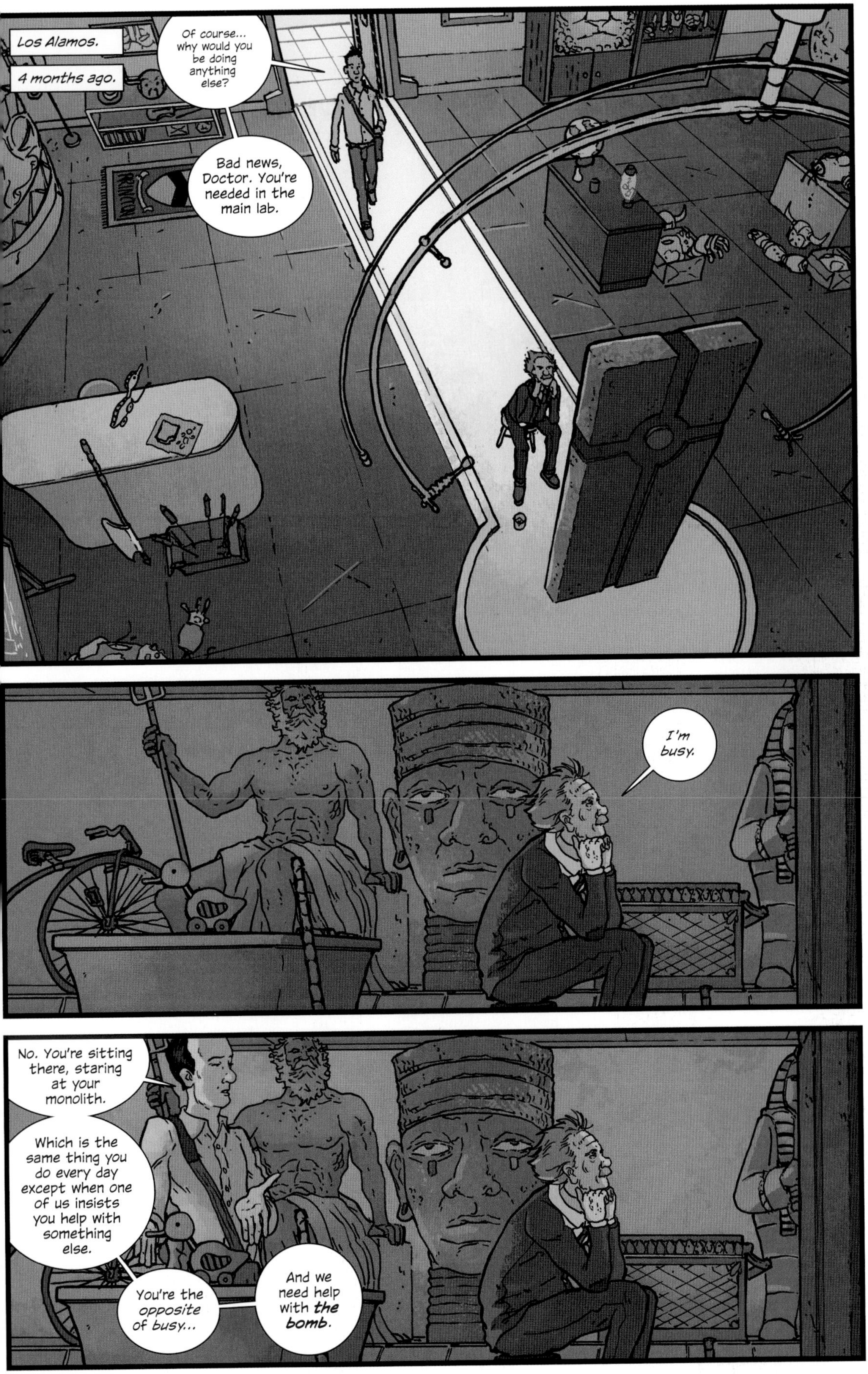
Los Alamos.
4 months ago.
Of course... why would you be doing anything else?
Bad news, Doctor. You're needed in the main lab.
I'm busy.
No. You're sitting there, staring at your monolith.
Which is the same thing you do every day except when one of us insists you help with something else.
You're the *opposite* of busy...
And we need help with ***the bomb***.

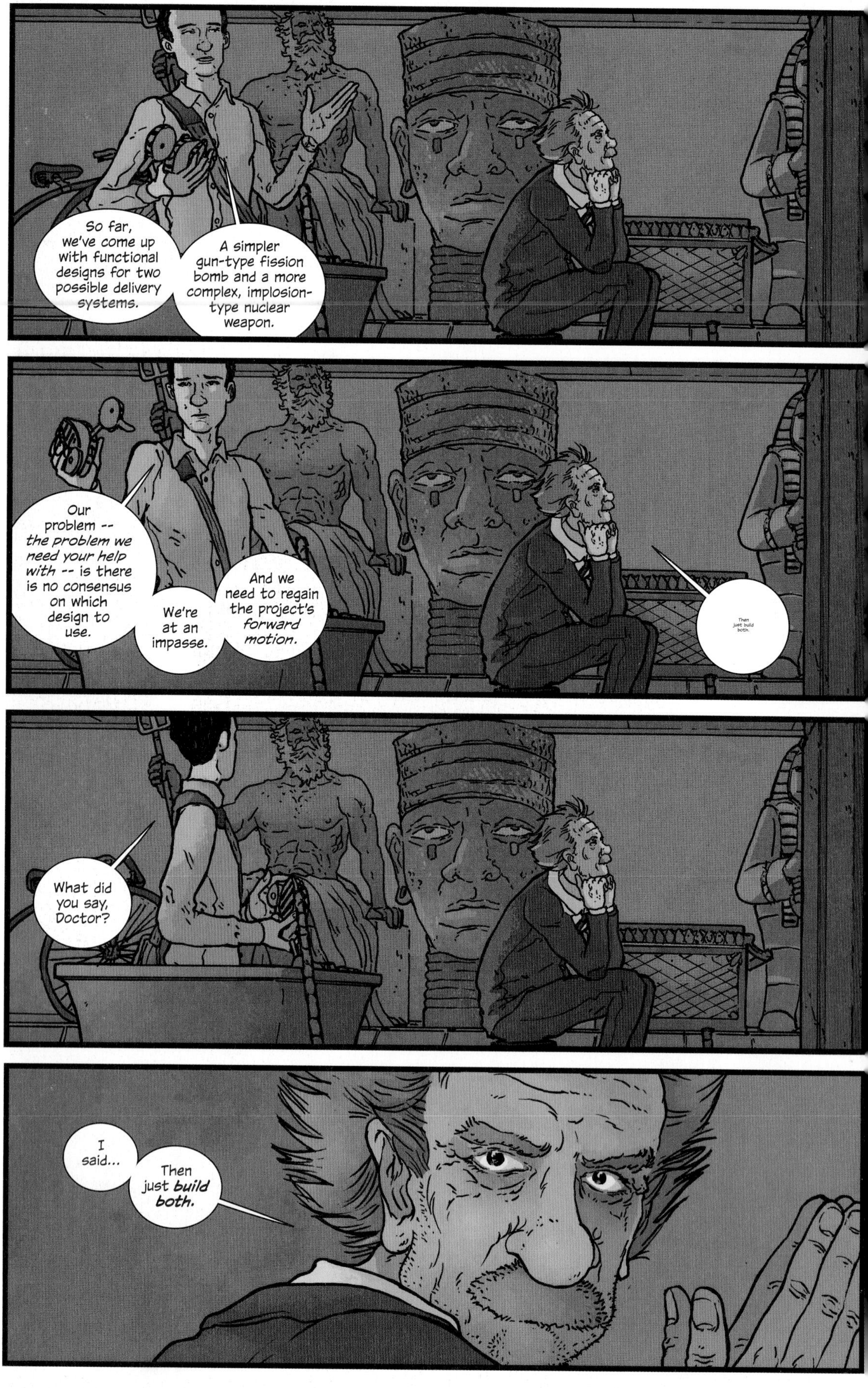
So far, we've come up with functional designs for two possible delivery systems.
A simpler gun-type fission bomb and a more complex, implosion-type nuclear weapon.
Our problem -- *the problem we need your help with* -- is there is no consensus on which design to use.
We're at an impasse.
And we need to regain the project's *forward motion.*
Then just build both.
What did you say, Doctor?
I said...
Then just ***build both.***

"THE BOMB MADE US RECKLESS. IT MADE US ARROGANT. IT MADE US STOP BELIEVING IN THE POSSIBILITY THAT ANYTHING COULD BE DONE.

INSTEAD, WE KNEW IT."

CLAVIS AUREA
THE RECORDED FEYNMAN

VOL. 1

03

THE
BOMB

"WHAT AM I GUILTY OF?

AN INTIMATE FAMILIARITY WITH THE NECESSITY OF FICTION. TRUTH IS MY WIFE, BUT LIES ARE MY MISTRESS. "

CLAVIS AUREA
THE RECORDED FEYNMAN | **VOL. 4**

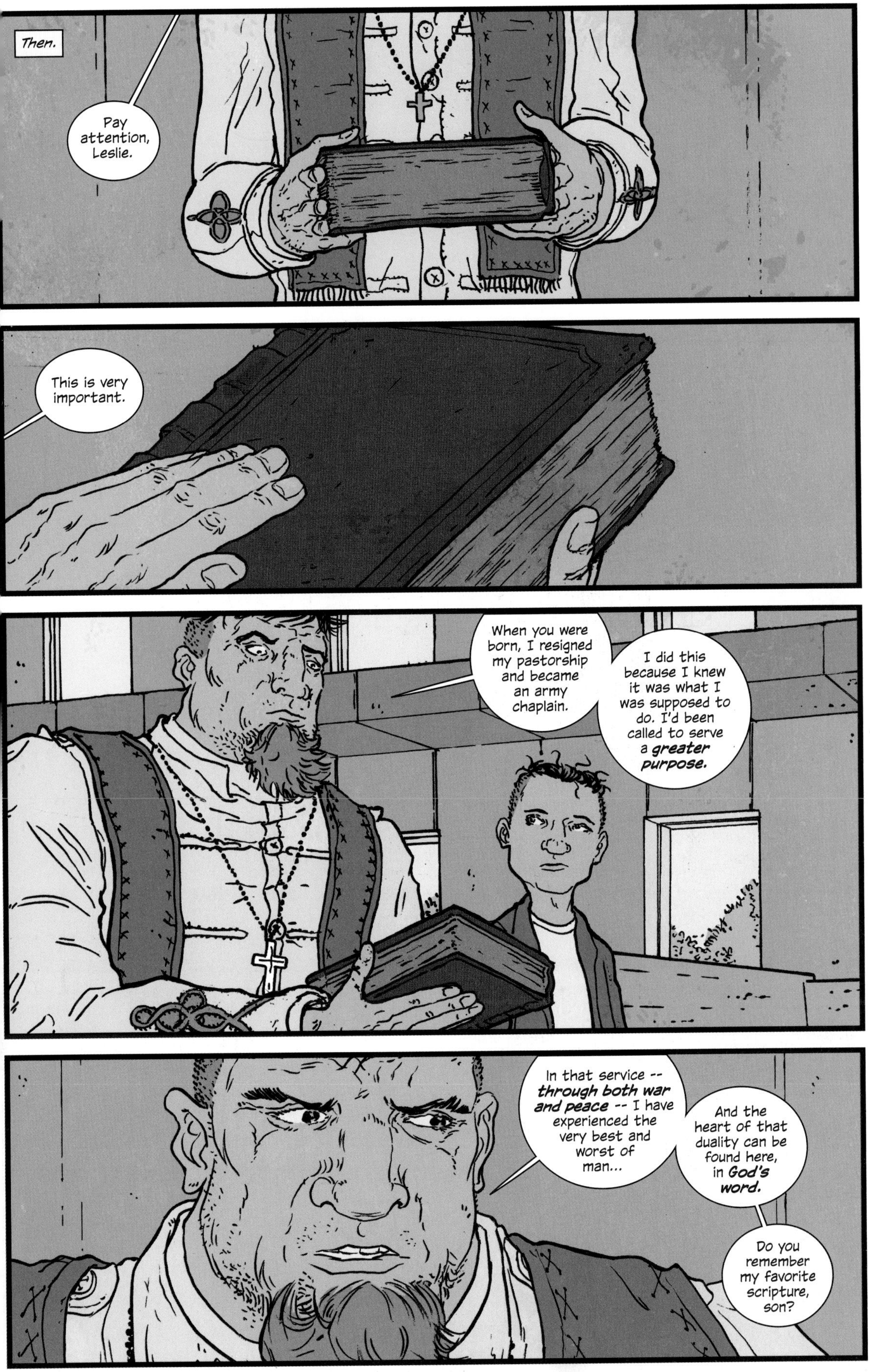
Then.
Pay attention, Leslie.
This is very important.
When you were born, I resigned my pastorship and became an army chaplain.
I did this because I knew it was what I was supposed to do. I'd been called to serve a **greater purpose.**
In that service -- ***through both war and peace*** -- I have experienced the very best and worst of man...
And the heart of that duality can be found here, in ***God's word.***
Do you remember my favorite scripture, son?

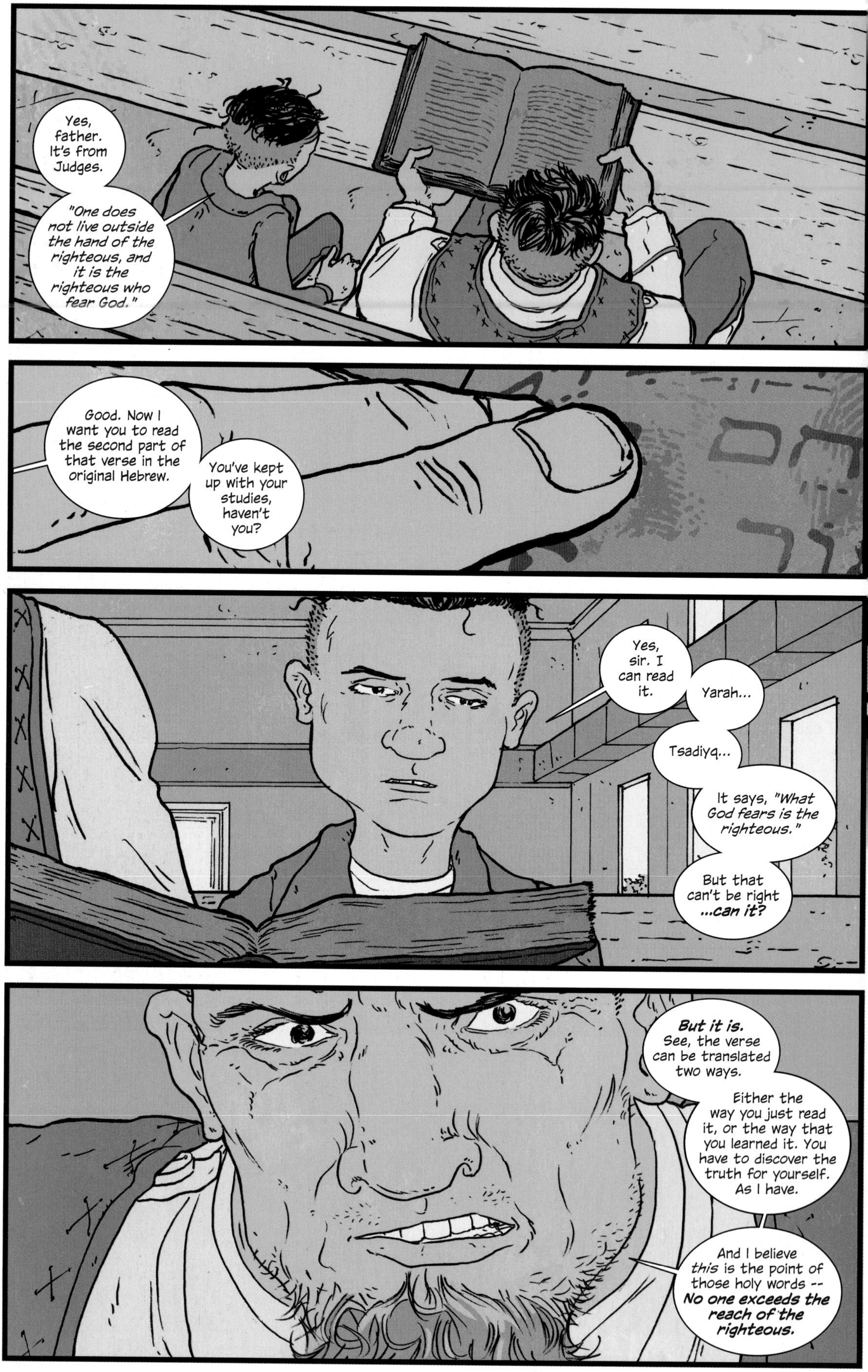
Yes, father. It's from Judges.
"One does not live outside the hand of the righteous, and it is the righteous who fear God."
Good. Now I want you to read the second part of that verse in the original Hebrew.
You've kept up with your studies, haven't you?
Yes, sir. I can read it.
Yarah...
Tsadiyq...
It says, "What God fears is the righteous."
But that can't be right ...can it?
But it is. See, the verse can be translated two ways.
Either the way you just read it, or the way that you learned it. You have to discover the truth for yourself. As I have.
And I believe this is the point of those holy words -- No one exceeds the reach of the righteous.

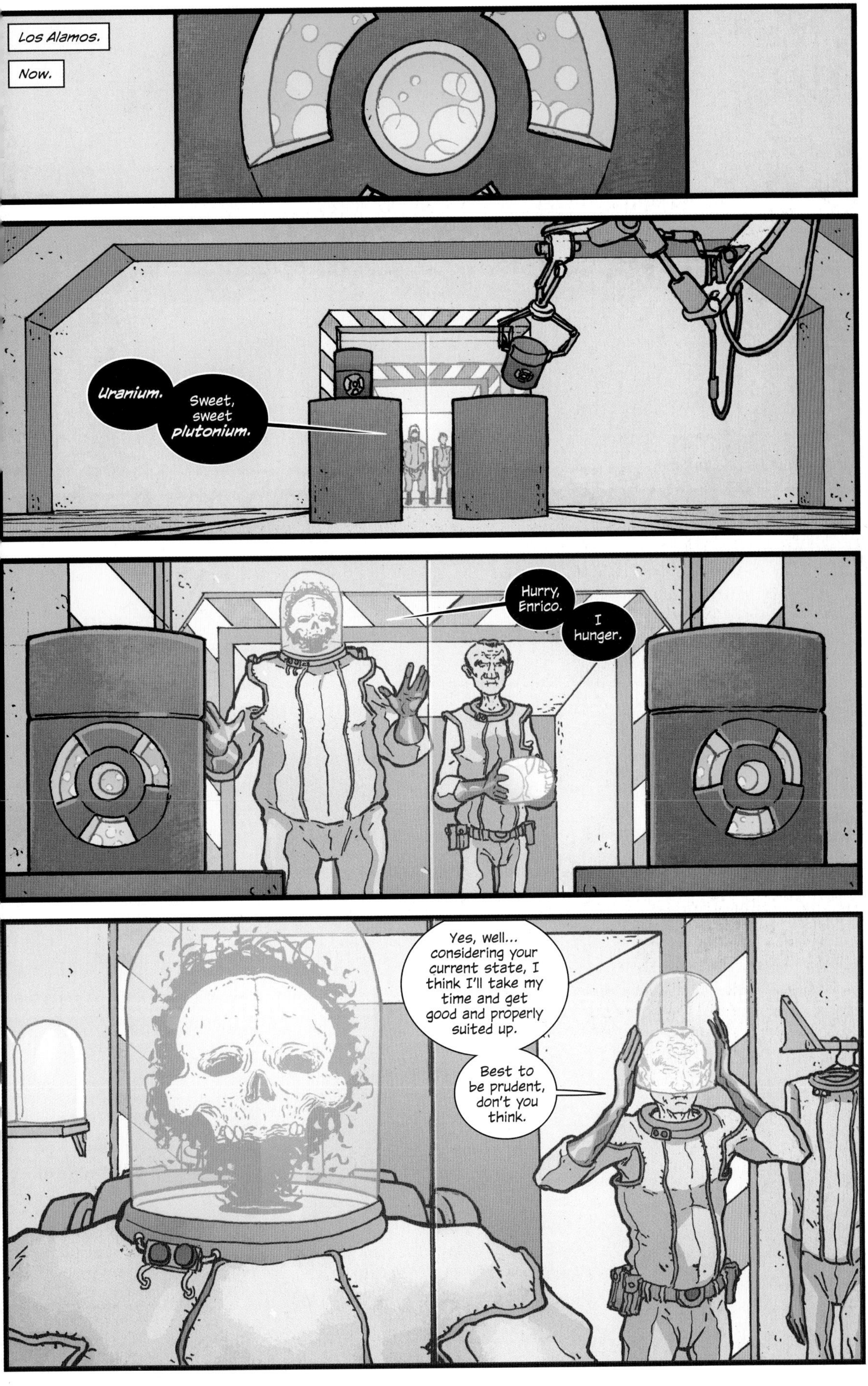

Los Alamos.
Now.
Uranium.
Sweet, sweet plutonium.
Hurry, Enrico.
I hunger.
Yes, well... considering your current state, I think I'll take my time and get good and properly suited up.
Best to be prudent, don't you think.

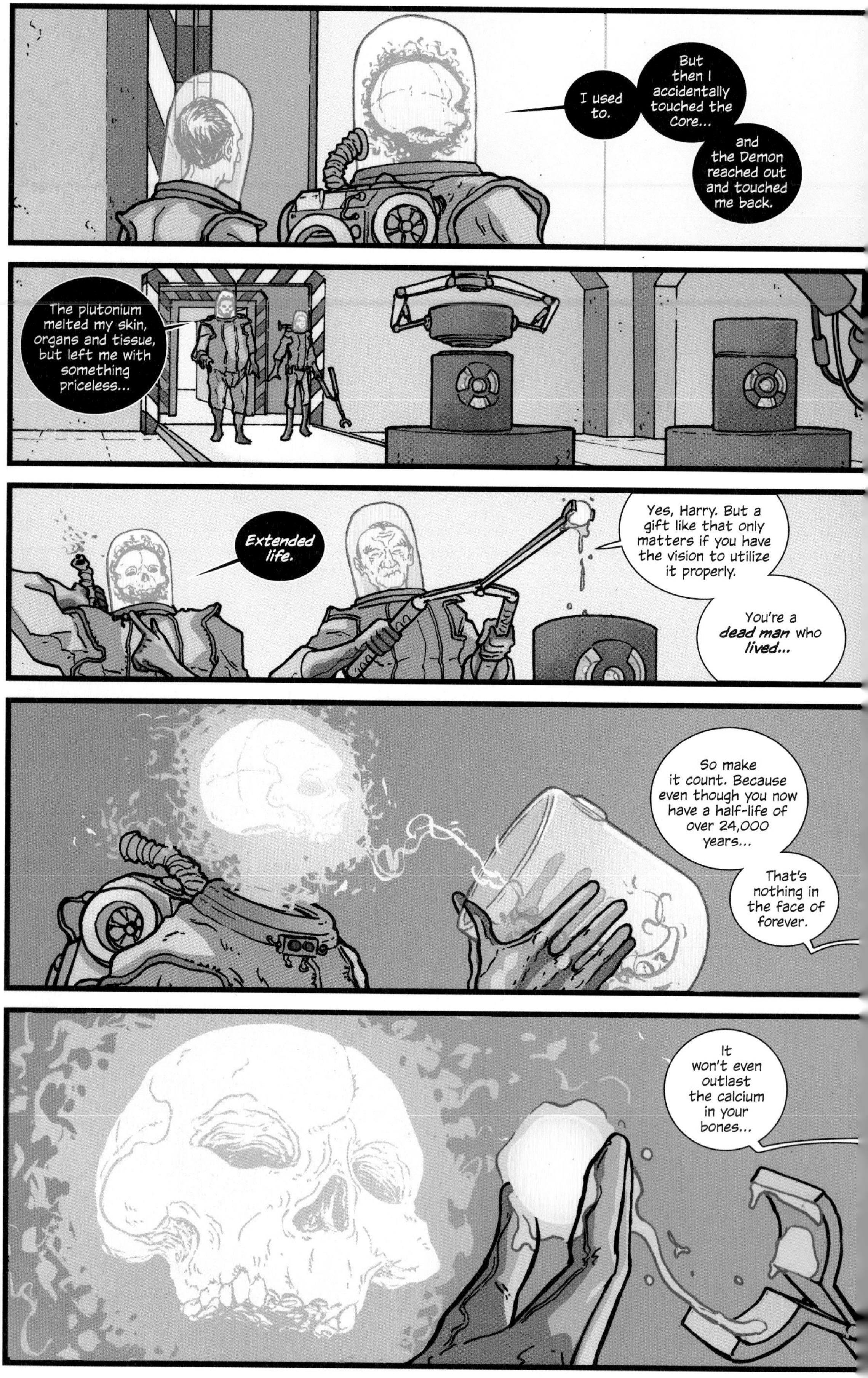

I used to.
But then I accidentally touched the Core...
and the Demon reached out and touched me back.
The plutonium melted my skin, organs and tissue, but left me with something priceless...
Extended life.
Yes, Harry. But a gift like that only matters if you have the vision to utilize it properly.
You're a dead man who lived...
So make it count. Because even though you now have a half-life of over 24,000 years...
That's nothing in the face of forever.
It won't even outlast the calcium in your bones...

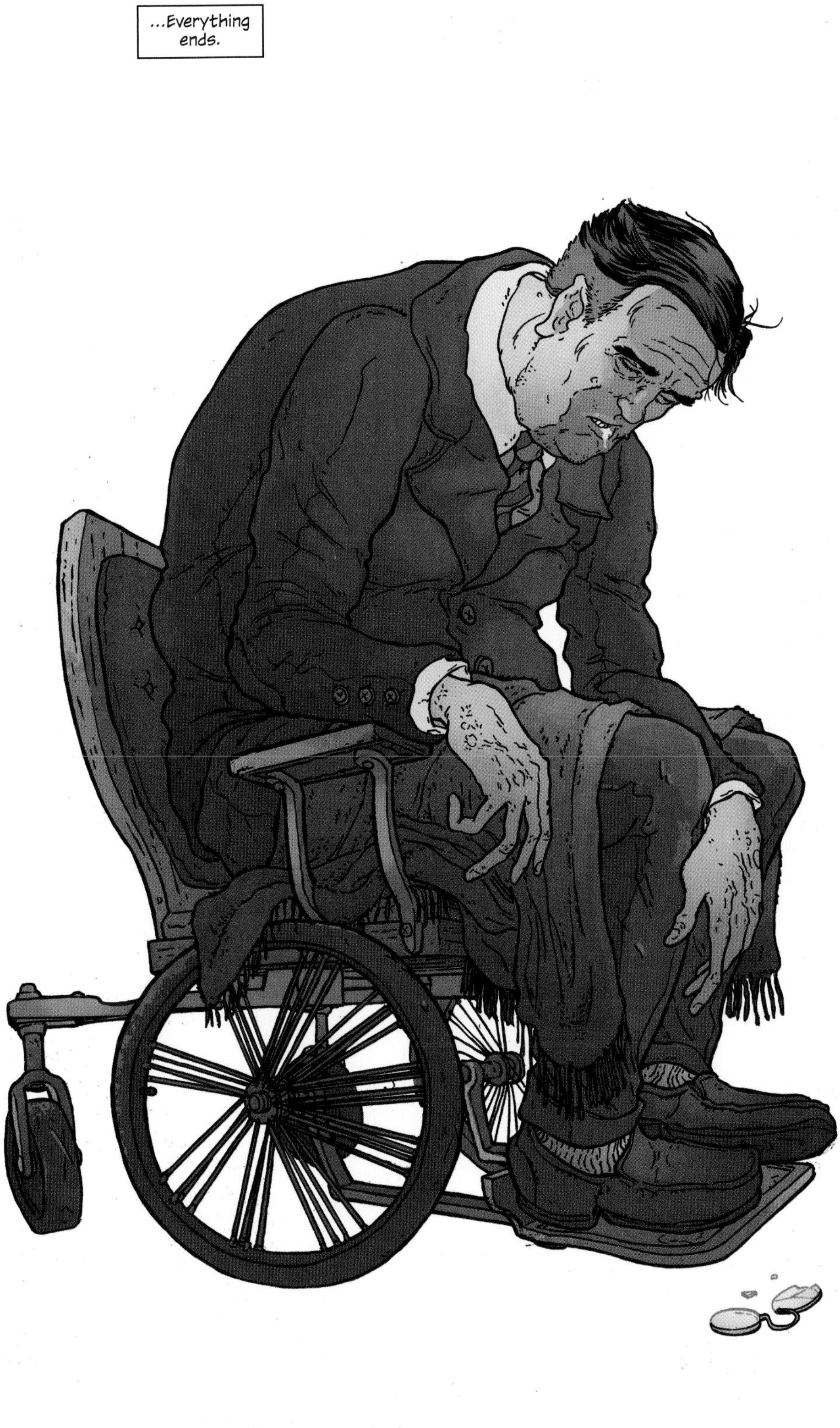
...Everything ends.

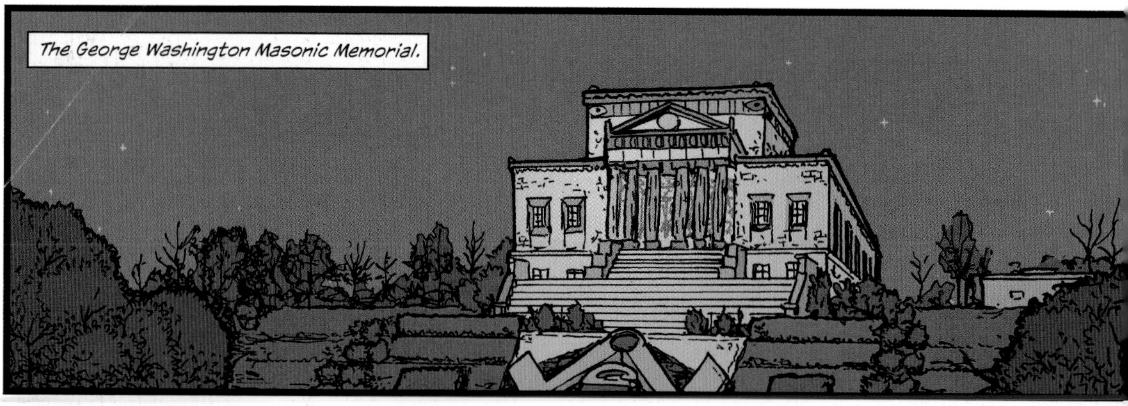
The George Washington Masonic Memorial.

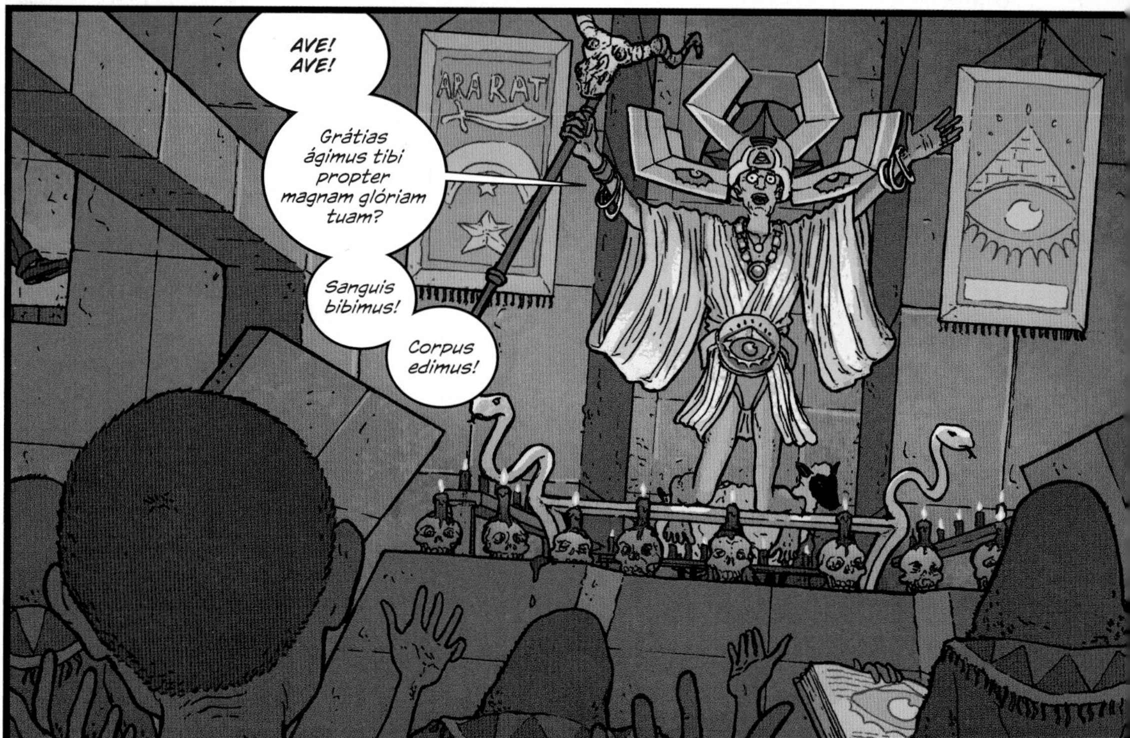
AVE! AVE!
Grátias ágimus tibi propter magnam glóriam tuam?
Sanguis bibimus!
Corpus edimus!
ARARAT

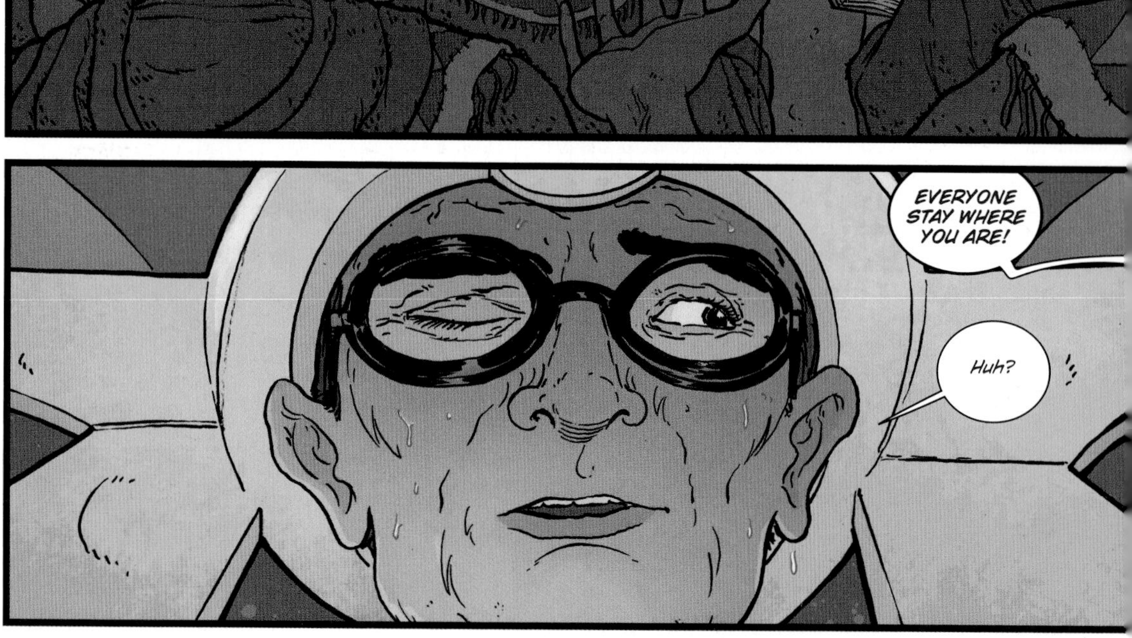
EVERYONE STAY WHERE YOU ARE!
Huh?

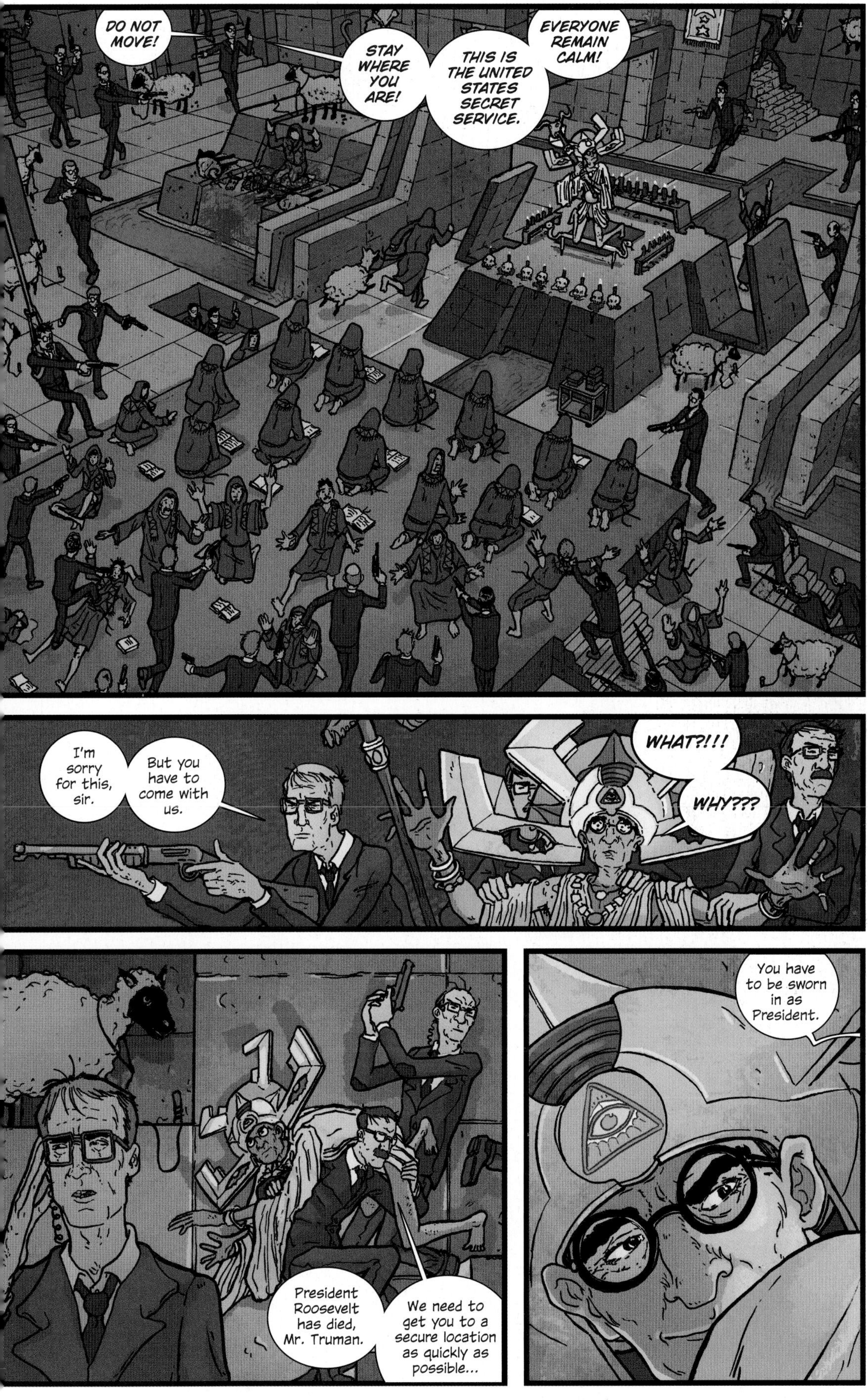
DO NOT MOVE!
STAY WHERE YOU ARE!
THIS IS THE UNITED STATES SECRET SERVICE.
EVERYONE REMAIN CALM!
I'm sorry for this, sir.
But you have to come with us.
WHAT?!!!
WHY???
President Roosevelt has died, Mr. Truman.
We need to get you to a secure location as quickly as possible...
You have to be sworn in as President.

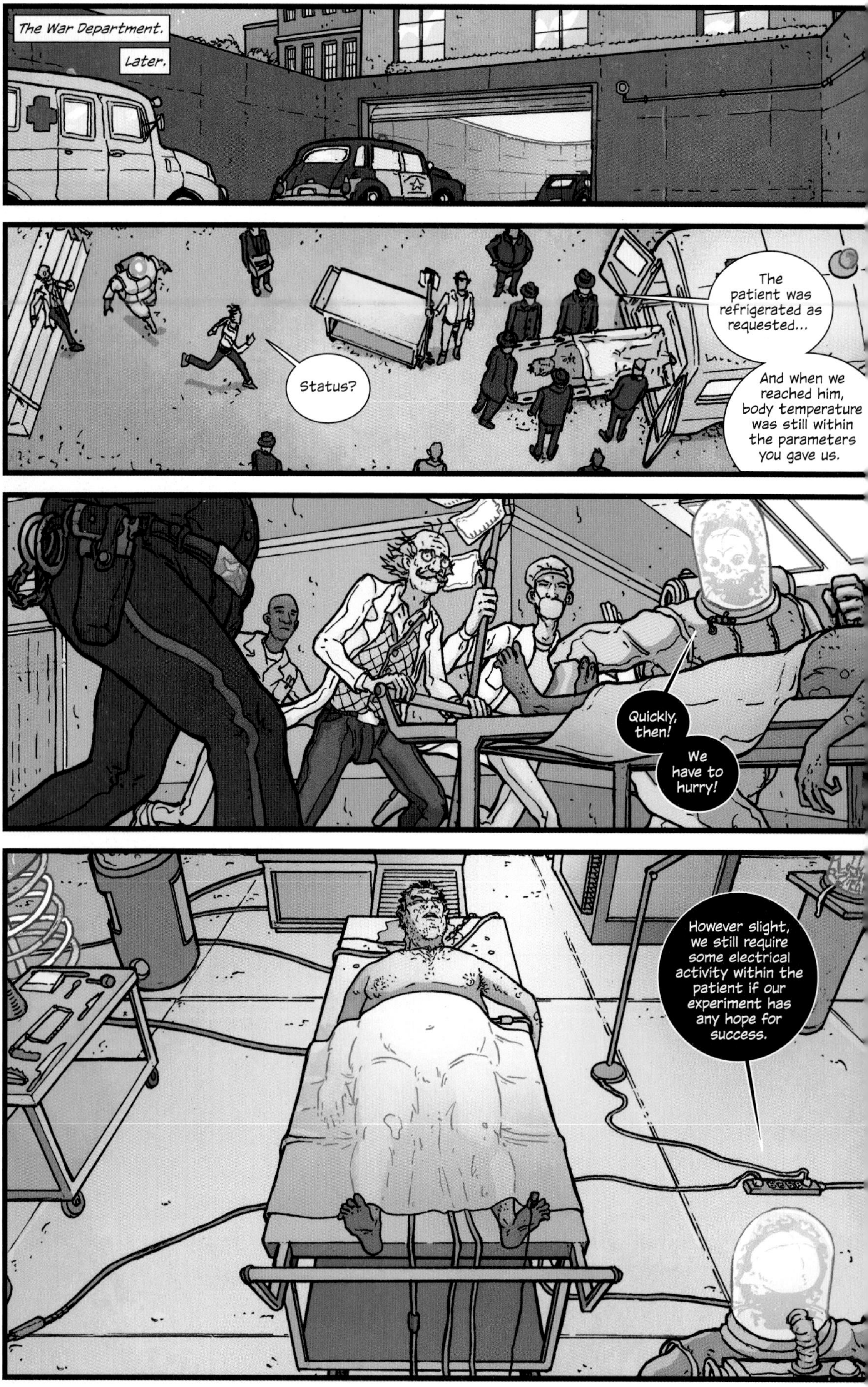
The War Department.
Later.
Status?
The patient was refrigerated as requested...
And when we reached him, body temperature was still within the parameters you gave us.
Quickly, then!
We have to hurry!
However slight, we still require some electrical activity within the patient if our experiment has any hope for success.

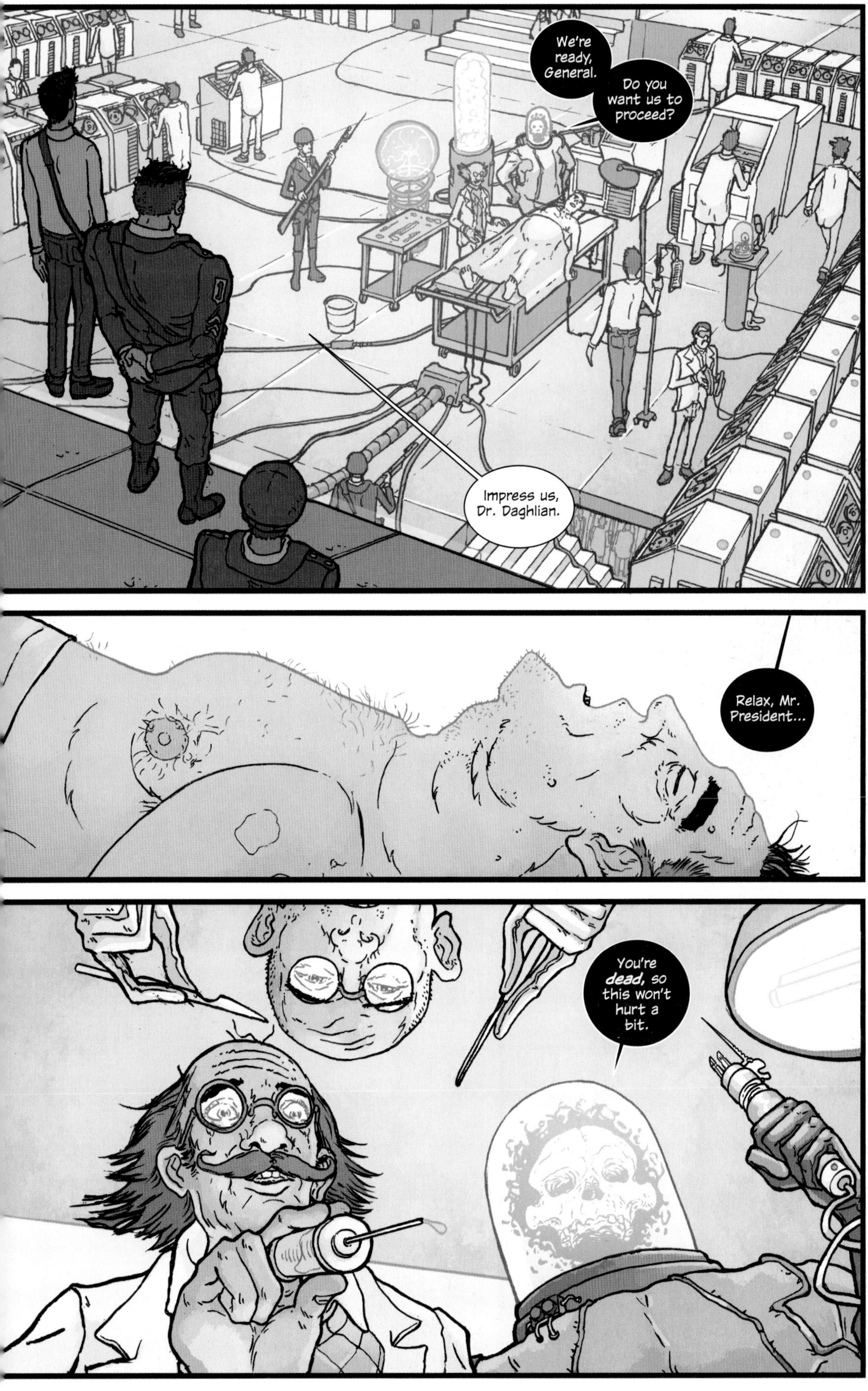
We're ready, General.
Do you want us to proceed?
Impress us, Dr. Daghlian.
Relax, Mr. President...
You're *dead,* so this won't hurt a bit.

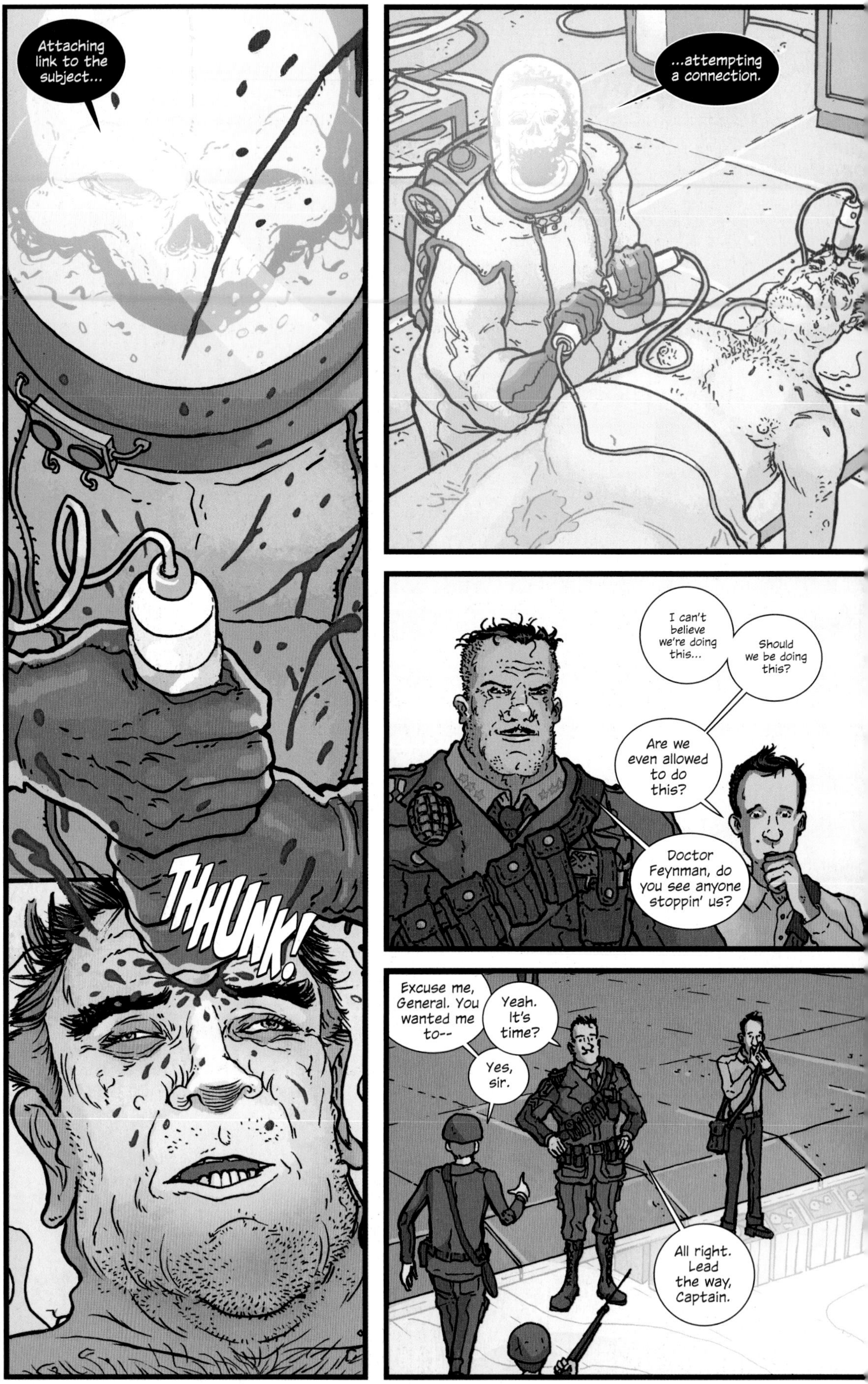
Attaching link to the subject...
...attempting a connection.
THHUNK!
I can't believe we're doing this...
Should we be doing this?
Are we even allowed to do this?
Doctor Feynman, do you see anyone stoppin' us?
Excuse me, General. You wanted me to--
Yeah. It's time?
Yes, sir.
All right. Lead the way, Captain.

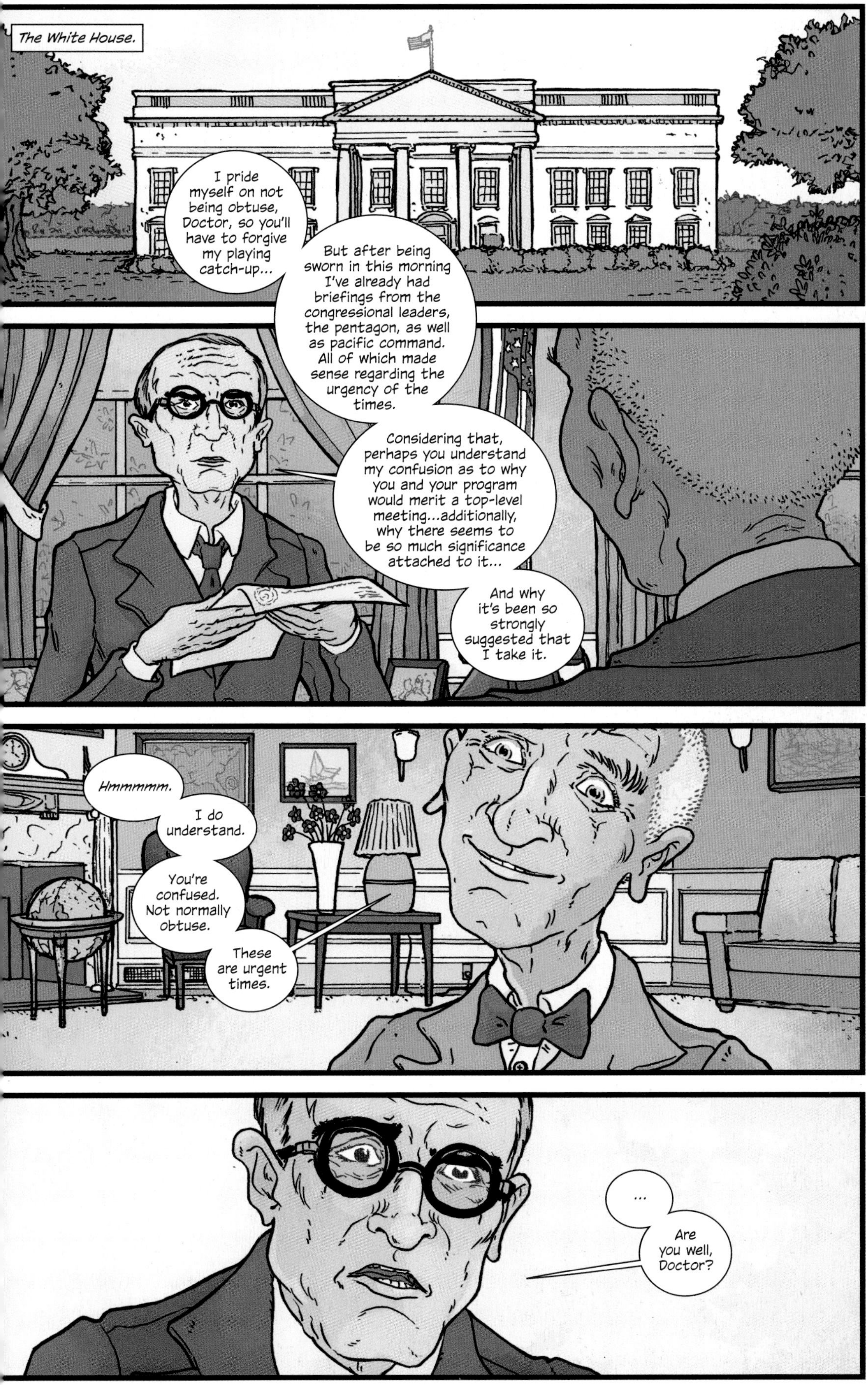
The White House.
I pride myself on not being obtuse, Doctor, so you'll have to forgive my playing catch-up...
But after being sworn in this morning I've already had briefings from the congressional leaders, the pentagon, as well as pacific command. All of which made sense regarding the urgency of the times.
Considering that, perhaps you understand my confusion as to why you and your program would merit a top-level meeting...additionally, why there seems to be so much significance attached to it...
And why it's been so strongly suggested that I take it.
Hmmmmm.
I do understand.
You're confused. Not normally obtuse.
These are urgent times.
...
Are you well, Doctor?

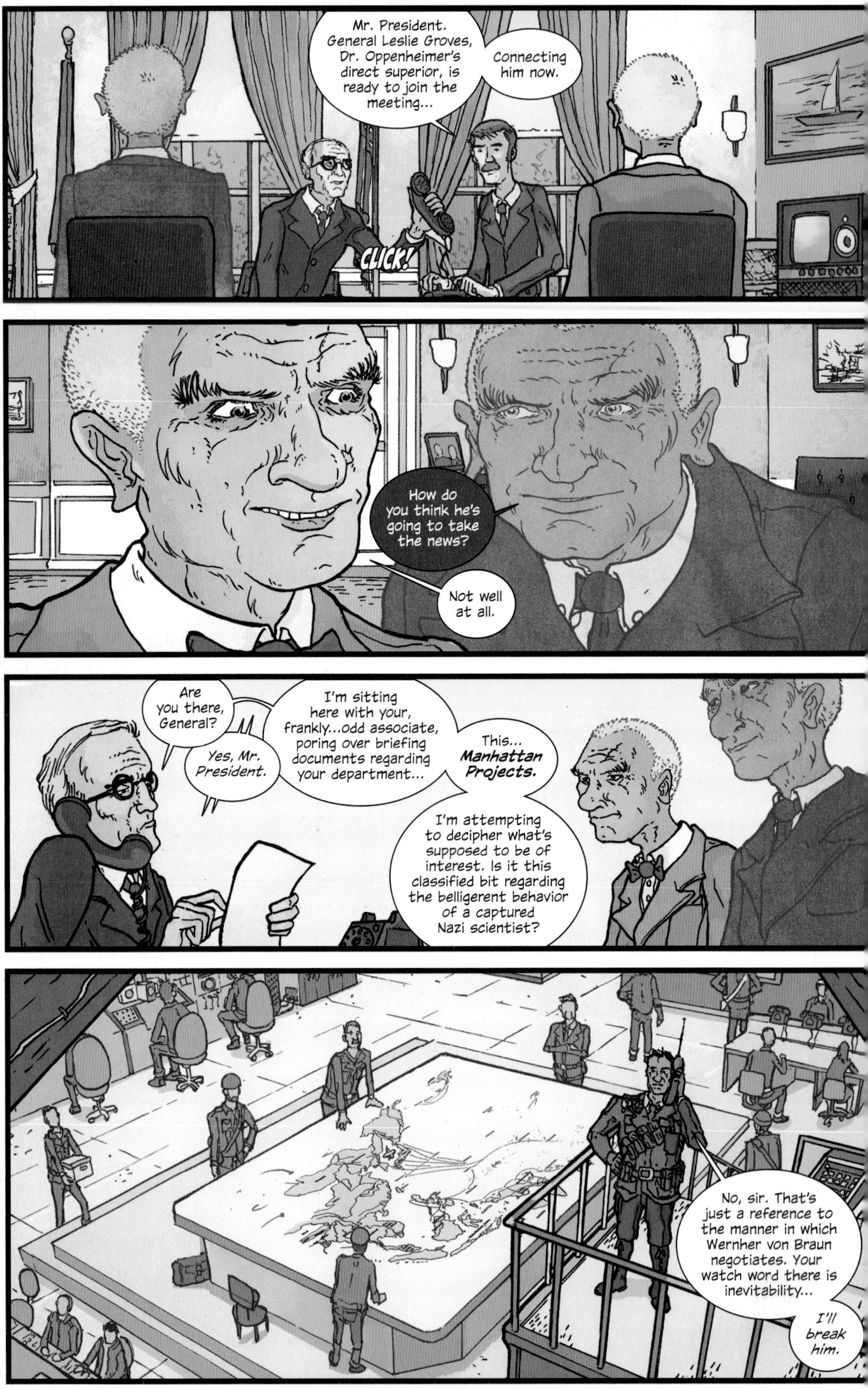

Mr. President. General Leslie Groves, Dr. Oppenheimer's direct superior, is ready to join the meeting...
Connecting him now.
CLICK!
How do you think he's going to take the news?
Not well at all.
Are you there, General?
Yes, Mr. President.
I'm sitting here with your, frankly...odd associate, poring over briefing documents regarding your department...
This... ***Manhattan Projects.***
I'm attempting to decipher what's supposed to be of interest. Is it this classified bit regarding the belligerent behavior of a captured Nazi scientist?
No, sir. That's just a reference to the manner in which Wernher von Braun negotiates. Your watch word there is inevitability...
I'll break him.

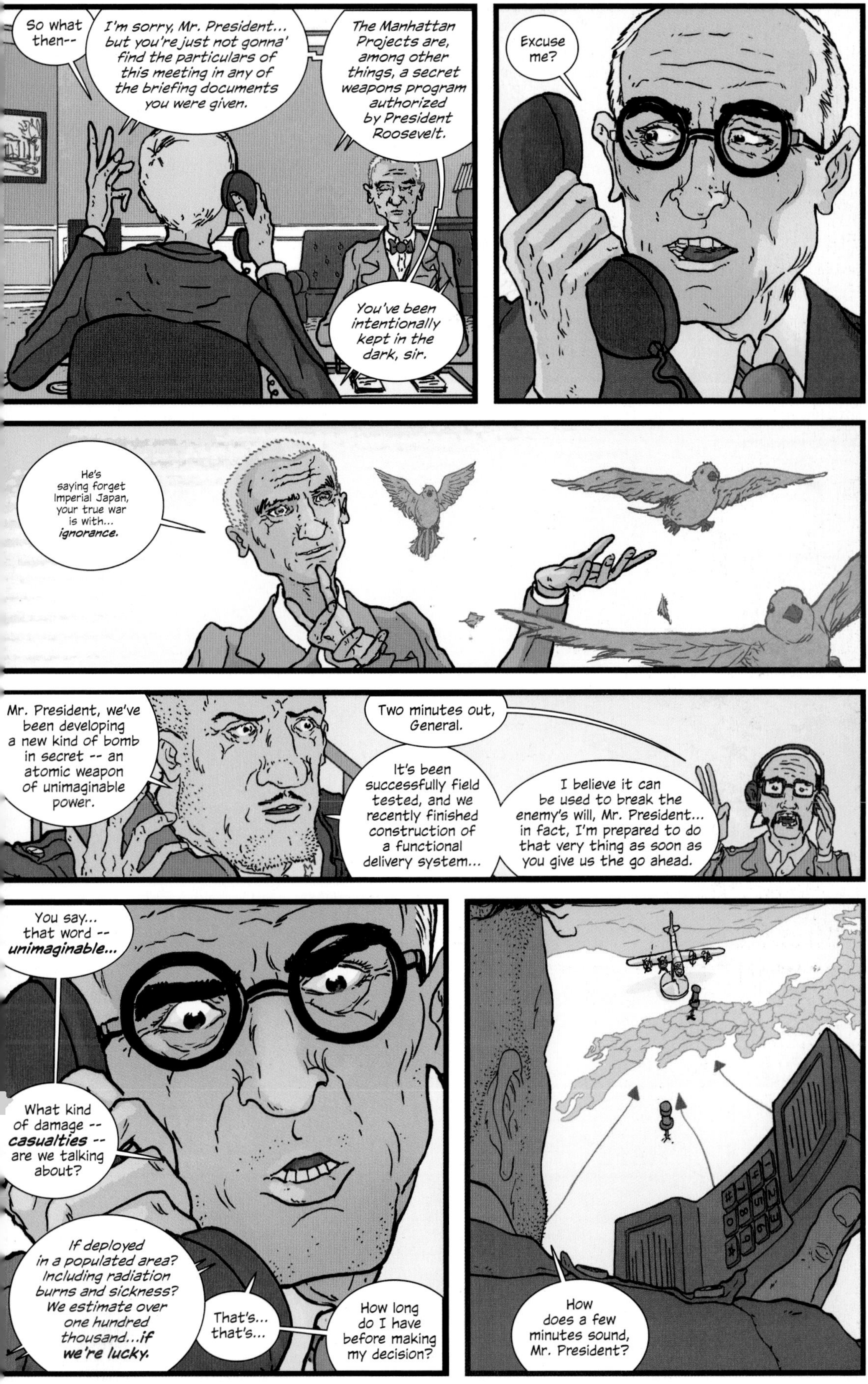
So what then--
I'm sorry, Mr. President... but you're just not gonna' find the particulars of this meeting in any of the briefing documents you were given.
The Manhattan Projects are, among other things, a secret weapons program authorized by President Roosevelt.
You've been intentionally kept in the dark, sir.
Excuse me?
He's saying forget Imperial Japan, your true war is with... *ignorance.*
Mr. President, we've been developing a new kind of bomb in secret -- an atomic weapon of unimaginable power.
Two minutes out, General.
It's been successfully field tested, and we recently finished construction of a functional delivery system...
I believe it can be used to break the enemy's will, Mr. President... in fact, I'm prepared to do that very thing as soon as you give us the go ahead.
You say... that word -- ***unimaginable...***
What kind of damage -- ***casualties*** -- are we talking about?
If deployed in a populated area? Including radiation burns and sickness? We estimate over one hundred thousand... ***if we're lucky.***
That's... that's...
How long do I have before making my decision?
How does a few minutes sound, Mr. President?

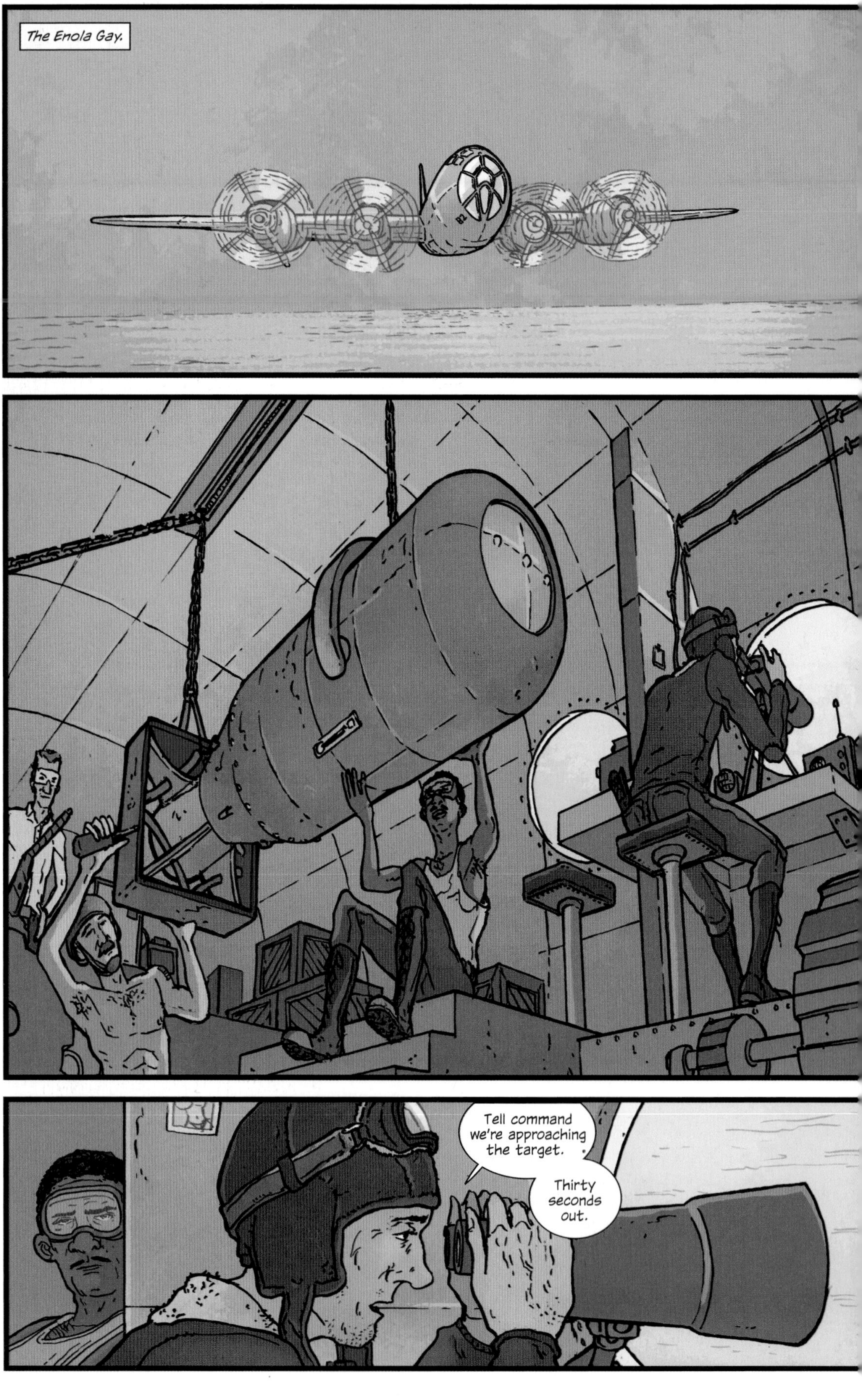
The Enola Gay.
Tell command we're approaching the target.
Thirty seconds out.

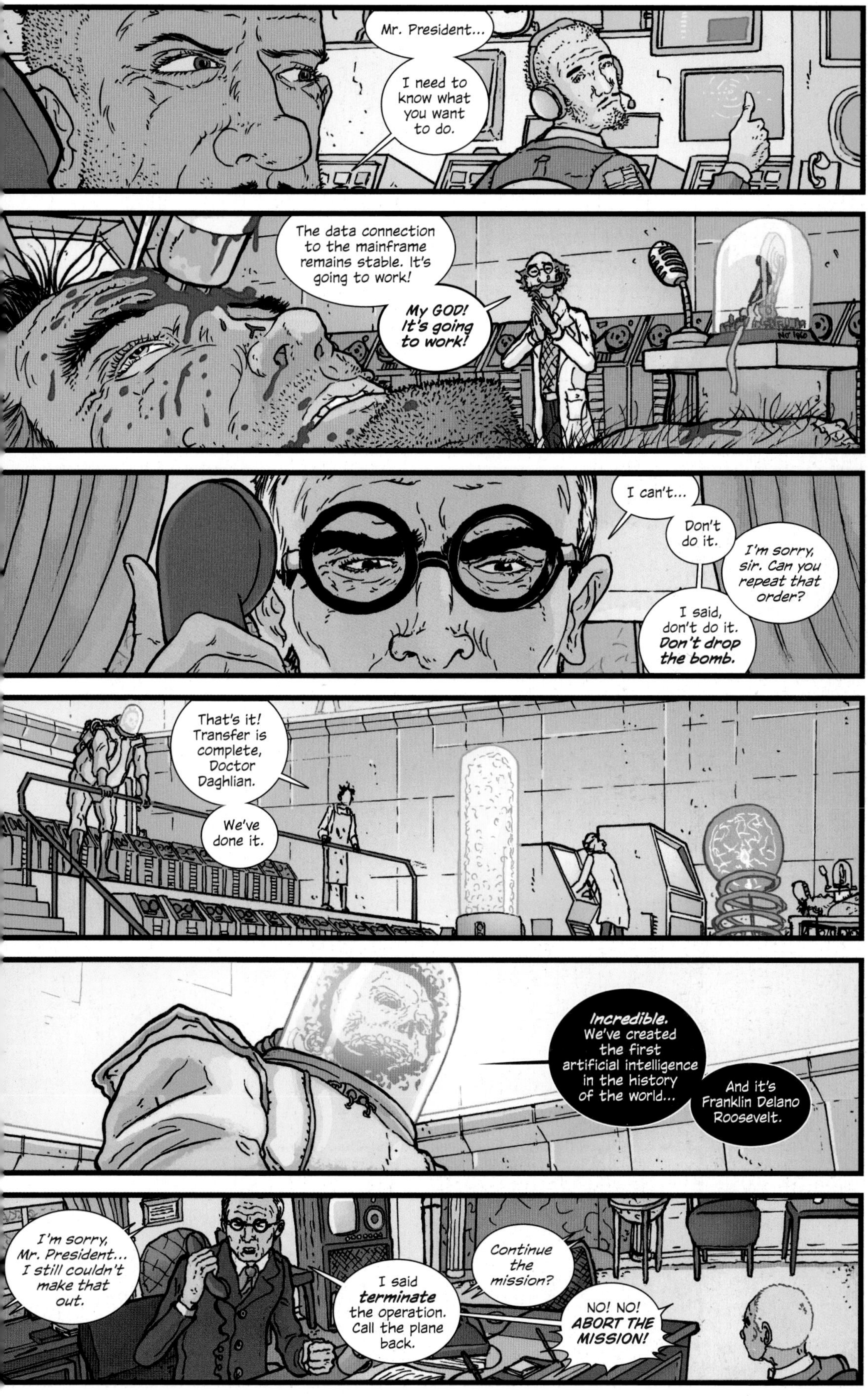
Mr. President...
I need to know what you want to do.
The data connection to the mainframe remains stable. It's going to work!
My GOD! It's going to work!
I can't...
Don't do it.
I'm sorry, sir. Can you repeat that order?
I said, don't do it. ***Don't drop the bomb.***
That's it! Transfer is complete, Doctor Daghlian.
We've done it.
Incredible. We've created the first artificial intelligence in the history of the world...
And it's Franklin Delano Roosevelt.
I'm sorry, Mr. President... I still couldn't make that out.
I said ***terminate*** the operation. Call the plane back.
Continue the mission?
NO! NO! ***ABORT THE MISSION!***

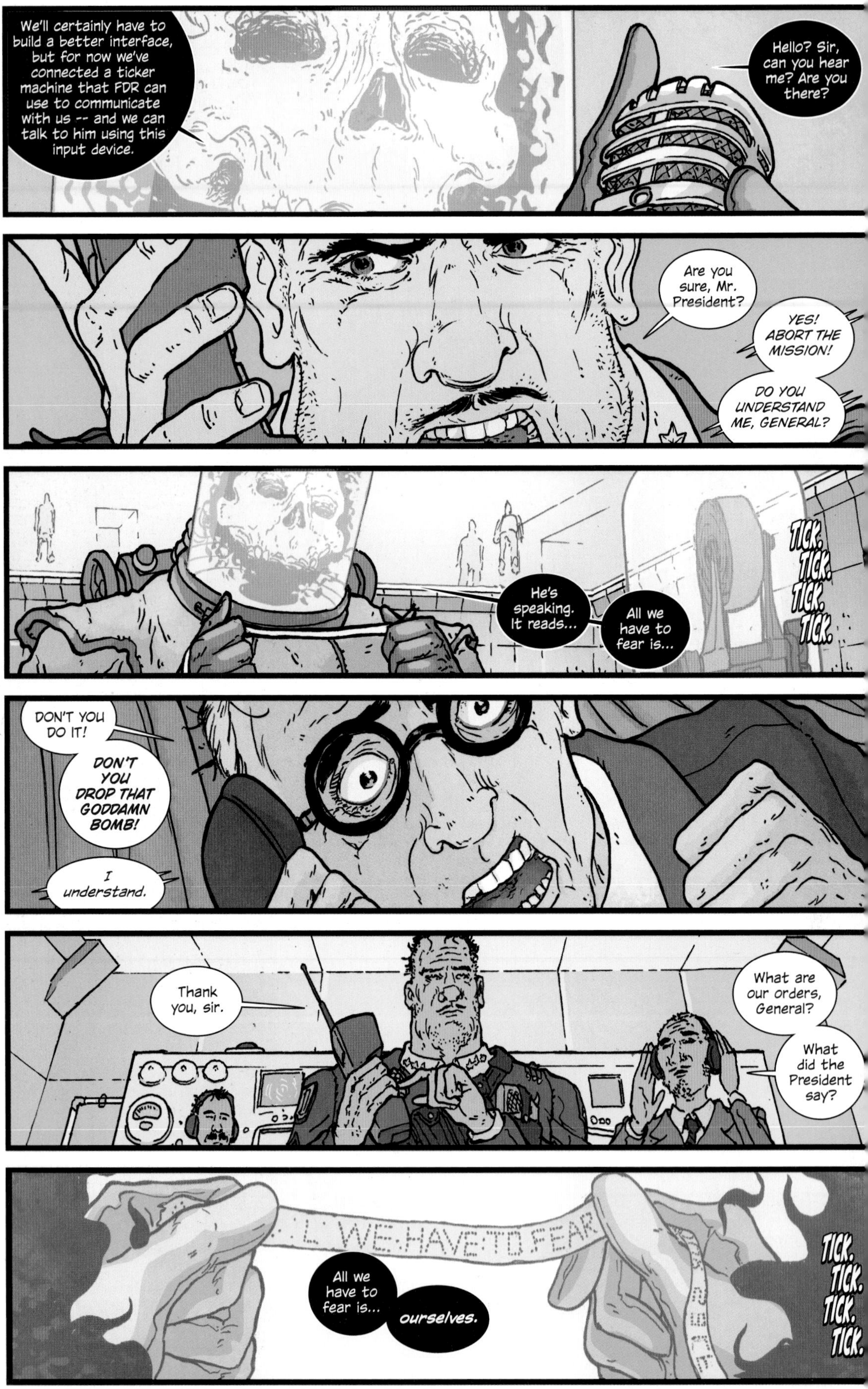

We'll certainly have to build a better interface, but for now we've connected a ticker machine that FDR can use to communicate with us -- and we can talk to him using this input device.
Hello? Sir, can you hear me? Are you there?
Are you sure, Mr. President?
YES! ABORT THE MISSION!
DO YOU UNDERSTAND ME, GENERAL?
He's speaking. It reads...
All we have to fear is...
TICK. TICK. TICK. TICK.
DON'T YOU DO IT!
DON'T YOU DROP THAT GODDAMN BOMB!
I understand.
Thank you, sir.
What are our orders, General?
What did the President say?
...L WE HAVE TO FEAR
All we have to fear is...
ourselves.
TICK. TICK. TICK. TICK.

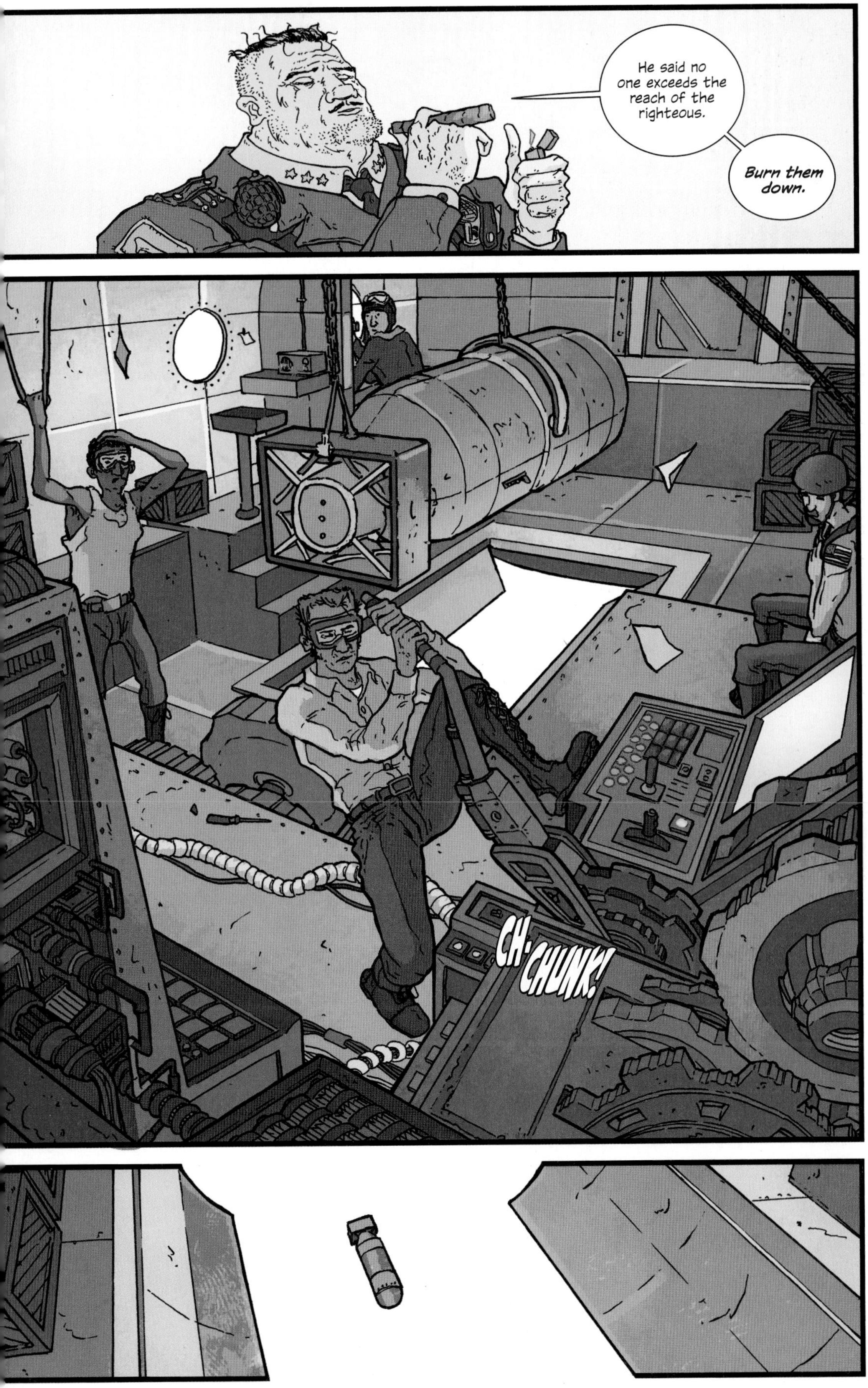
He said no one exceeds the reach of the righteous.
Burn them down.
CH-CHUNK!

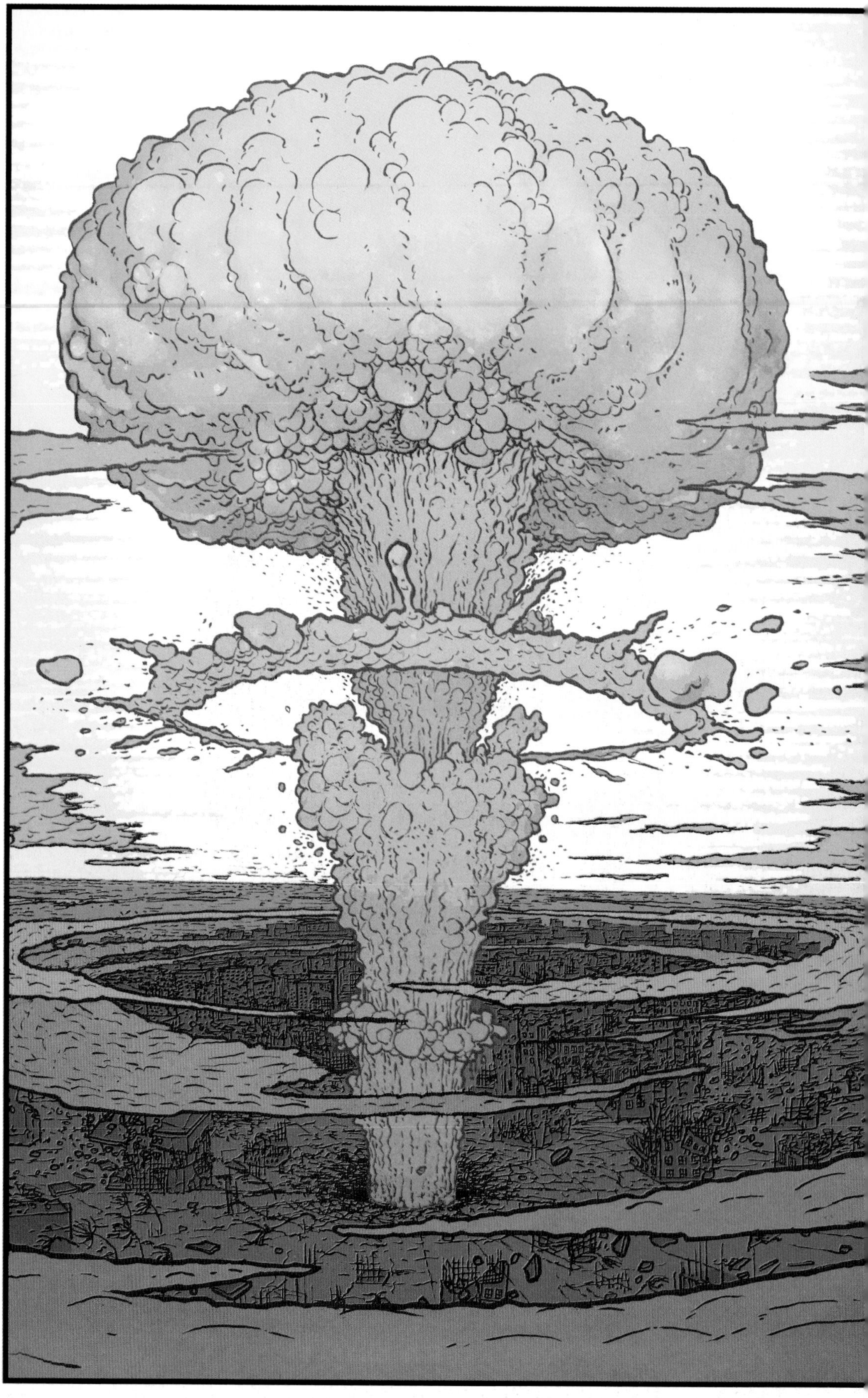

"AFTER HIROSHIMA, AT THE URGING OF GENERAL GROVES AND DIRECTOR OPPENHEIMER, THE FDR ARTIFICIAL INTELLIGENCE ESTABLISHED A SHADOW GOVERNMENT OF THE UNITED STATES."

CLAVIS AUREA
THE RECORDED FEYNMAN

VOL. 1

THE DOOR OPENED
WIDER

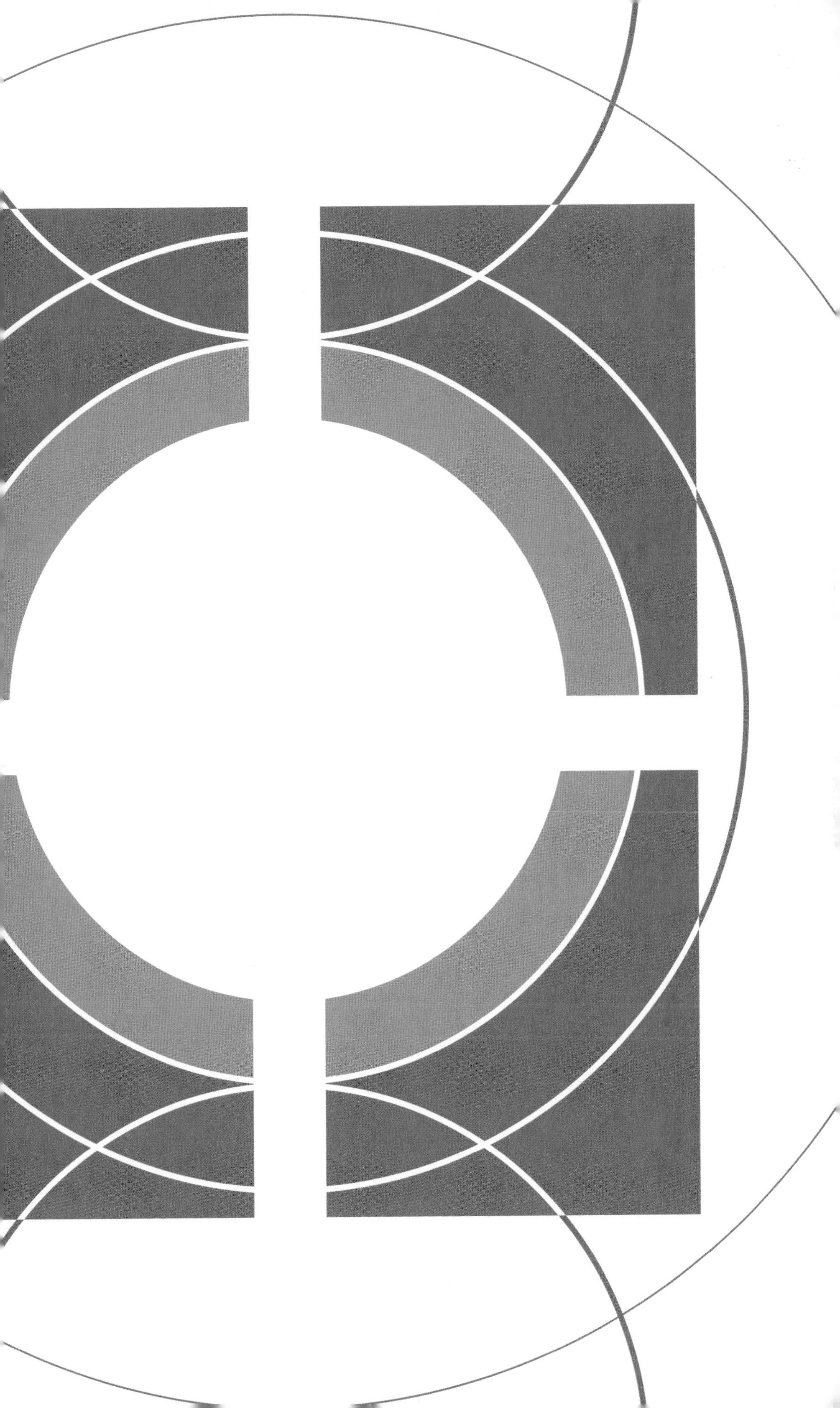

"A HUMAN BEING IS A PART OF THE WHOLE, CALLED BY US 'UNIVERSE', A PART LIMITED IN TIME AND SPACE. "

- ALBERT EINSTEIN

CLAVIS AUREA
THE RECORDED FEYNMAN | **VOL. 1**

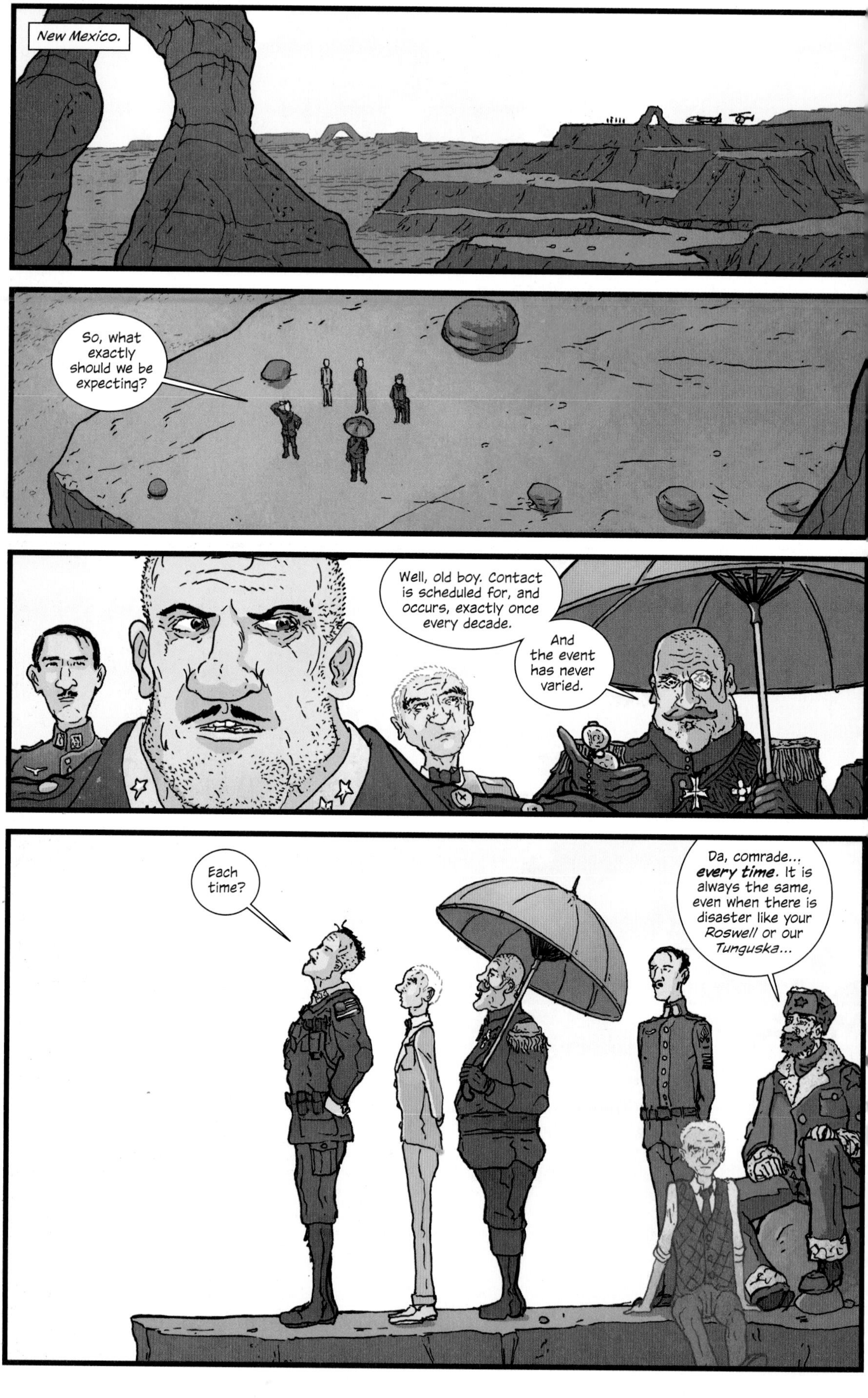
New Mexico.
So, what exactly should we be expecting?
Well, old boy. Contact is scheduled for, and occurs, exactly once every decade.
And the event has never varied.
Each time?
Da, comrade... **every time**. It is always the same, even when there is disaster like your *Roswell* or our *Tunguska*...

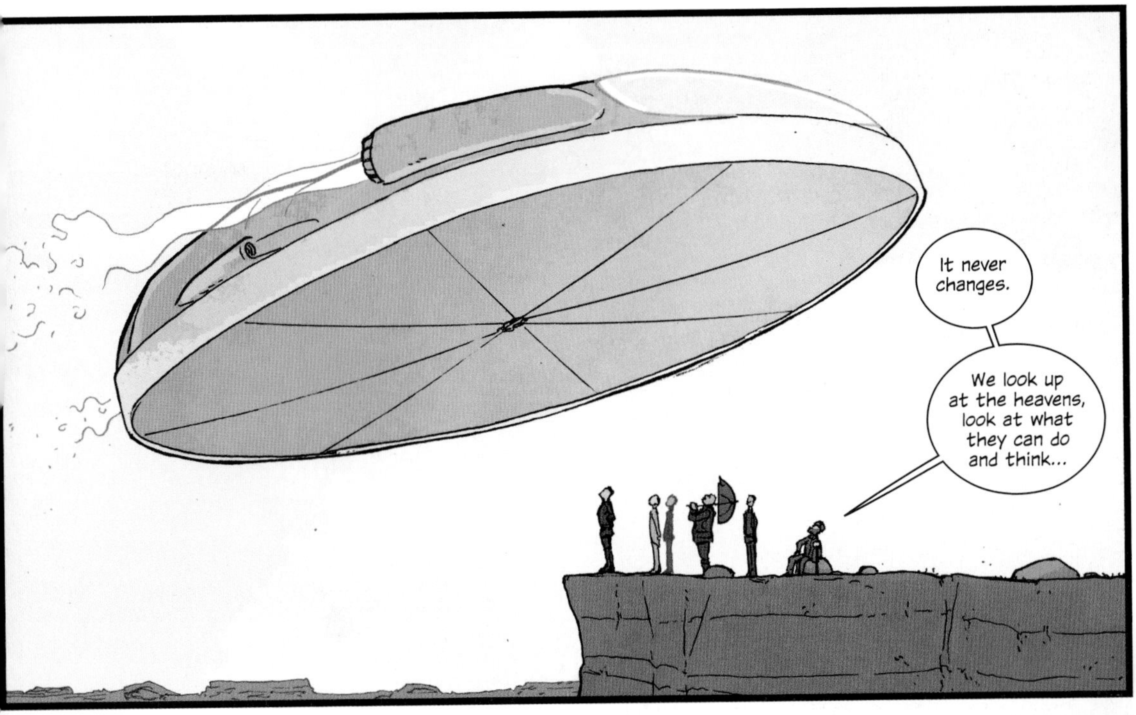
It never changes.
We look up at the heavens, look at what they can do and think...

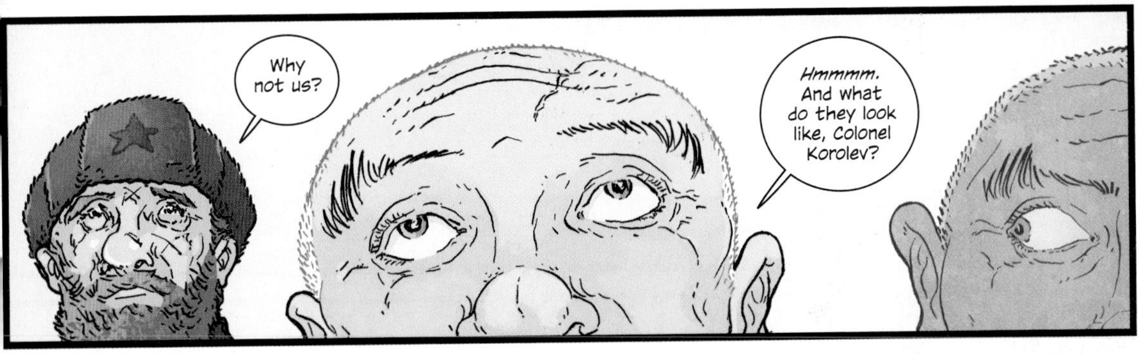
Why not us?
Hmmmm. And what do they look like, Colonel Korolev?

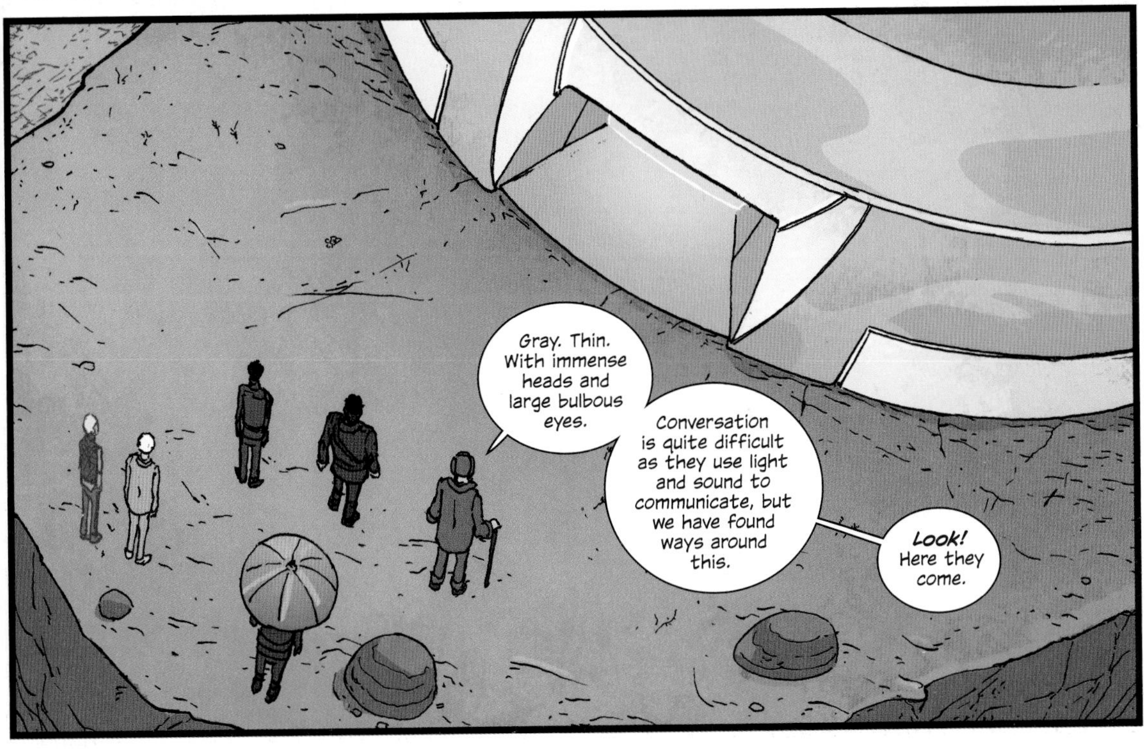
Gray. Thin. With immense heads and large bulbous eyes.
Conversation is quite difficult as they use light and sound to communicate, but we have found ways around this.
Look! Here they come.

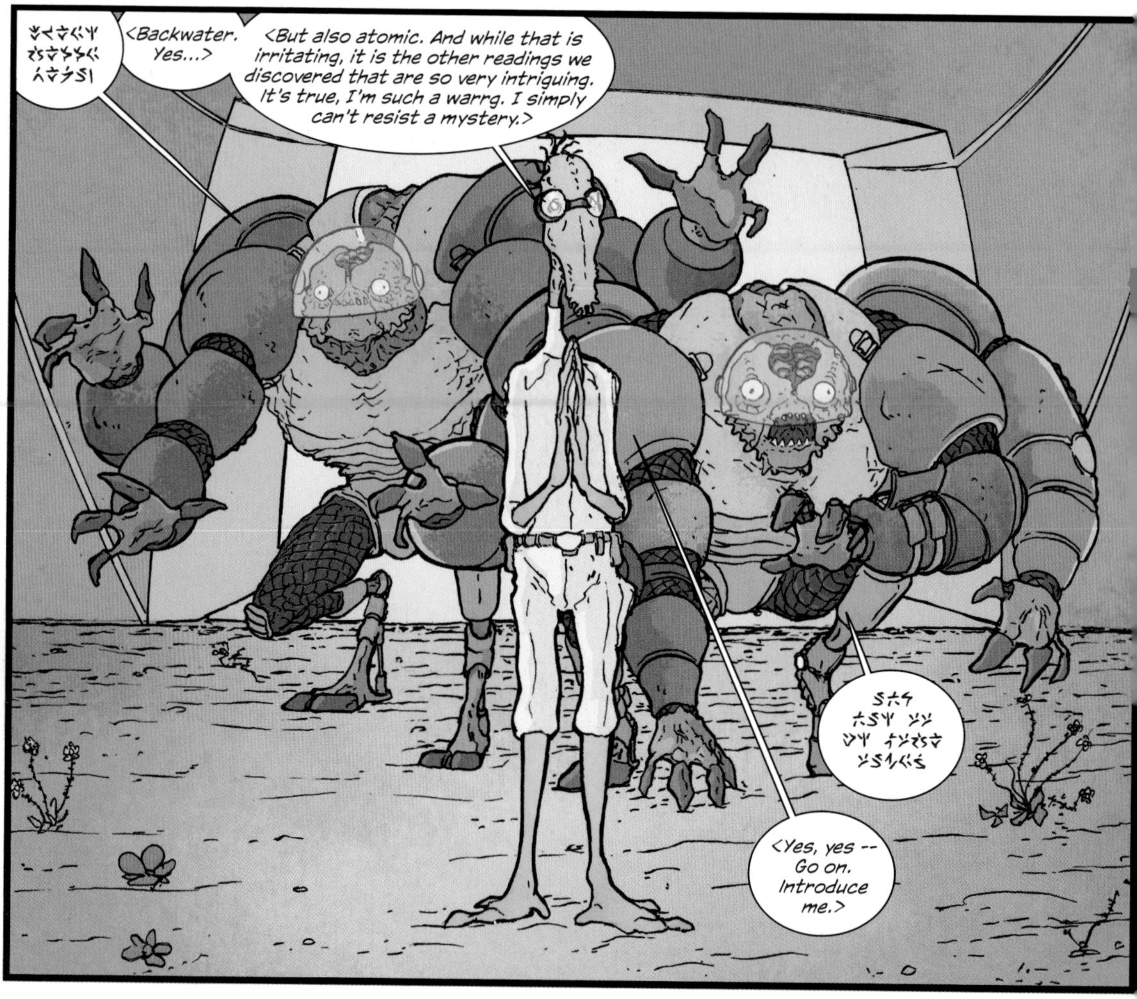
<Backwater. Yes...>
<But also atomic. And while that is irritating, it is the other readings we discovered that are so very intriguing. It's true, I'm such a warrg. I simply can't resist a mystery.>
<Yes, yes -- Go on. Introduce me.>

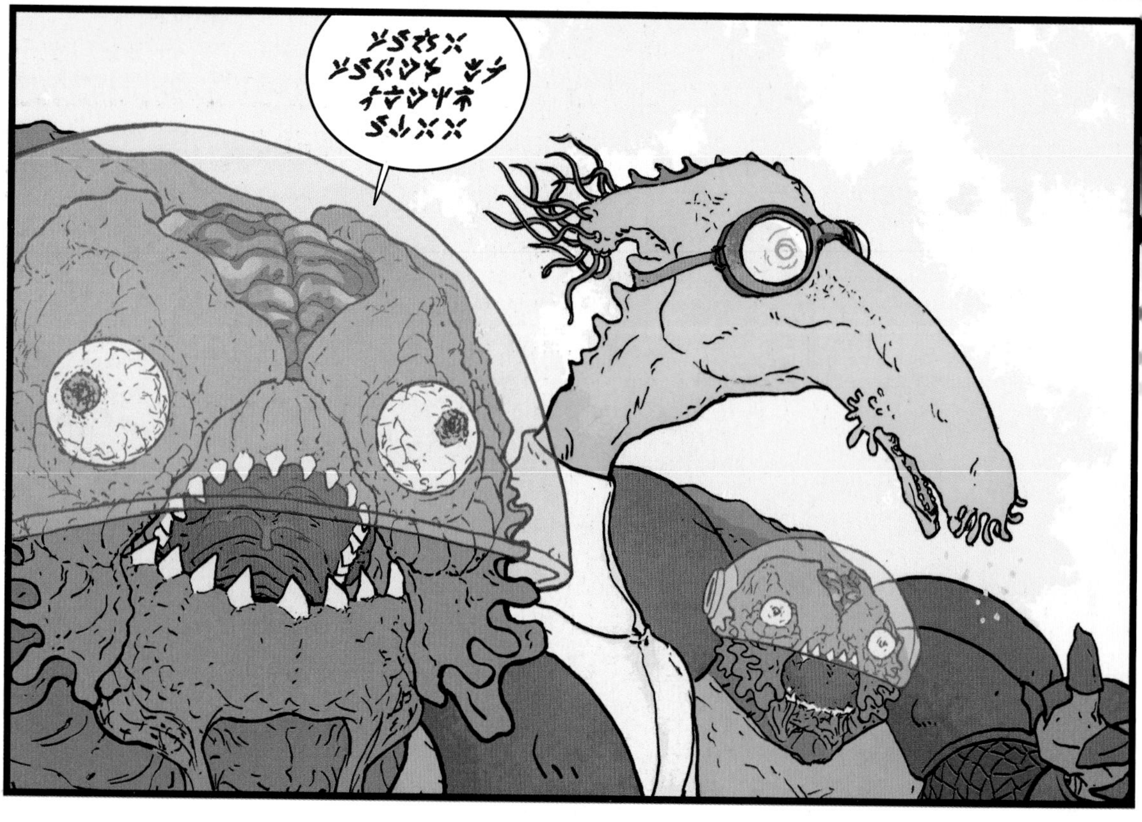

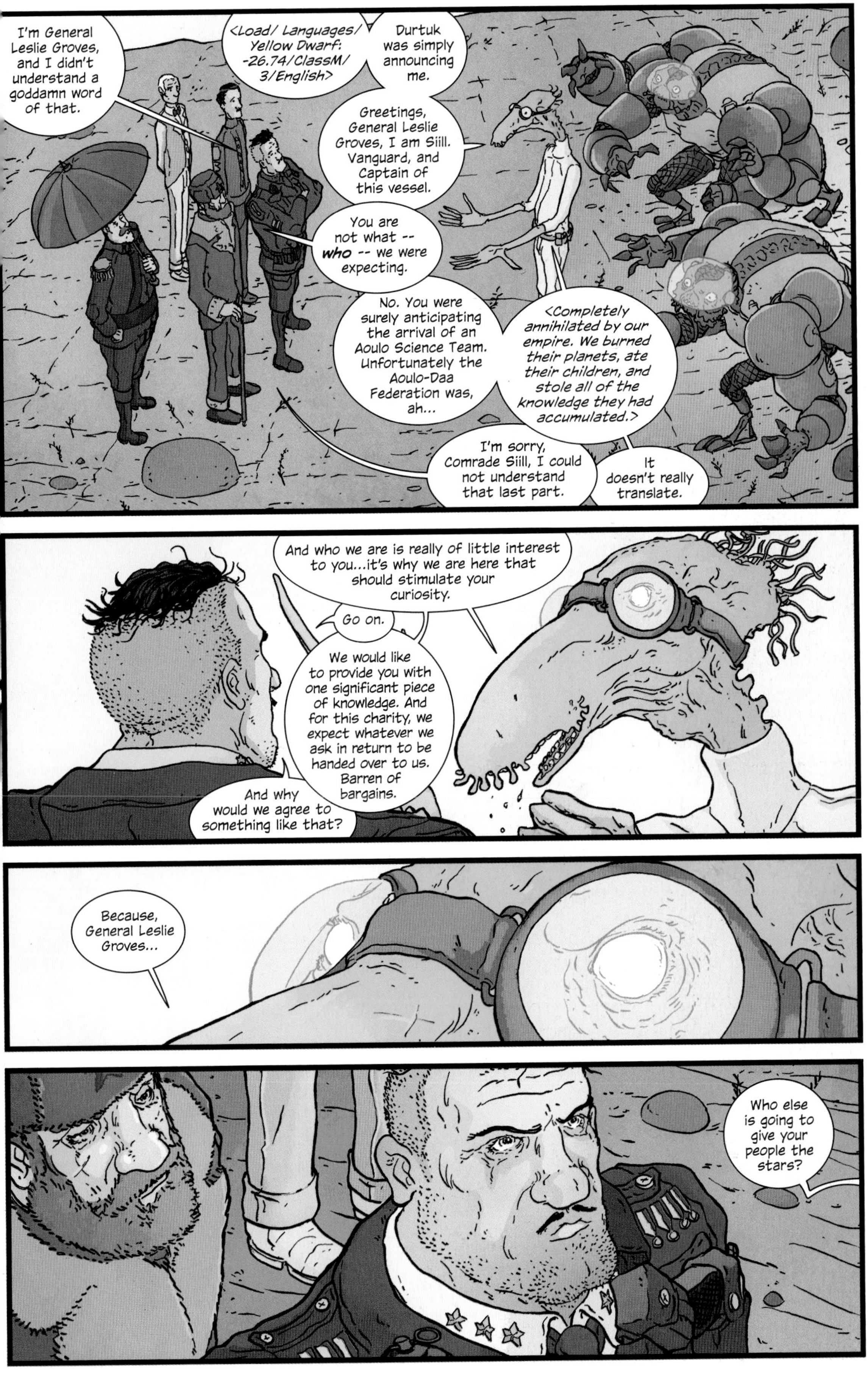
I'm General Leslie Groves, and I didn't understand a goddamn word of that.
<Load/ Languages/ Yellow Dwarf: -26.74/ClassM/ 3/English>
Durtuk was simply announcing me.
Greetings, General Leslie Groves, I am Siill. Vanguard, and Captain of this vessel.
You are not what -- who -- we were expecting.
No. You were surely anticipating the arrival of an Aoulo Science Team. Unfortunately the Aoulo-Daa Federation was, ah...
<Completely annihilated by our empire. We burned their planets, ate their children, and stole all of the knowledge they had accumulated.>
I'm sorry, Comrade Siill, I could not understand that last part.
It doesn't really translate.
And who we are is really of little interest to you...it's why we are here that should stimulate your curiosity.
Go on.
We would like to provide you with one significant piece of knowledge. And for this charity, we expect whatever we ask in return to be handed over to us. Barren of bargains.
And why would we agree to something like that?
Because, General Leslie Groves...
Who else is going to give your people the stars?

04

THE
ROSE BRIDGE

"IMAGINATION IS MORE IMPORTANT THAN KNOWLEDGE. FOR KNOWLEDGE IS LIMITED, WHEREAS IMAGINATION EMBRACES THE ENTIRE WORLD, STIMULATING PROGRESS, GIVING BIRTH TO EVOLUTION."

- ALBERT EINSTEIN

CLAVIS AUREA
THE RECORDED FEYNMAN | **VOL. 1**

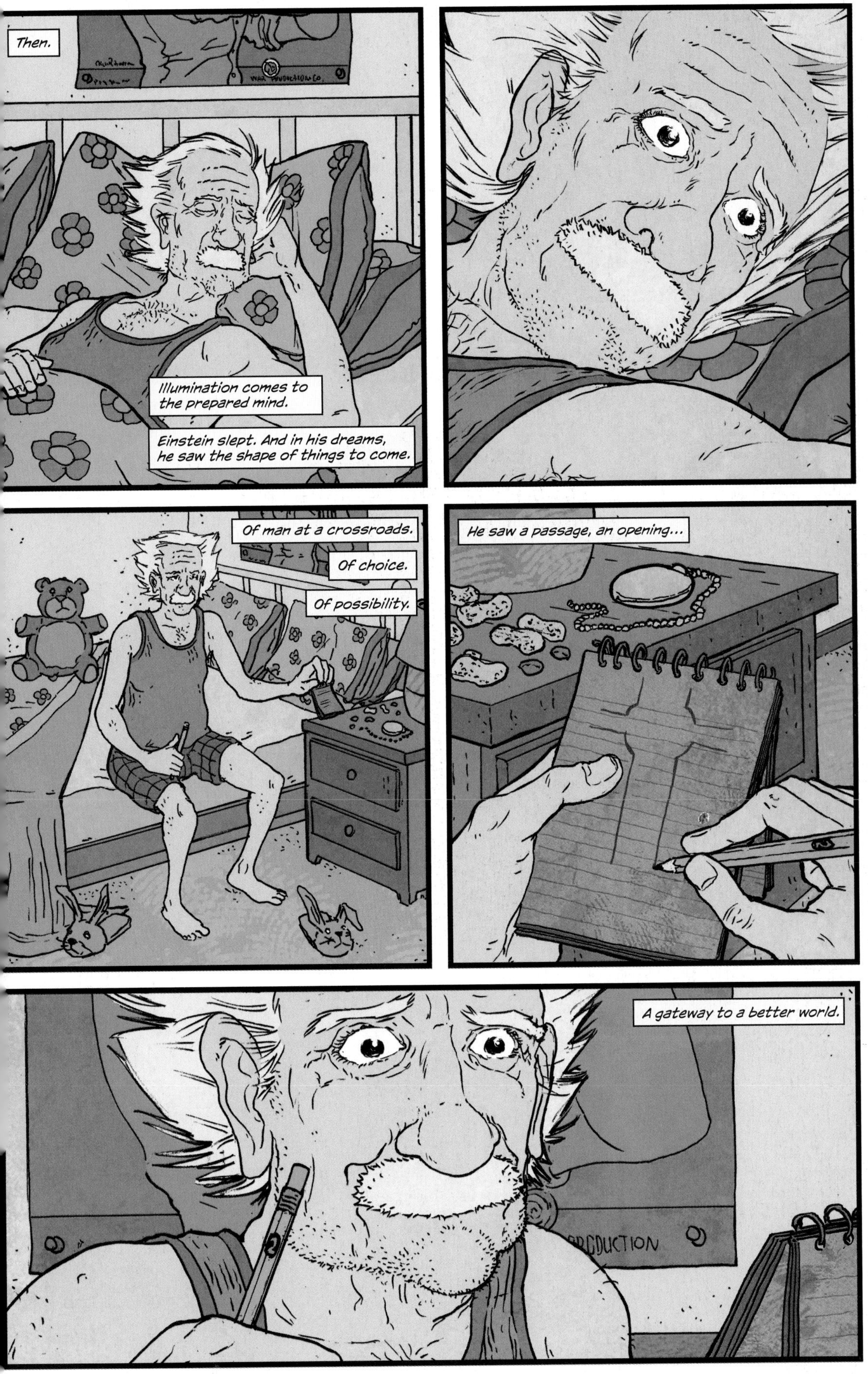
Then.
Illumination comes to the prepared mind.
Einstein slept. And in his dreams, he saw the shape of things to come.
Of man at a crossroads.
Of choice.
Of possibility.
He saw a passage, an opening...
A gateway to a better world.

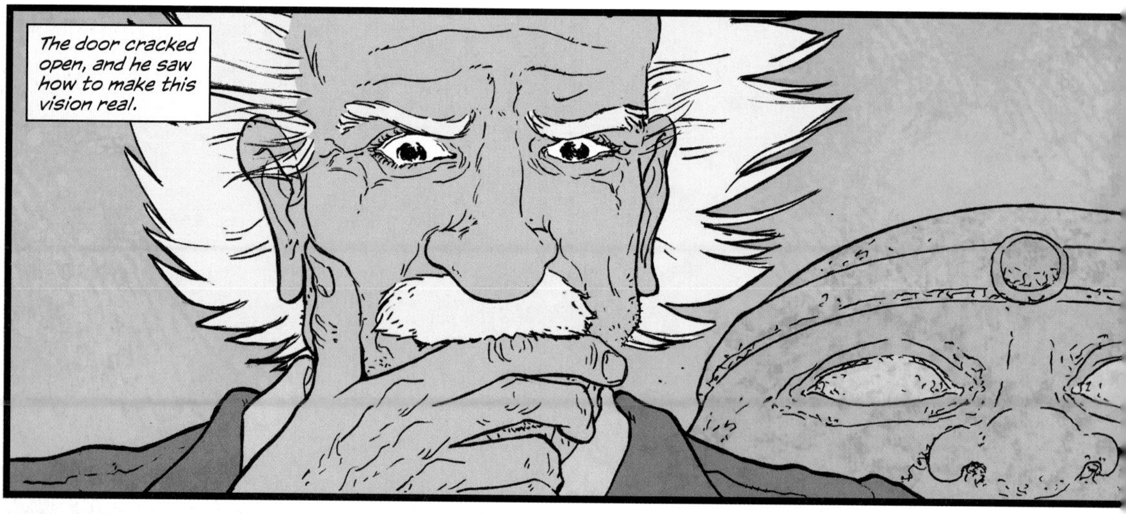
The door cracked open, and he saw how to make this vision real.

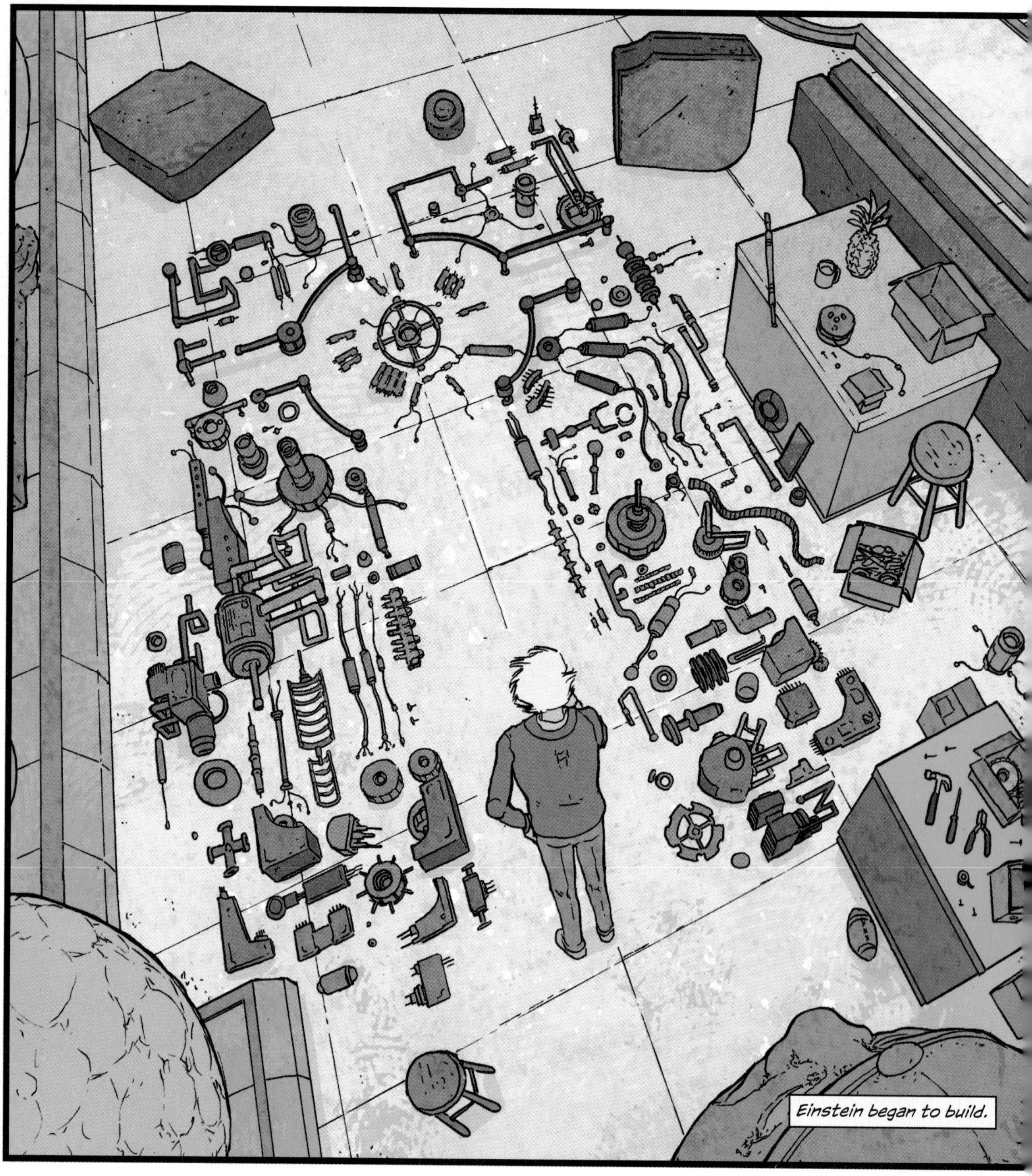
Einstein began to build.

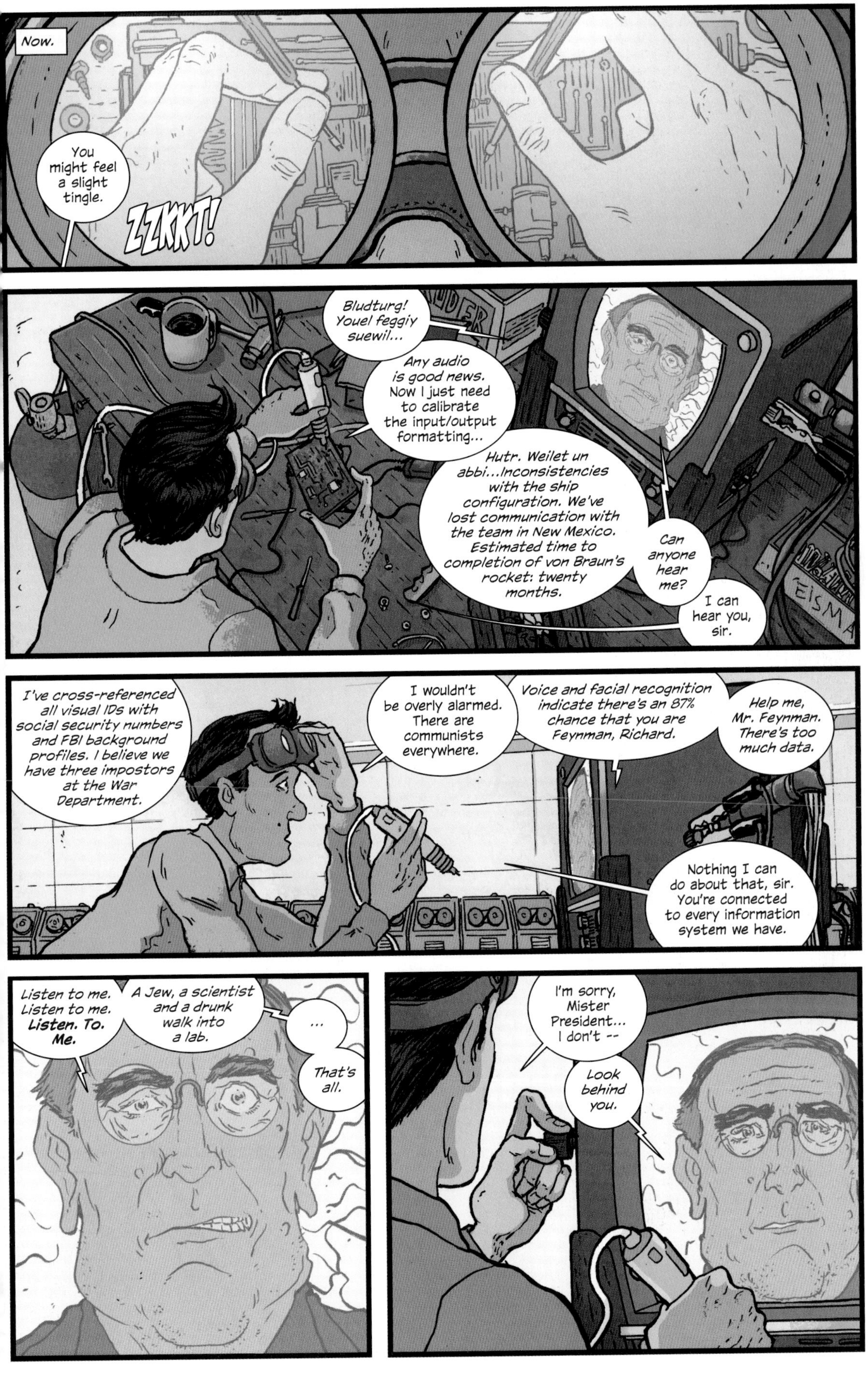
Now.
You might feel a slight tingle.
ZZKKT!
Bludturg! Youel feggiy suewil...
Any audio is good news. Now I just need to calibrate the input/output formatting...
Hutr. Weilet un abbi...Inconsistencies with the ship configuration. We've lost communication with the team in New Mexico. Estimated time to completion of von Braun's rocket: twenty months.
Can anyone hear me?
I can hear you, sir.
I've cross-referenced all visual IDs with social security numbers and FBI background profiles. I believe we have three impostors at the War Department.
I wouldn't be overly alarmed. There are communists everywhere.
Voice and facial recognition indicate there's an 87% chance that you are Feynman, Richard.
Help me, Mr. Feynman. There's too much data.
Nothing I can do about that, sir. You're connected to every information system we have.
Listen to me. Listen to me. **Listen. To. Me.**
A Jew, a scientist and a drunk walk into a lab.
...
That's all.
I'm sorry, Mister President... I don't --
Look behind you.

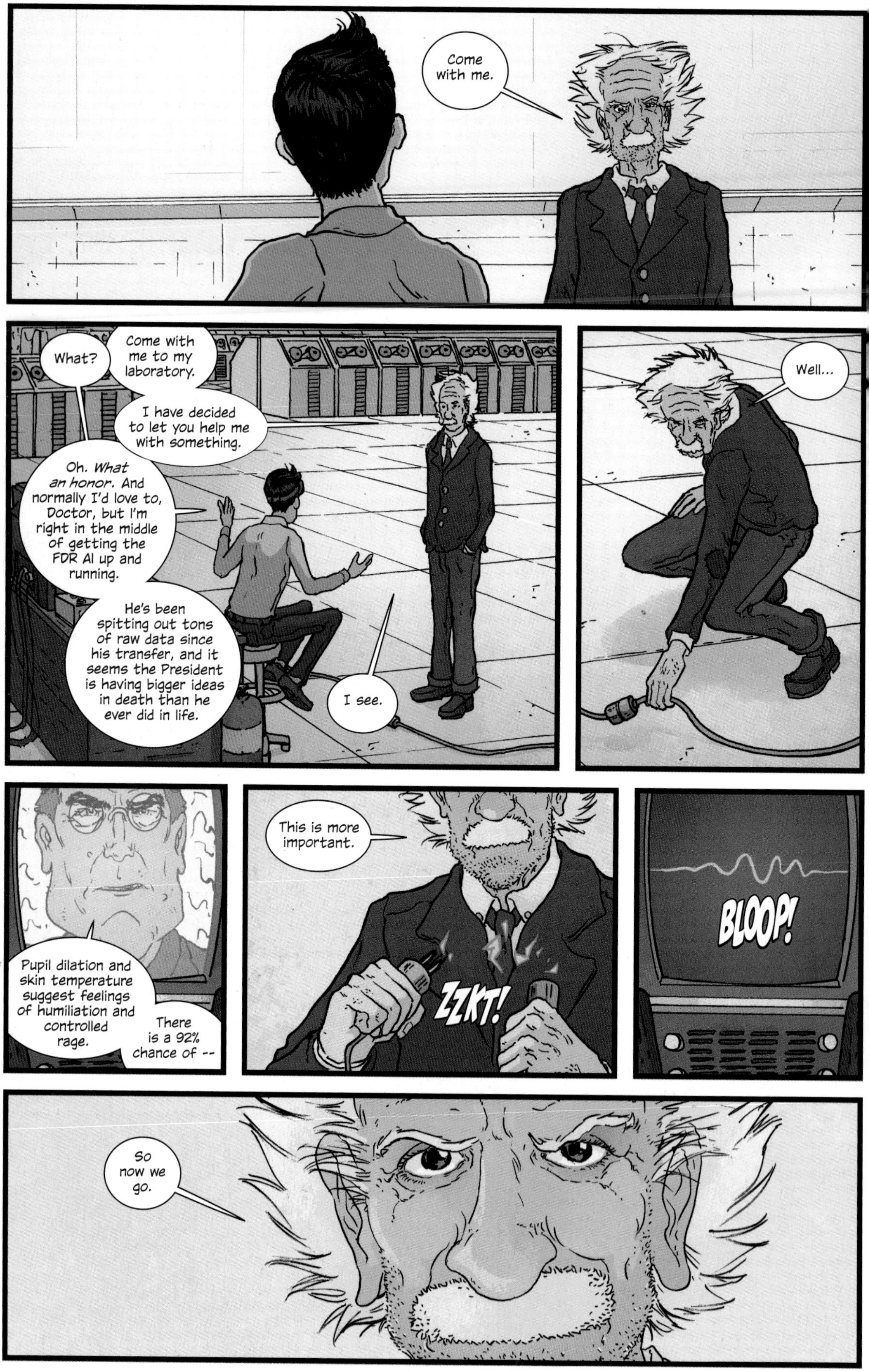
Come with me.
What?
Come with me to my laboratory.
I have decided to let you help me with something.
Oh. *What an honor.* And normally I'd love to, Doctor, but I'm right in the middle of getting the FDR AI up and running.
He's been spitting out tons of raw data since his transfer, and it seems the President is having bigger ideas in death than he ever did in life.
I see.
Well...
Pupil dilation and skin temperature suggest feelings of humiliation and controlled rage.
There is a 92% chance of --
This is more important.
ZZKT!
BLOOP!
So now we go.

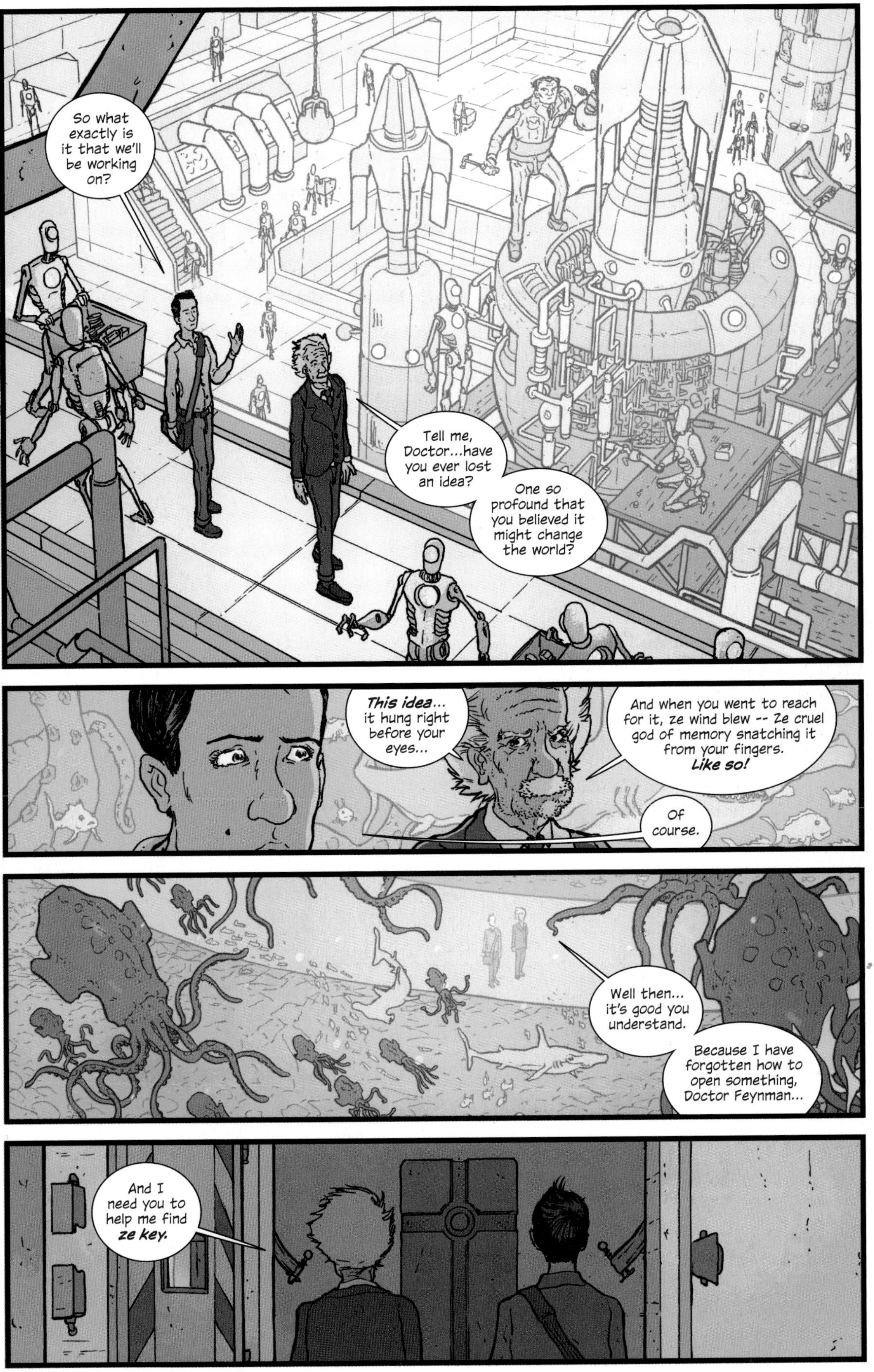
So what exactly is it that we'll be working on?
Tell me, Doctor...have you ever lost an idea?
One so profound that you believed it might change the world?
This idea... it hung right before your eyes...
And when you went to reach for it, ze wind blew -- Ze cruel god of memory snatching it from your fingers. Like so!
Of course.
Well then... it's good you understand.
Because I have forgotten how to open something, Doctor Feynman...
And I need you to help me find ze key.

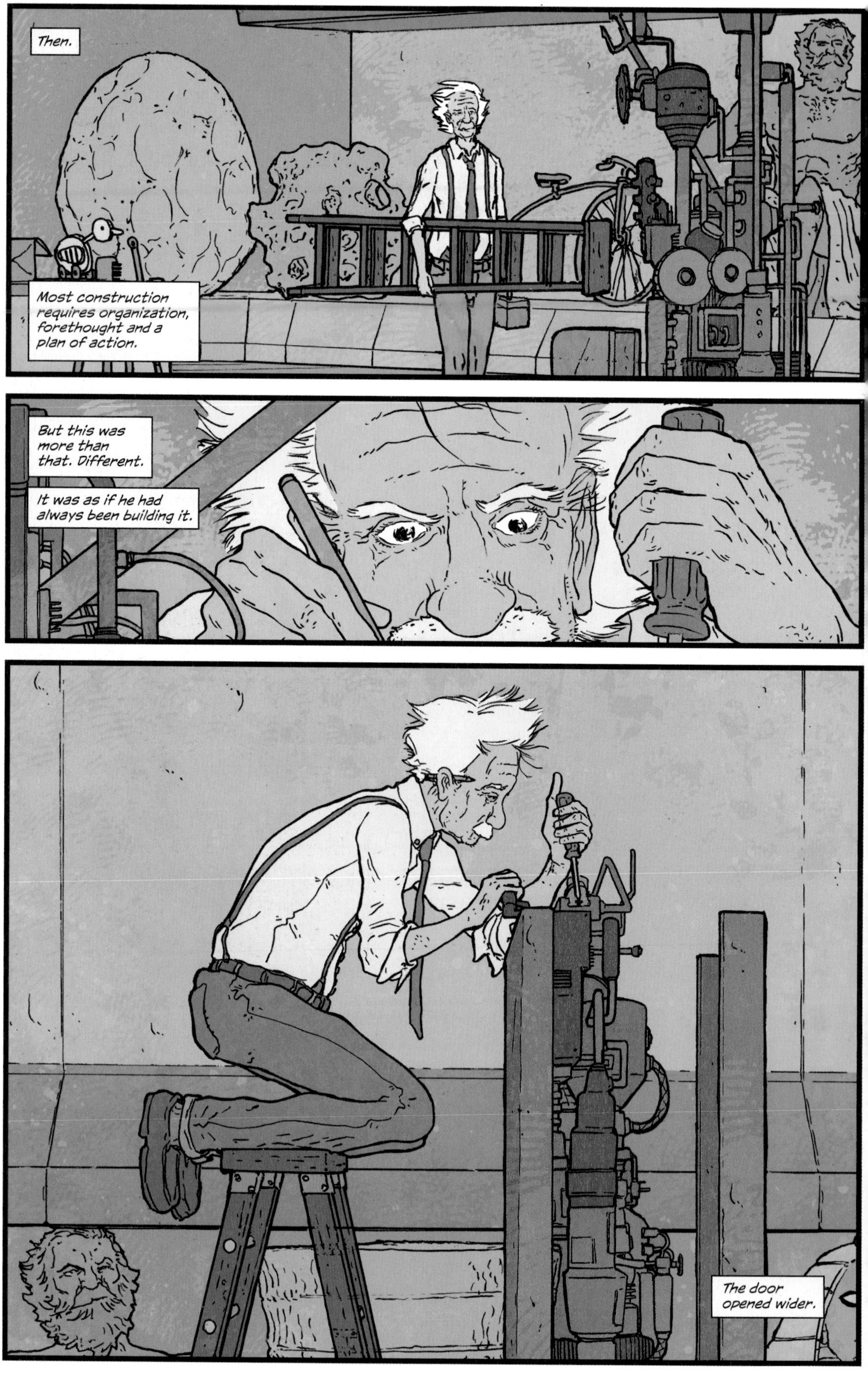
Then.
Most construction requires organization, forethought and a plan of action.
But this was more than that. Different.
It was as if he had always been building it.
The door opened wider.

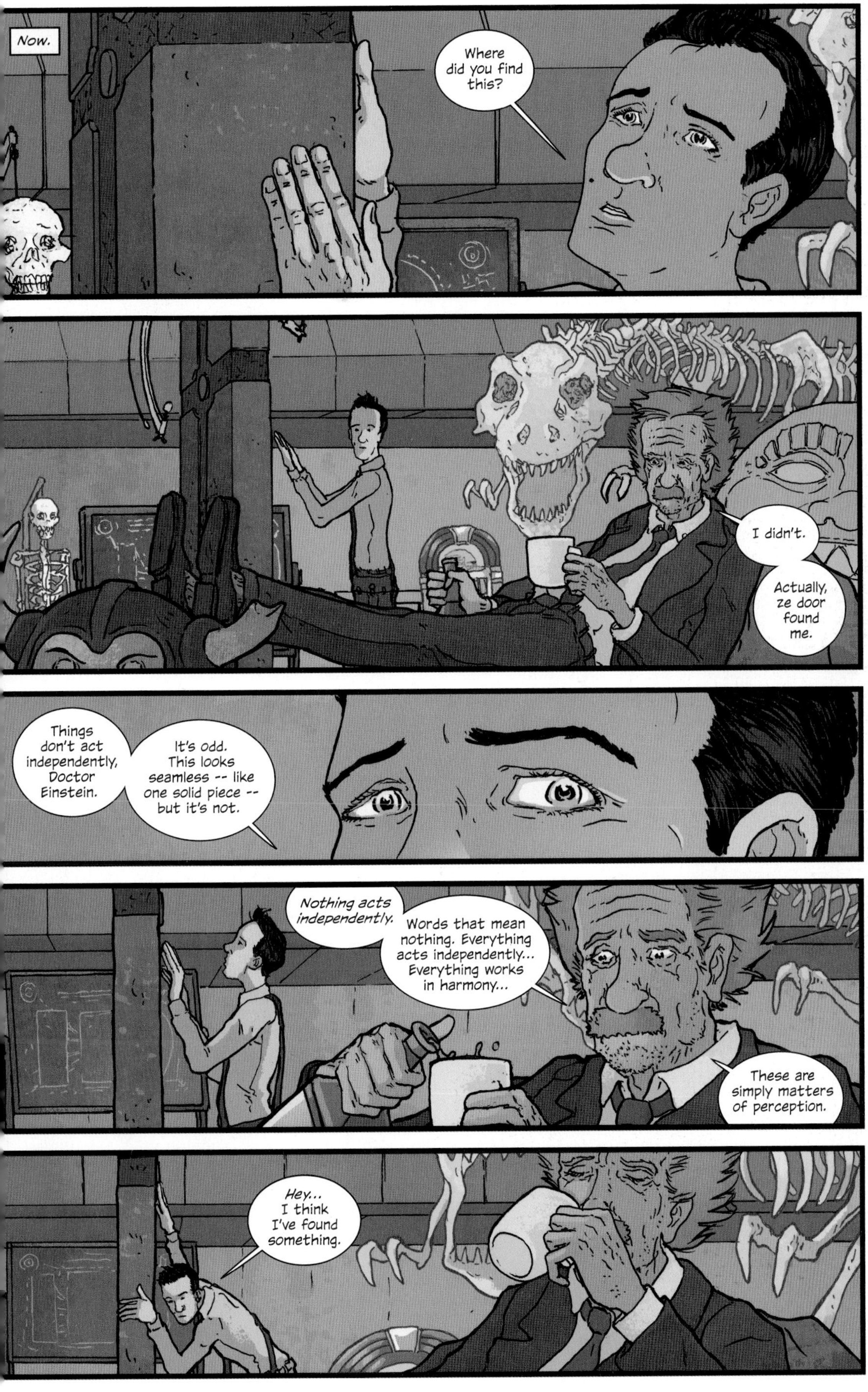

Now.
Where did you find this?
I didn't.
Actually, ze door found me.
Things don't act independently, Doctor Einstein.
It's odd. This looks seamless -- like one solid piece -- but it's not.
Nothing acts independently.
Words that mean nothing. Everything acts independently... Everything works in harmony...
These are simply matters of perception.
Hey... I think I've found something.

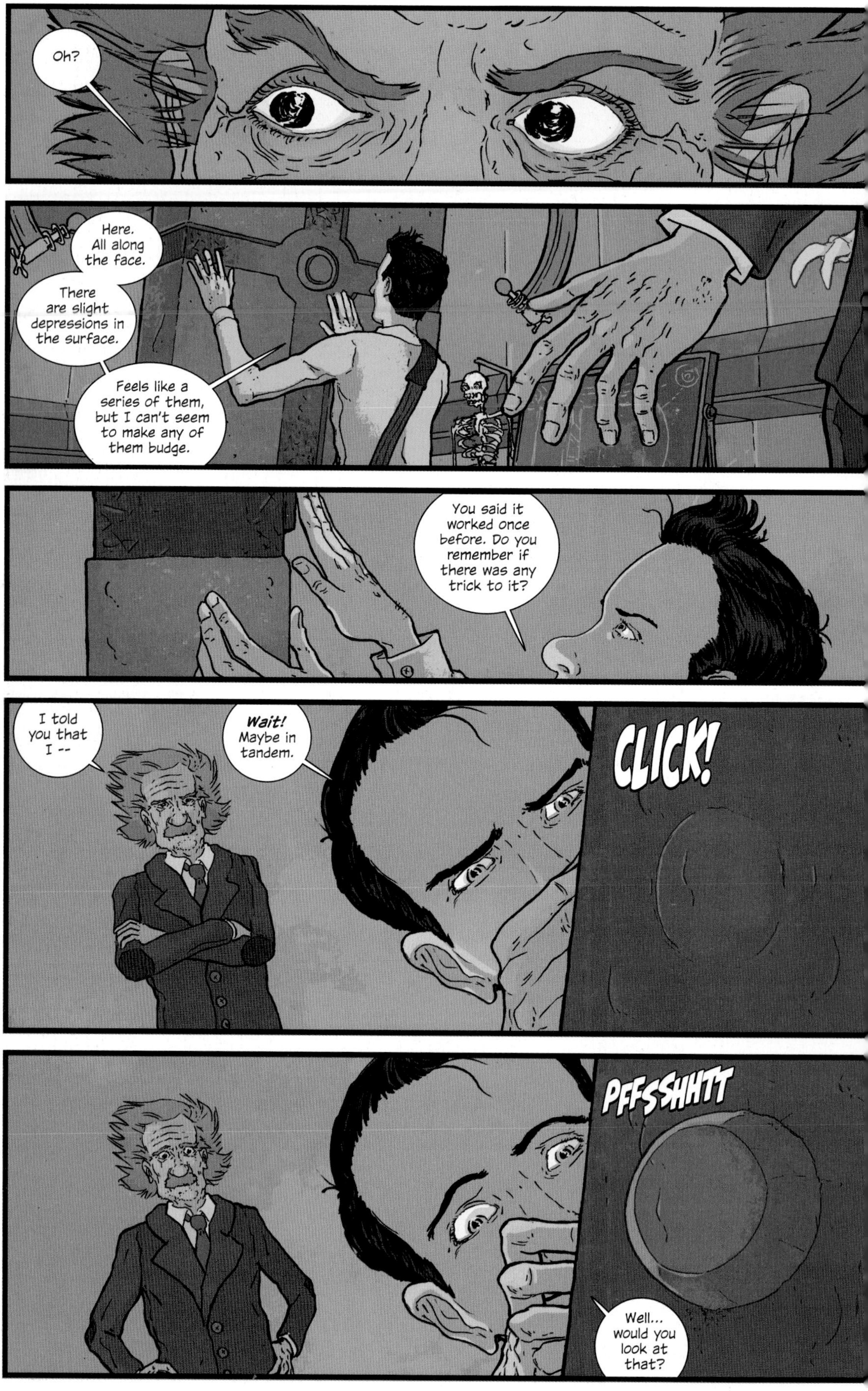

Oh?
Here. All along the face.
There are slight depressions in the surface.
Feels like a series of them, but I can't seem to make any of them budge.
You said it worked once before. Do you remember if there was any trick to it?
I told you that I --
Wait! Maybe in tandem.
CLICK!
PFFSSHHTT
Well... would you look at that?

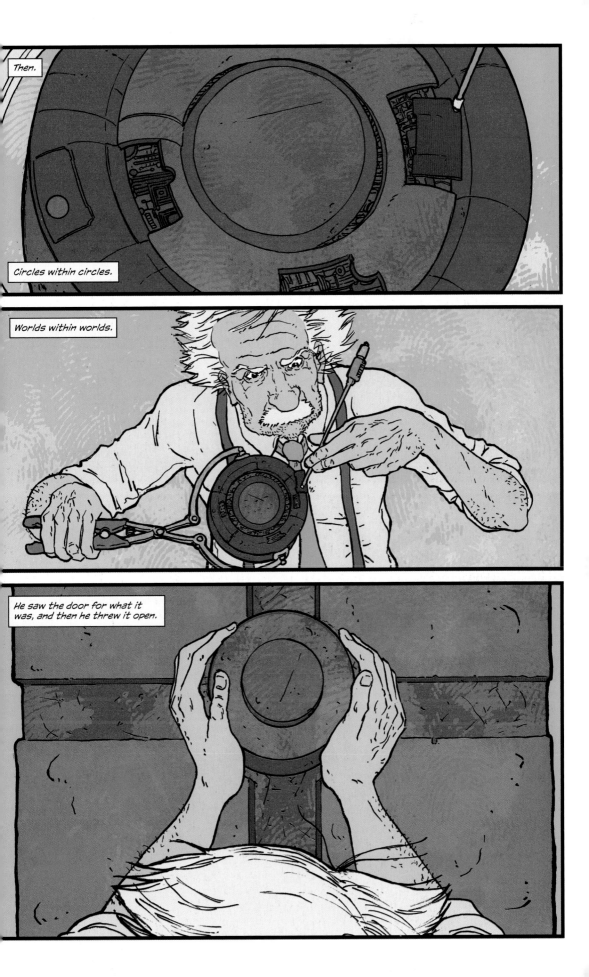

Then.

Circles within circles.

Worlds within worlds.

He saw the door for what it was, and then he threw it open.

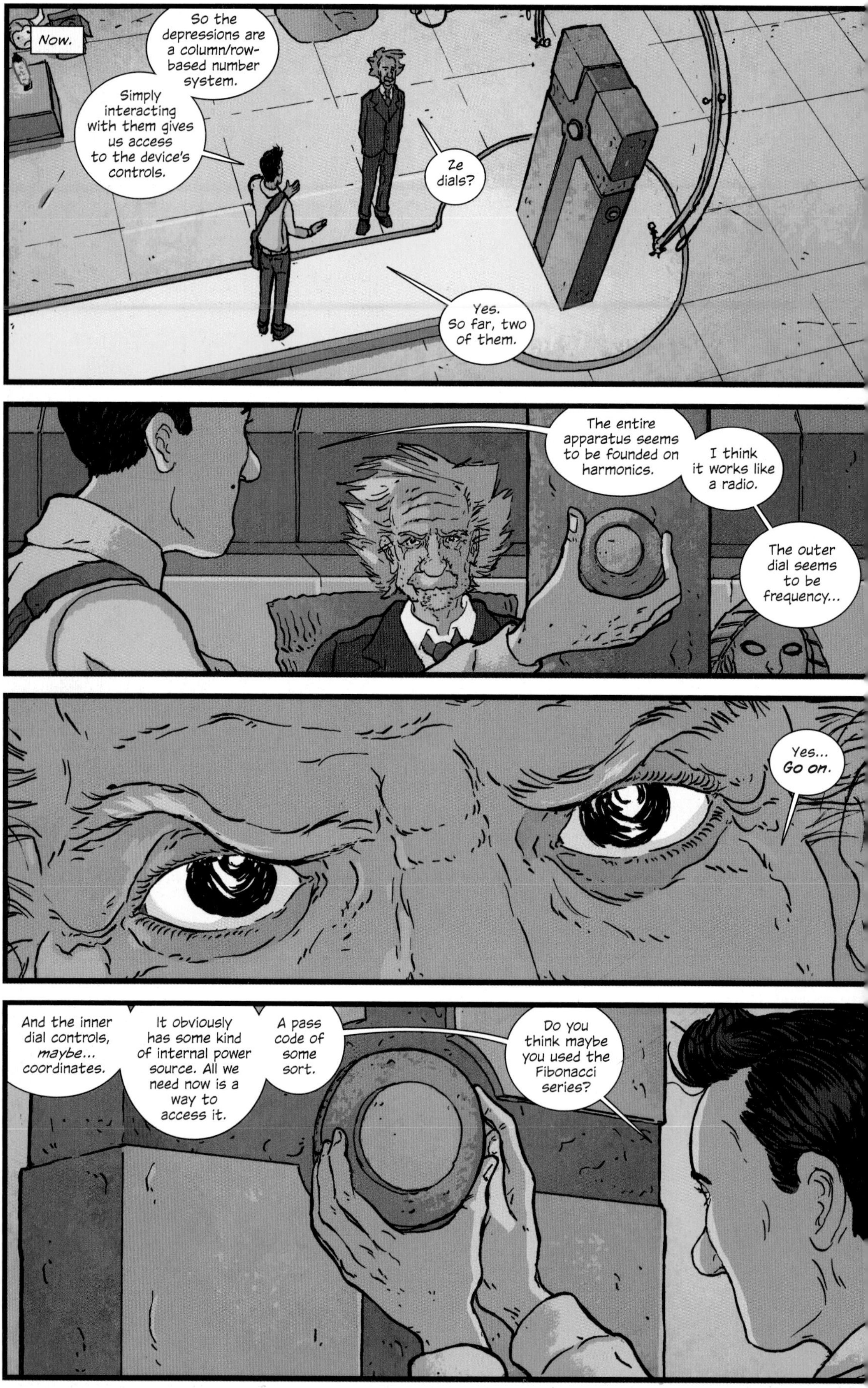
Now.
So the depressions are a column/row-based number system.
Simply interacting with them gives us access to the device's controls.
Ze dials?
Yes. So far, two of them.
The entire apparatus seems to be founded on harmonics.
I think it works like a radio.
The outer dial seems to be frequency...
Yes... *Go on.*
And the inner dial controls, *maybe*... coordinates.
It obviously has some kind of internal power source. All we need now is a way to access it.
A pass code of some sort.
Do you think maybe you used the Fibonacci series?

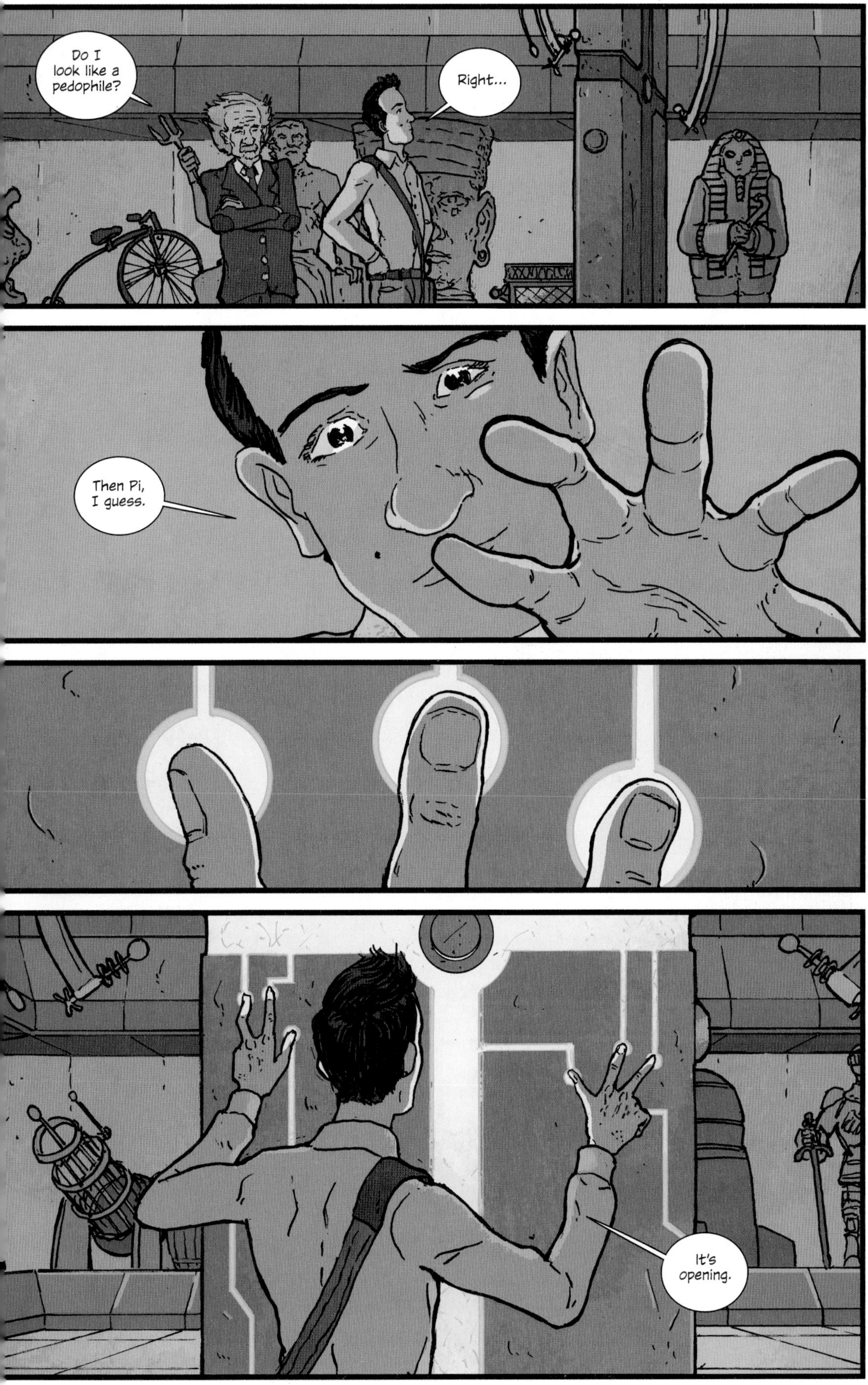
Do I look like a pedophile?
Right...
Then Pi, I guess.
It's opening.

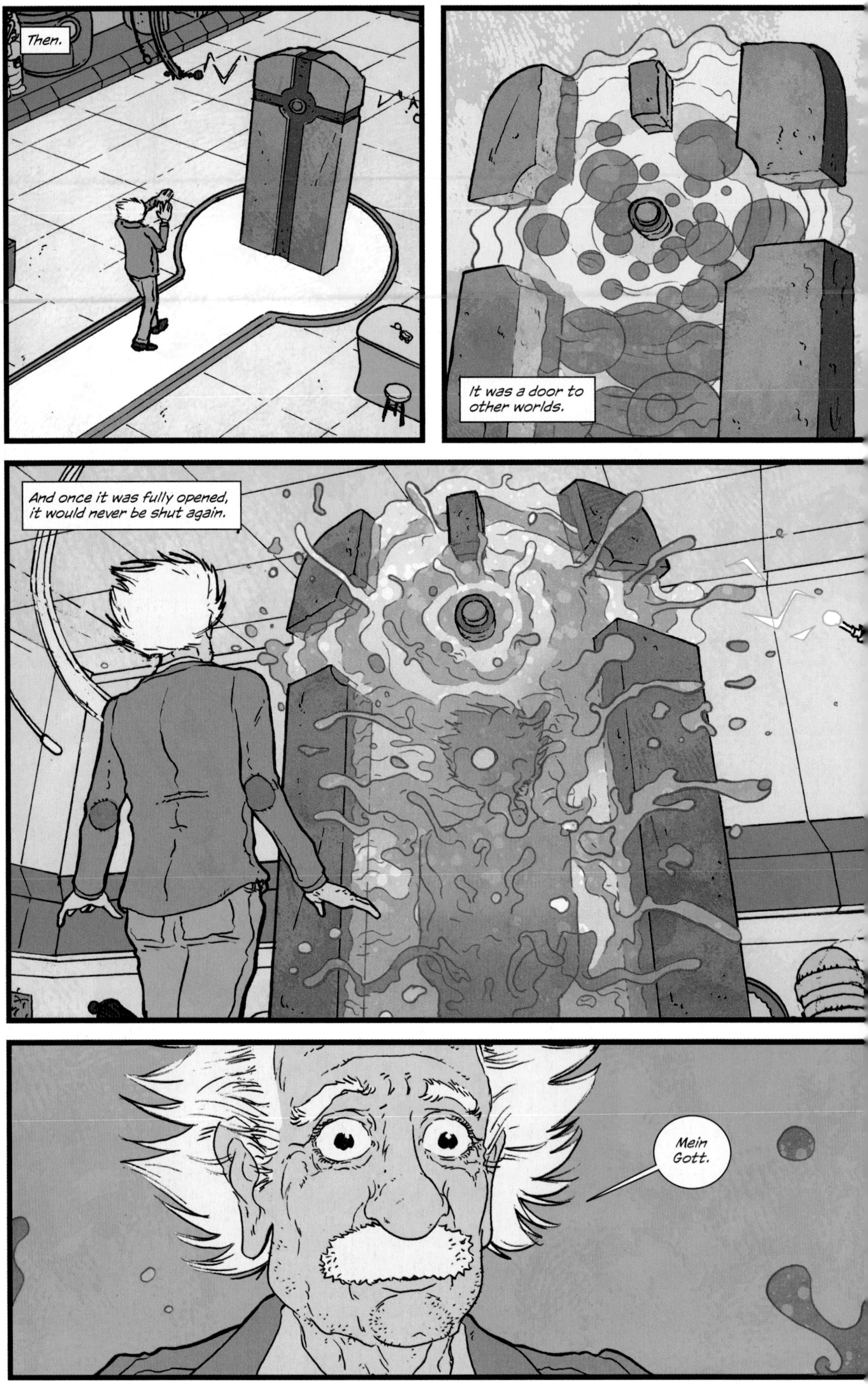
Then.
It was a door to other worlds.
And once it was fully opened, it would never be shut again.
Mein Gott.

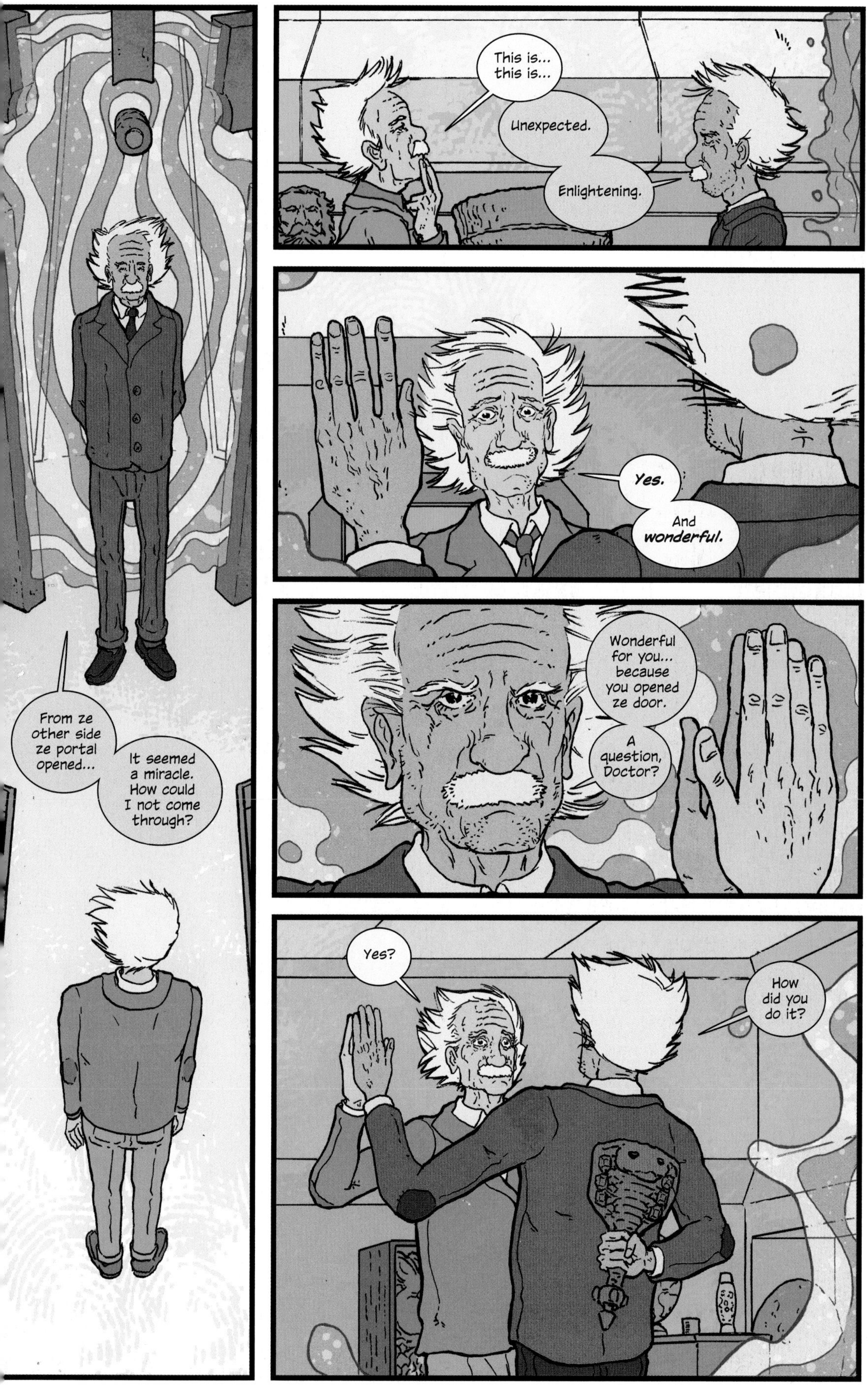
From ze other side ze portal opened...
It seemed a miracle. How could I not come through?
This is... this is...
Unexpected.
Enlightening.
Yes.
And wonderful.
Wonderful for you... because you opened ze door.
A question, Doctor?
Yes?
How did you do it?

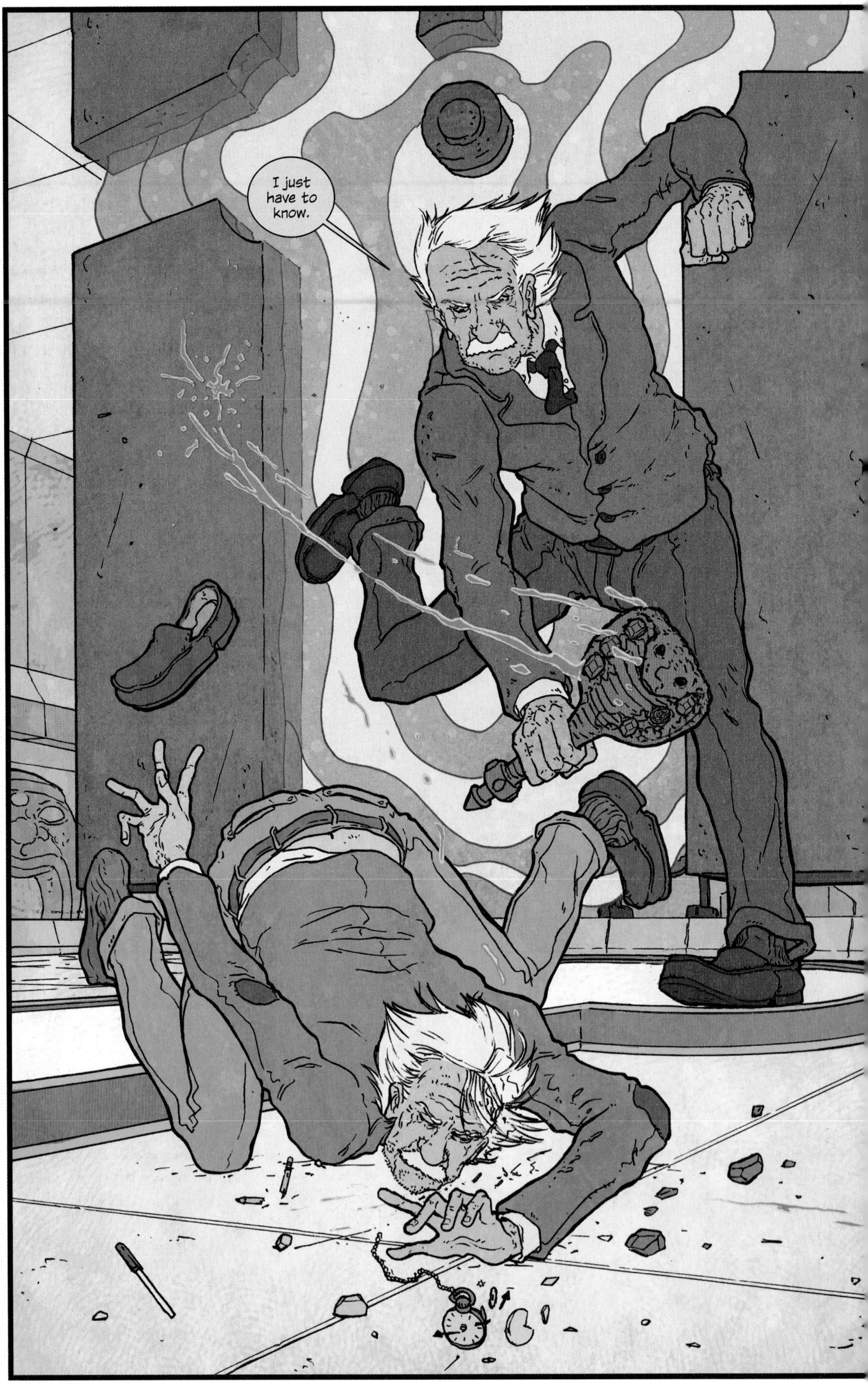
I just have to know.

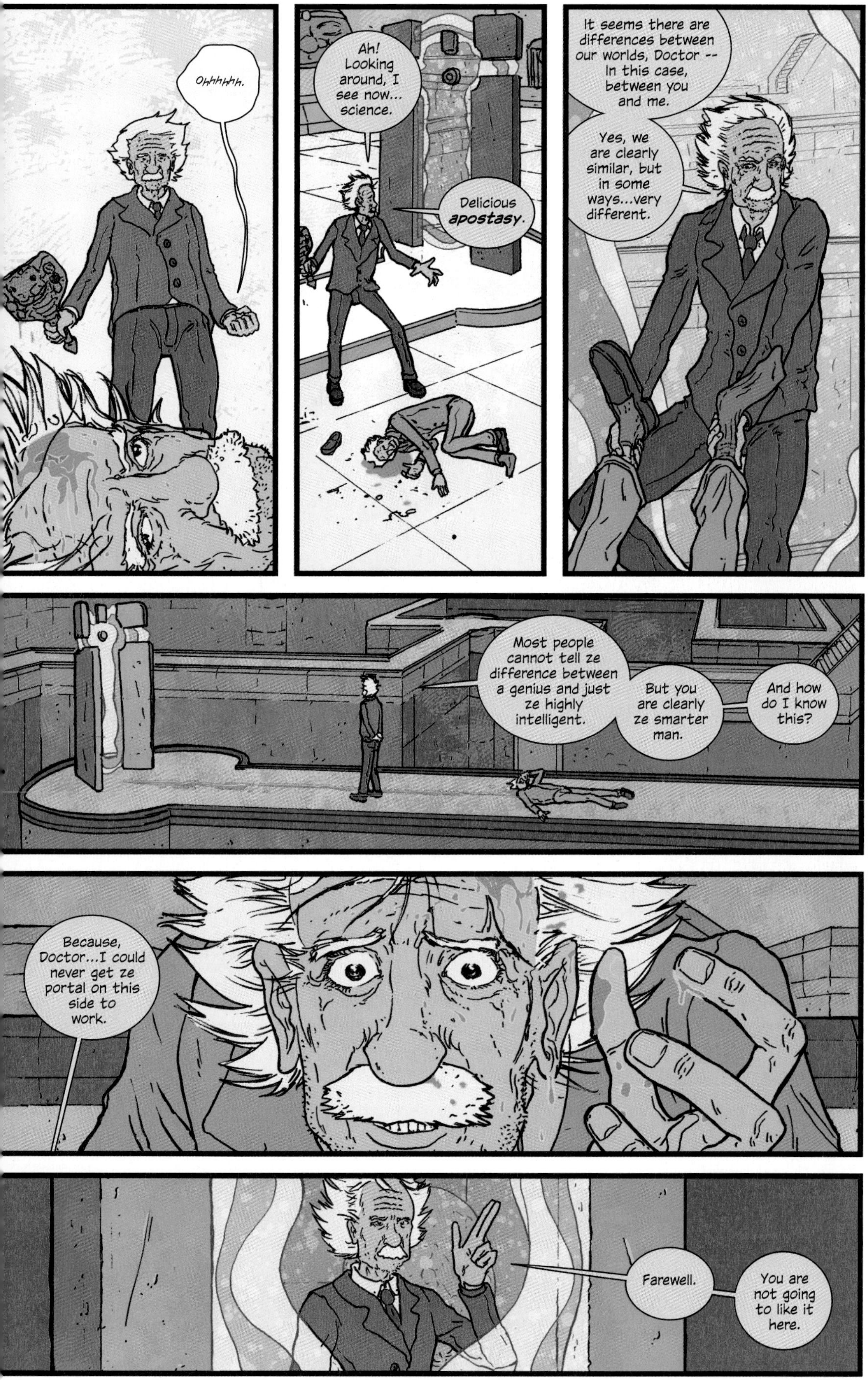
Ohhhhhh.
Ah! Looking around, I see now... science.
Delicious *apostasy*.
It seems there are differences between our worlds, Doctor -- In this case, between you and me.
Yes, we are clearly similar, but in some ways...very different.
Most people cannot tell ze difference between a genius and just ze highly intelligent.
But you are clearly ze smarter man.
And how do I know this?
Because, Doctor...I could never get ze portal on this side to work.
Farewell.
You are not going to like it here.

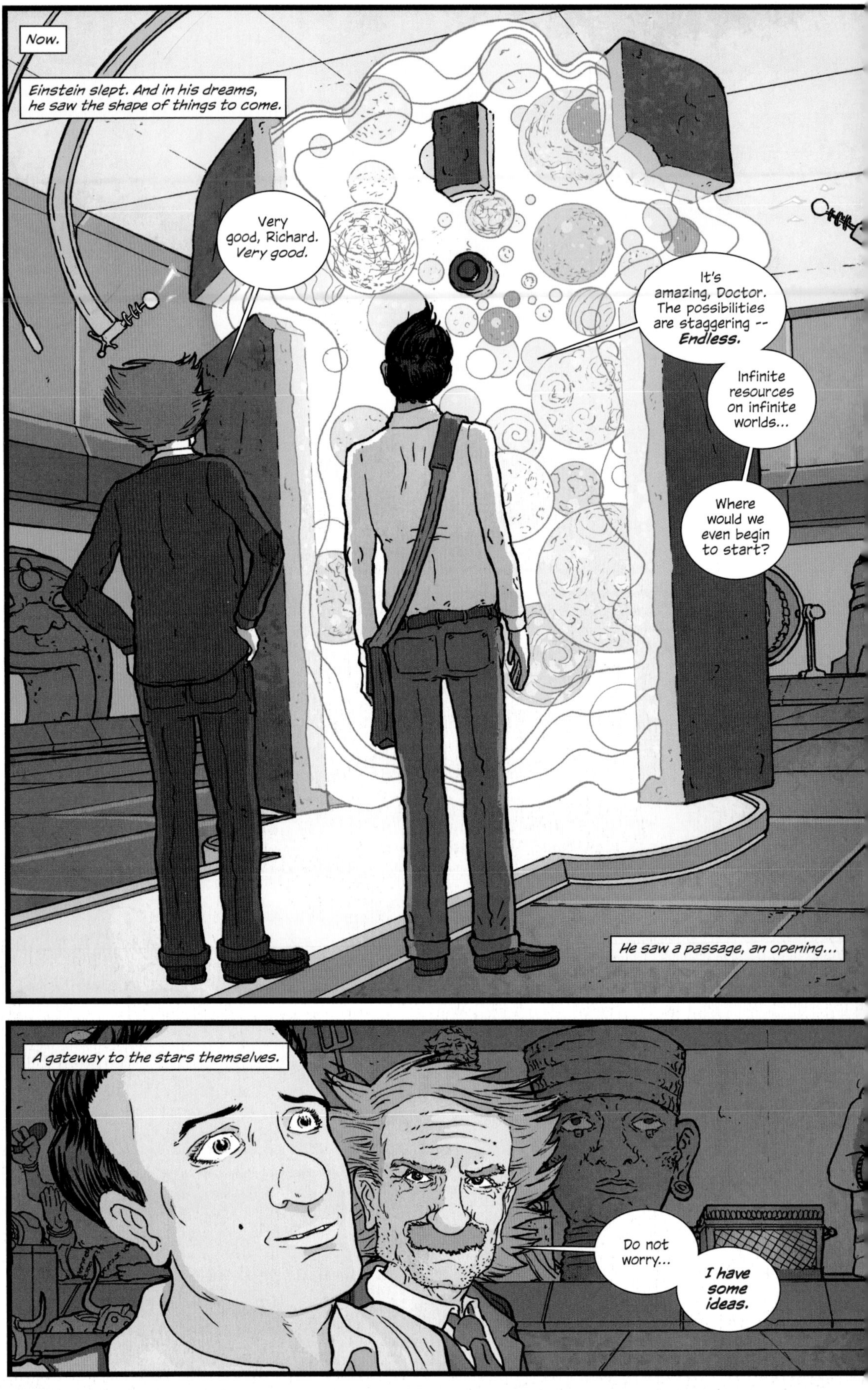
Now.
Einstein slept. And in his dreams, he saw the shape of things to come.
Very good, Richard. Very good.
It's amazing, Doctor. The possibilities are staggering -- Endless.
Infinite resources on infinite worlds...
Where would we even begin to start?
He saw a passage, an opening...
A gateway to the stars themselves.
Do not worry...
I have some ideas.

"THE UNIVERSE ASKED A QUESTION. I SIMPLY ANSWERED IT.

WHO COULD HAVE PREDICTED THE HELL THAT FOLLOWED?"

- ALBERT EINSTEIN

CLAVIS AUREA
THE RECORDED FEYNMAN | **VOL. 4**

THERE ARE NO PERFECT
ANSWERS

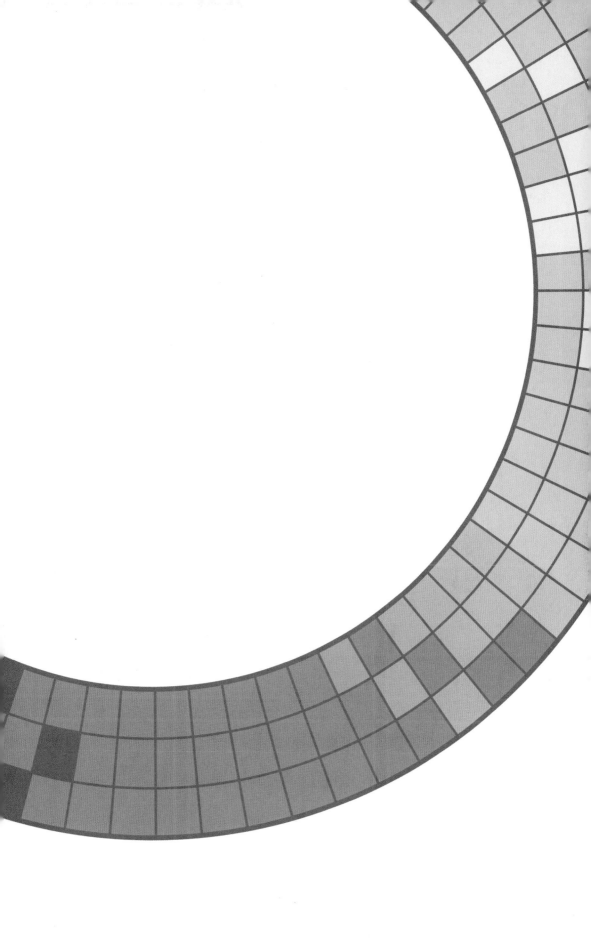

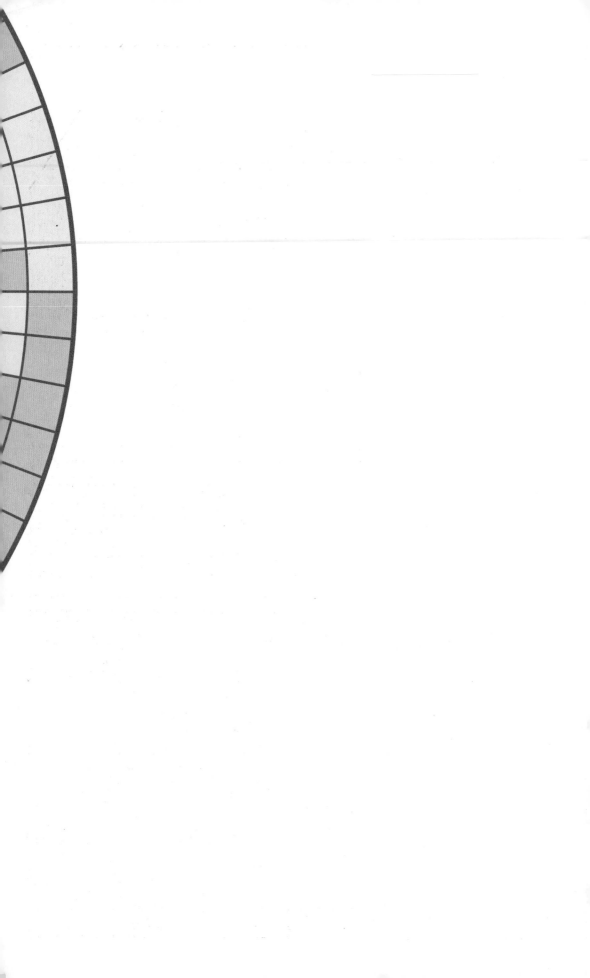

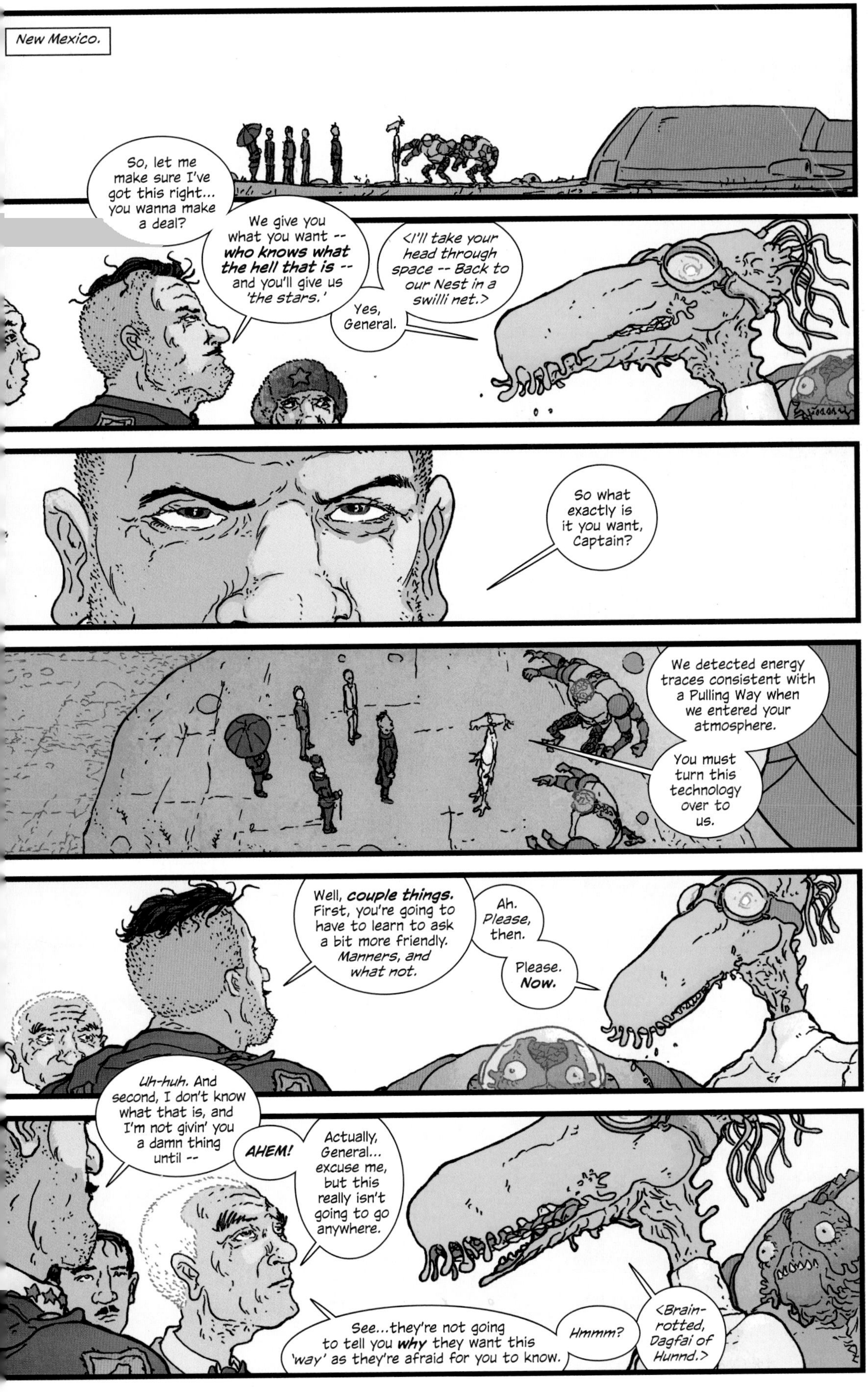
New Mexico.
So, let me make sure I've got this right... you wanna make a deal?
We give you what you want -- **who knows what the hell that is** -- and you'll give us 'the stars.'
Yes, General.
<I'll take your head through space -- Back to our Nest in a swilli net.>
So what exactly is it you want, Captain?
We detected energy traces consistent with a Pulling Way when we entered your atmosphere.
You must turn this technology over to us.
Well, **couple things.** First, you're going to have to learn to ask a bit more friendly. *Manners, and what not.*
Ah. *Please,* then.
Please. **Now.**
Uh-huh. And second, I don't know what that is, and I'm not givin' you a damn thing until --
AHEM!
Actually, General... excuse me, but this really isn't going to go anywhere.
See...they're not going to tell you **why** they want this 'way' as they're afraid for you to know.
Hmmm?
<Brain-rotted, Dagfai of Hunnd.>

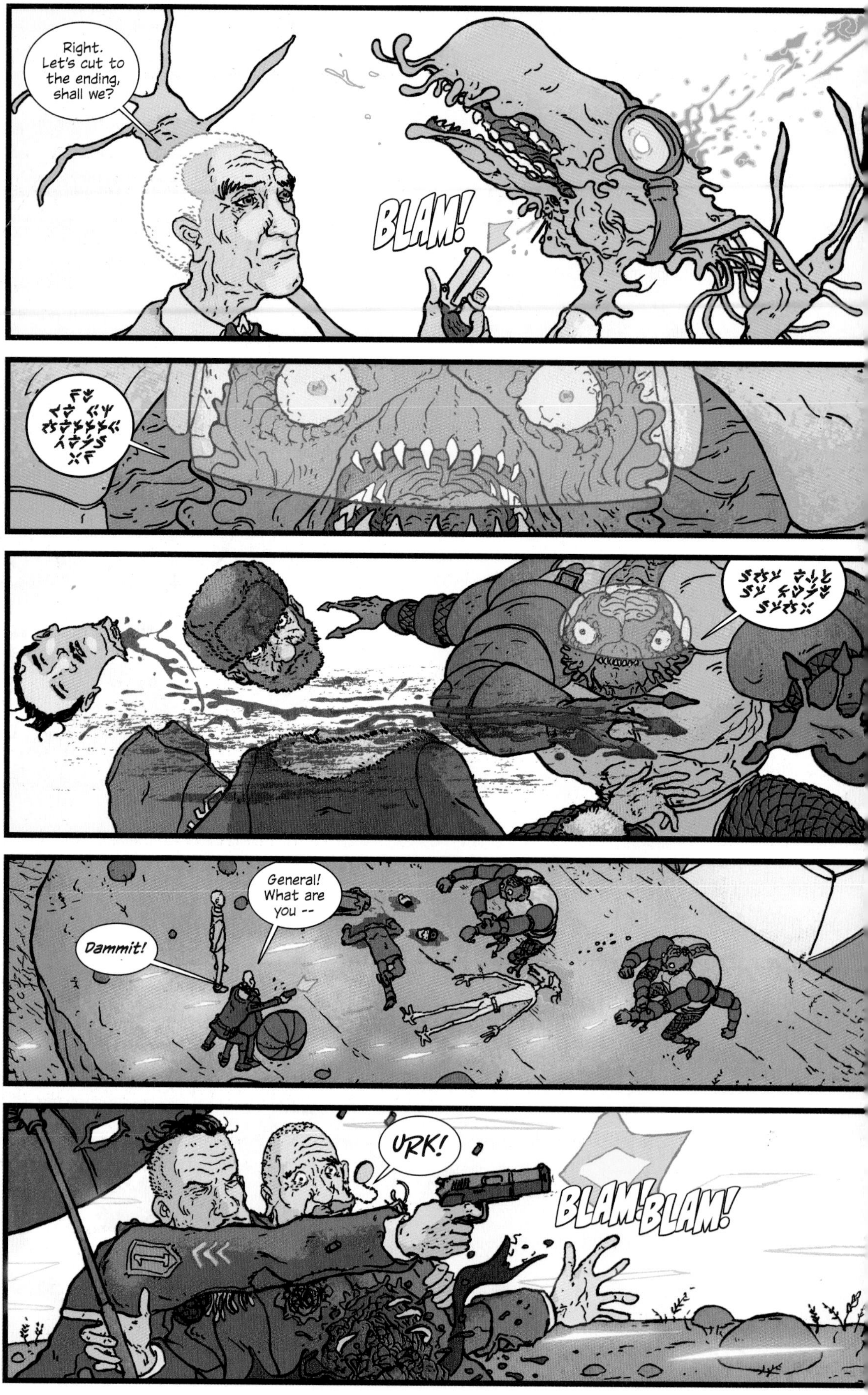
Right. Let's cut to the ending, shall we?
BLAM!
General! What are you --
Dammit!
URK!
BLAM! BLAM!

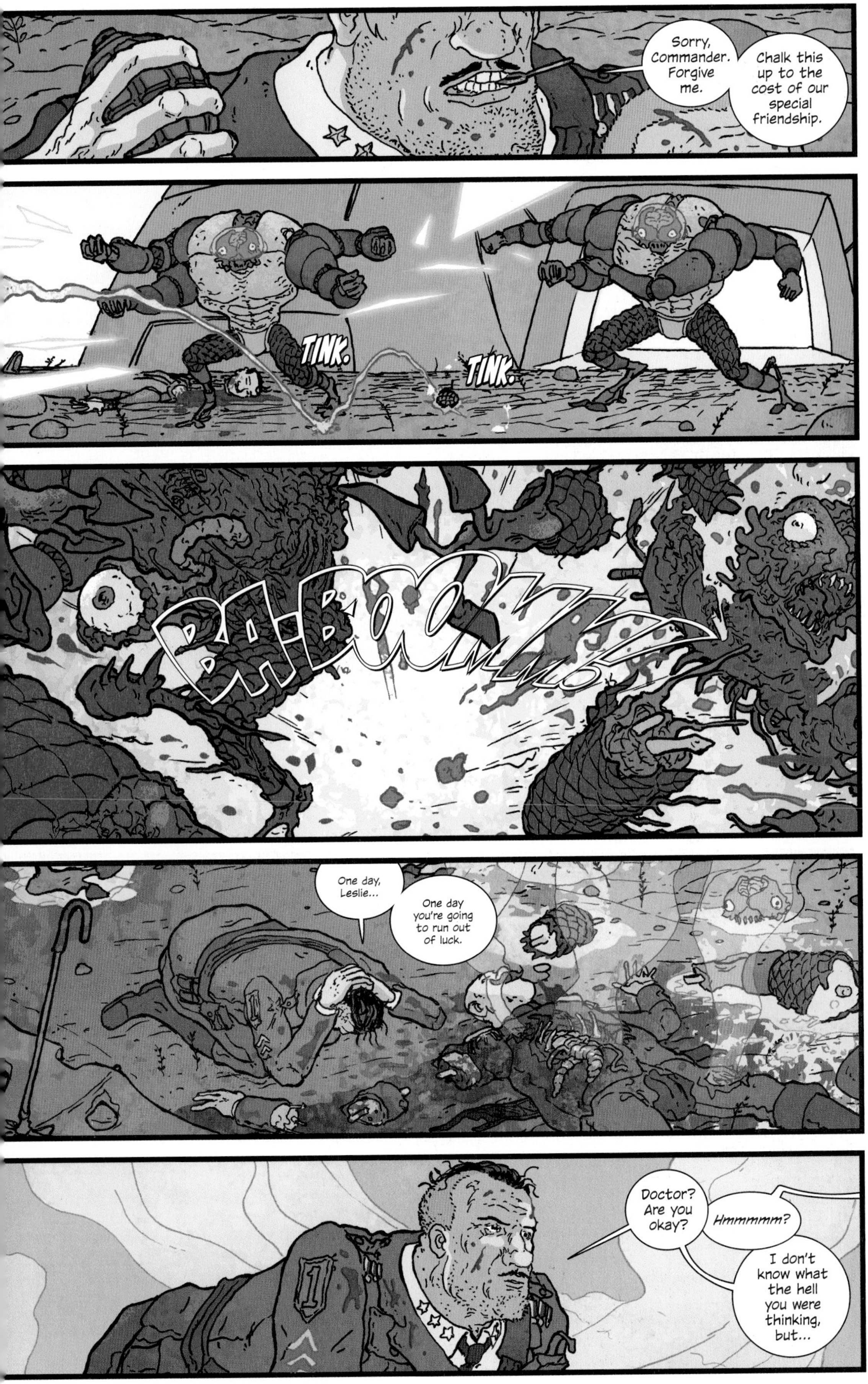
Sorry, Commander. Forgive me.
Chalk this up to the cost of our special friendship.
TINK.
TINK.
BA-BOOM!
One day, Leslie...
One day you're going to run out of luck.
Doctor? Are you okay?
Hmmmmm?
I don't know what the hell you were thinking, but...

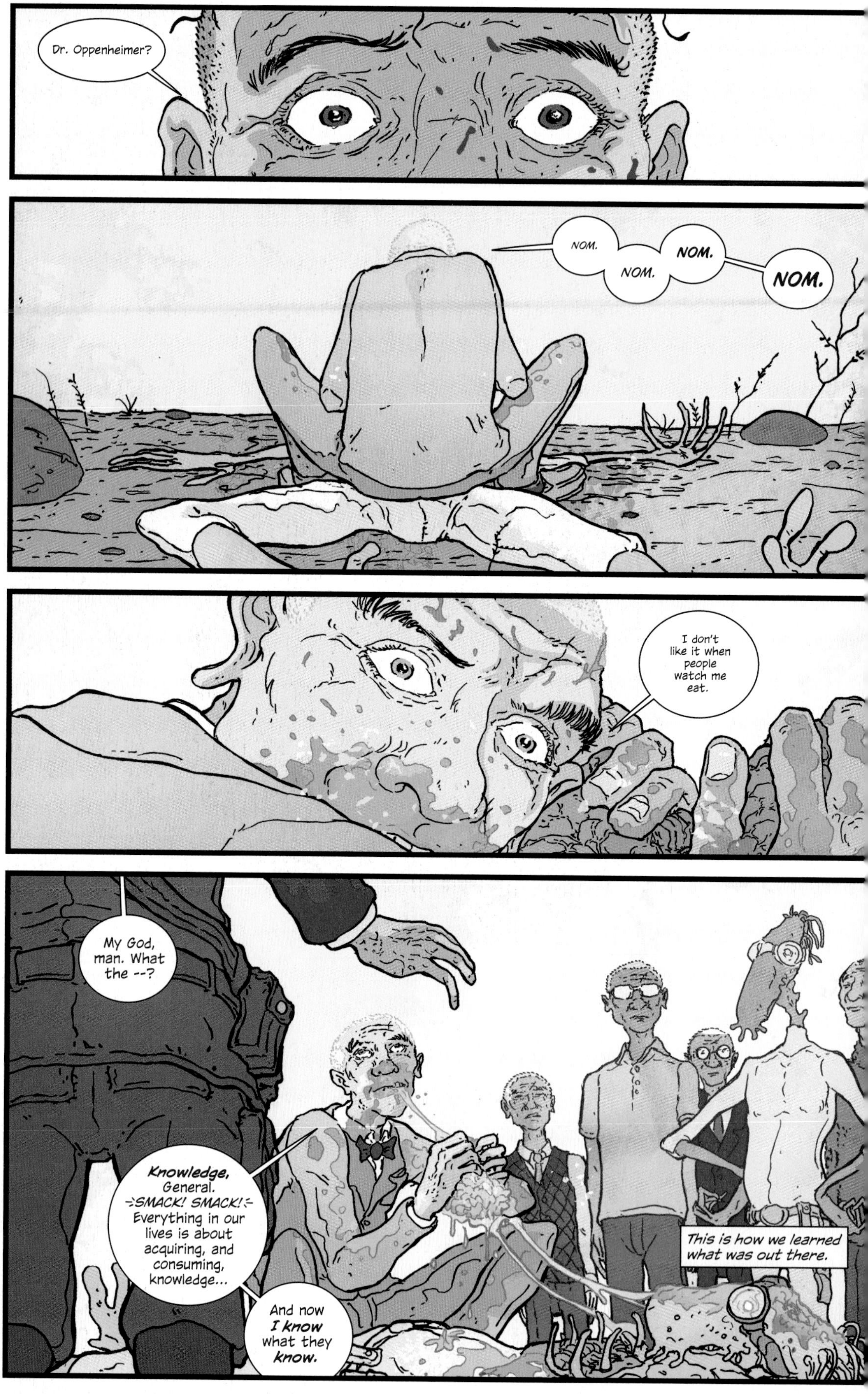
Dr. Oppenheimer?
NOM.
NOM.
NOM.
NOM.
I don't like it when people watch me eat.
My God, man. What the --?
Knowledge, General. -SMACK! SMACK!- Everything in our lives is about acquiring, and consuming, knowledge...
And now *I know* what they *know.*
This is how we learned what was out there.

"HMMMM?"

- OPPENHEIMER

CLAVIS AUREA
THE RECORDED FEYNMAN

VOL. 1

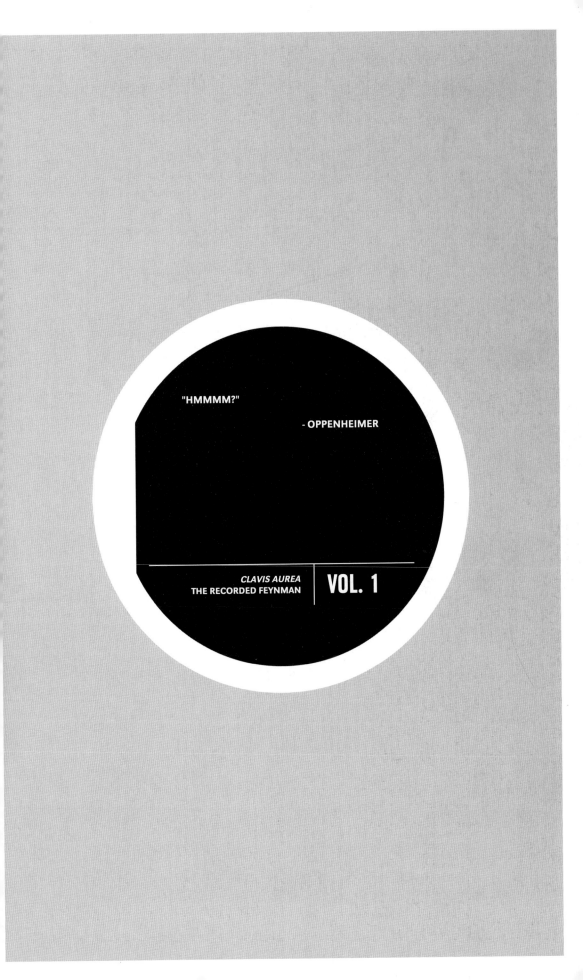

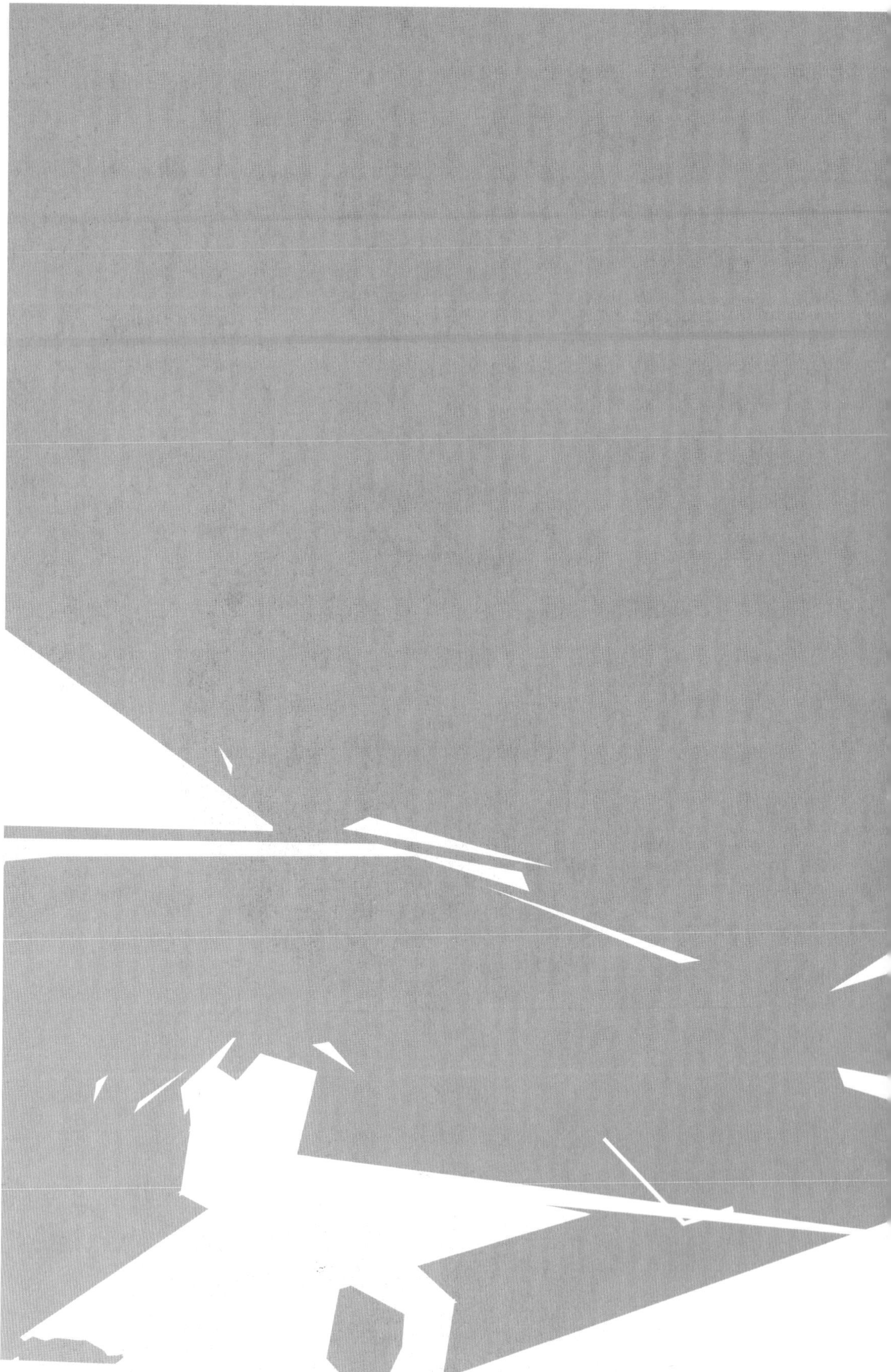

05

HORIZON

"WHAT I LEARNED WAS THE DIFFERENCE BETWEEN VALUE AND COST.

EVERY DECISION THAT FOLLOWED WAS SIMPLY A PRODUCT OF WEIGHING THE POTENTIAL PUNISHMENT."

CLAVIS AUREA
THE RECORDED FEYNMAN

VOL. 1

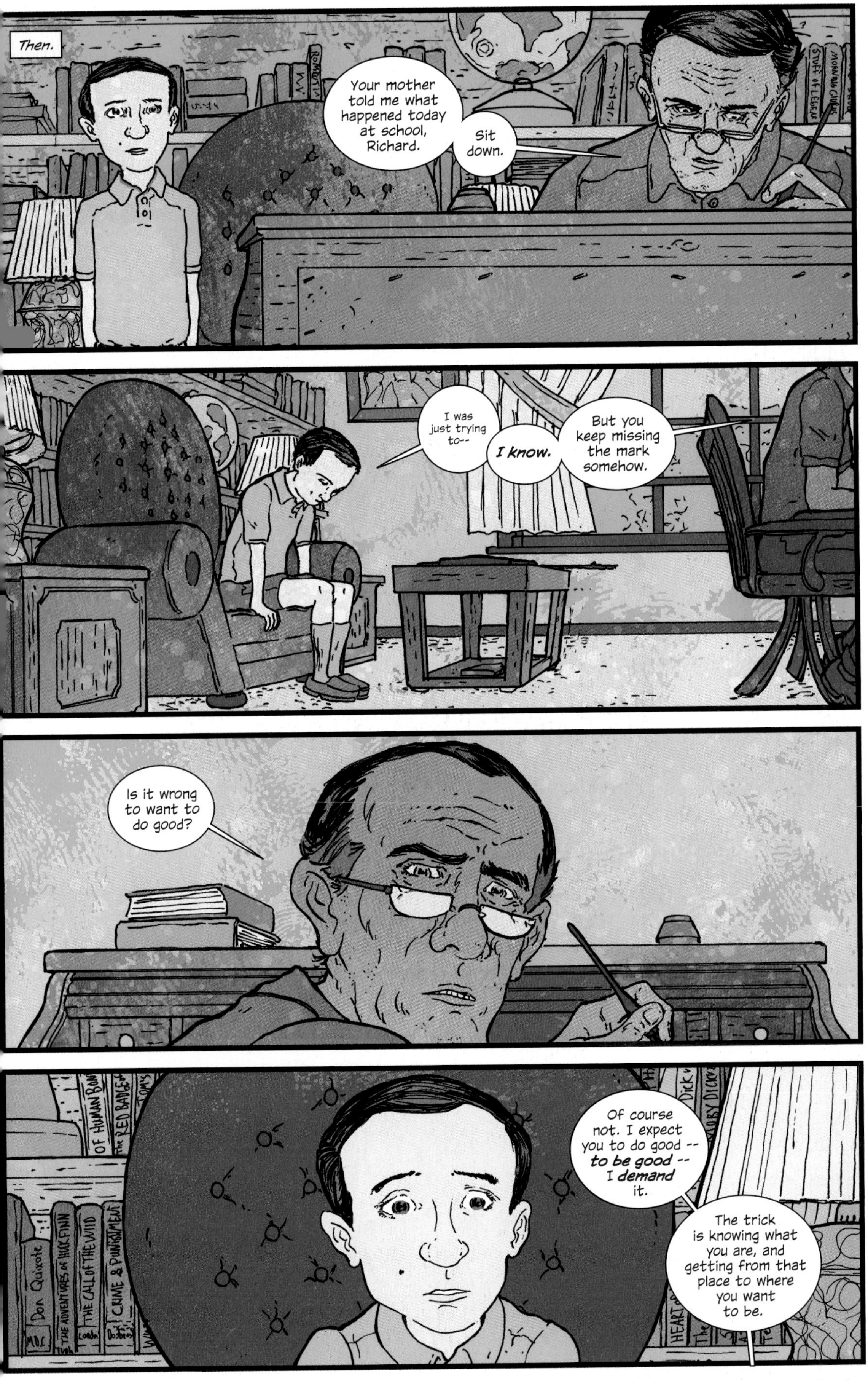
Then.
Your mother told me what happened today at school, Richard.
Sit down.
I was just trying to--
I know.
But you keep missing the mark somehow.
Is it wrong to want to do good?
Of course not. I expect you to do good -- ***to be good*** -- I ***demand*** it.
The trick is knowing what you are, and getting from that place to where you want to be.

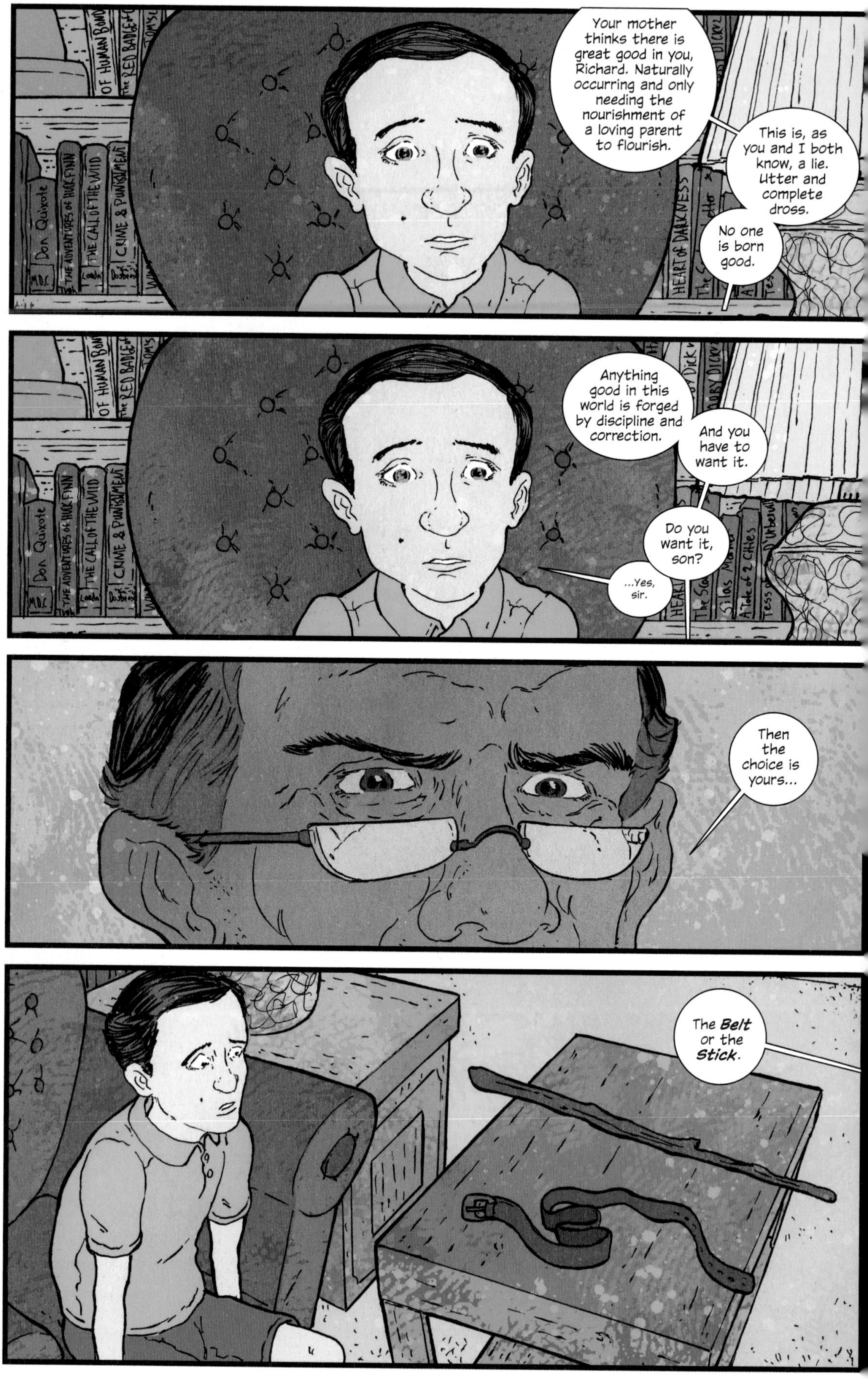

Your mother thinks there is great good in you, Richard. Naturally occurring and only needing the nourishment of a loving parent to flourish.
This is, as you and I both know, a lie. Utter and complete dross.
No one is born good.
Anything good in this world is forged by discipline and correction.
And you have to want it.
Do you want it, son?
...Yes, sir.
Then the choice is yours...
The **Belt** or the **Stick**.

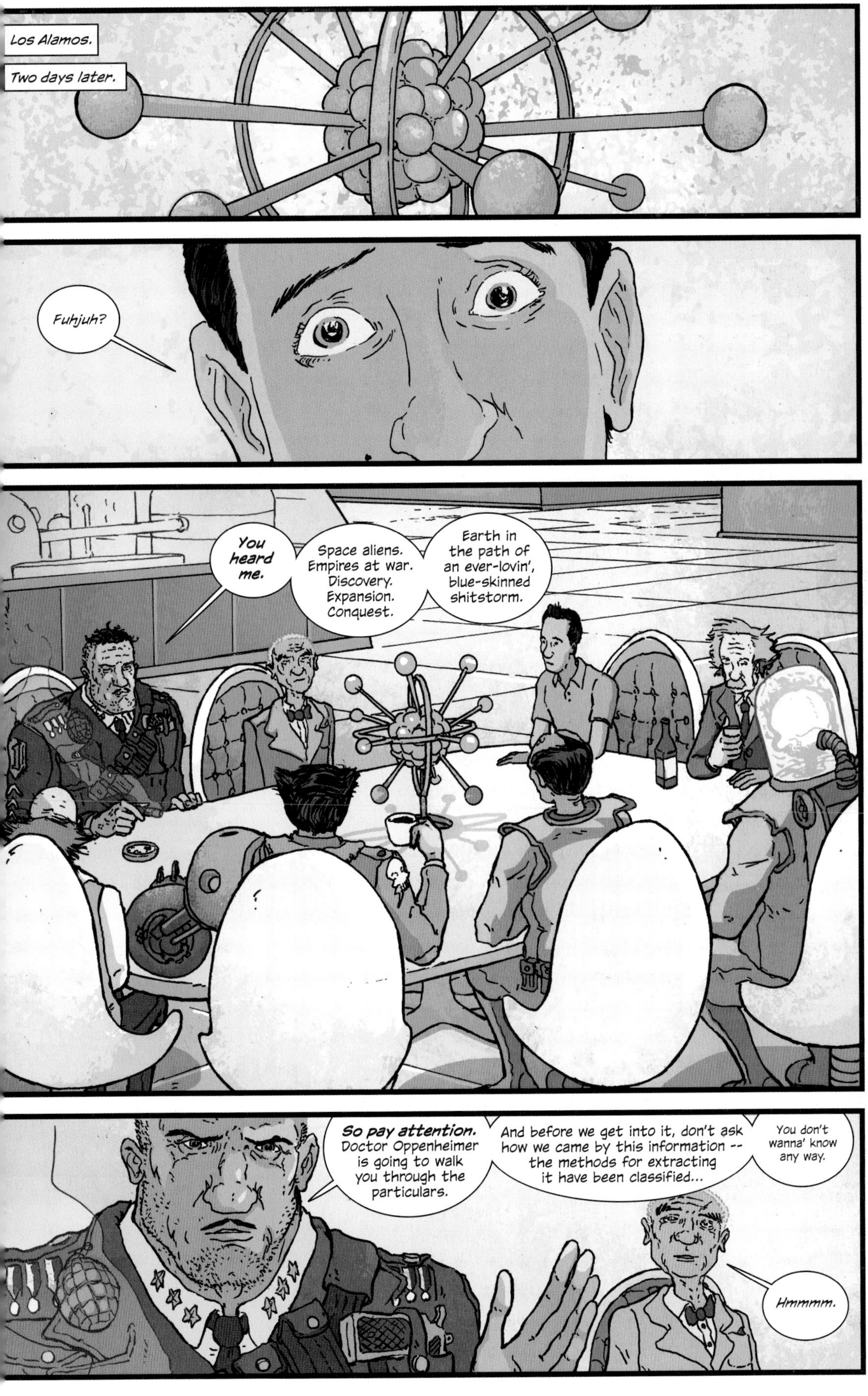

Los Alamos.
Two days later.
Fuhjuh?
You heard me.
Space aliens. Empires at war. Discovery. Expansion. Conquest.
Earth in the path of an ever-lovin', blue-skinned shitstorm.
So pay attention. Doctor Oppenheimer is going to walk you through the particulars.
And before we get into it, don't ask how we came by this information -- the methods for extracting it have been classified...
You don't wanna' know any way.
Hmmmm.

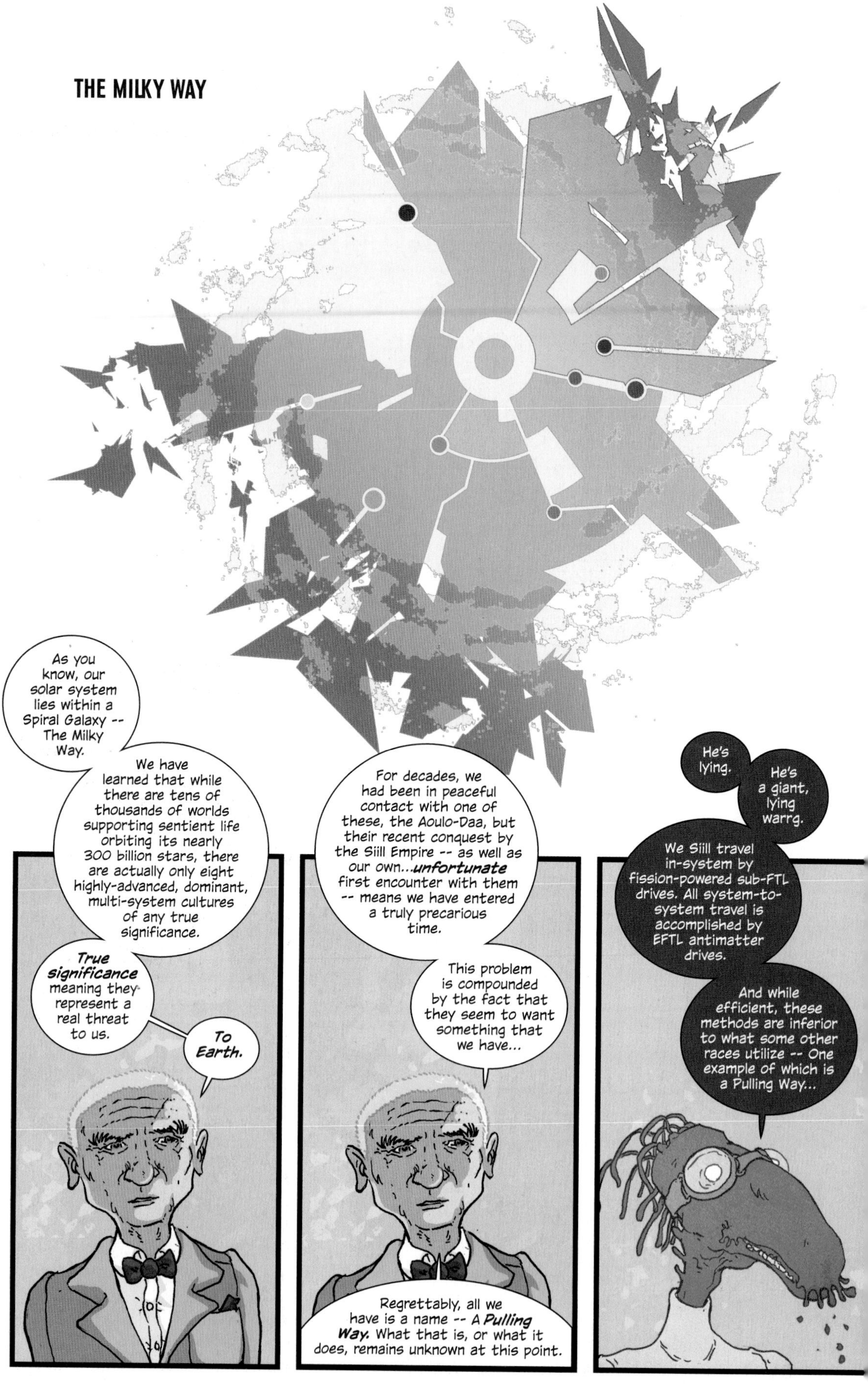
THE MILKY WAY
As you know, our solar system lies within a Spiral Galaxy -- The Milky Way.
We have learned that while there are tens of thousands of worlds supporting sentient life orbiting its nearly 300 billion stars, there are actually only eight highly-advanced, dominant, multi-system cultures of any true significance.
True significance meaning they represent a real threat to us.
To Earth.
For decades, we had been in peaceful contact with one of these, the Aoulo-Daa, but their recent conquest by the Siill Empire -- as well as our own... *unfortunate* first encounter with them -- means we have entered a truly precarious time.
This problem is compounded by the fact that they seem to want something that we have...
Regrettably, all we have is a name -- A *Pulling Way.* What that is, or what it does, remains unknown at this point.
He's lying.
He's a giant, lying warrg.
We Siill travel in-system by fission-powered sub-FTL drives. All system-to-system travel is accomplished by EFTL antimatter drives.
And while efficient, these methods are inferior to what some other races utilize -- One example of which is a Pulling Way...

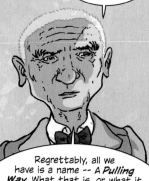

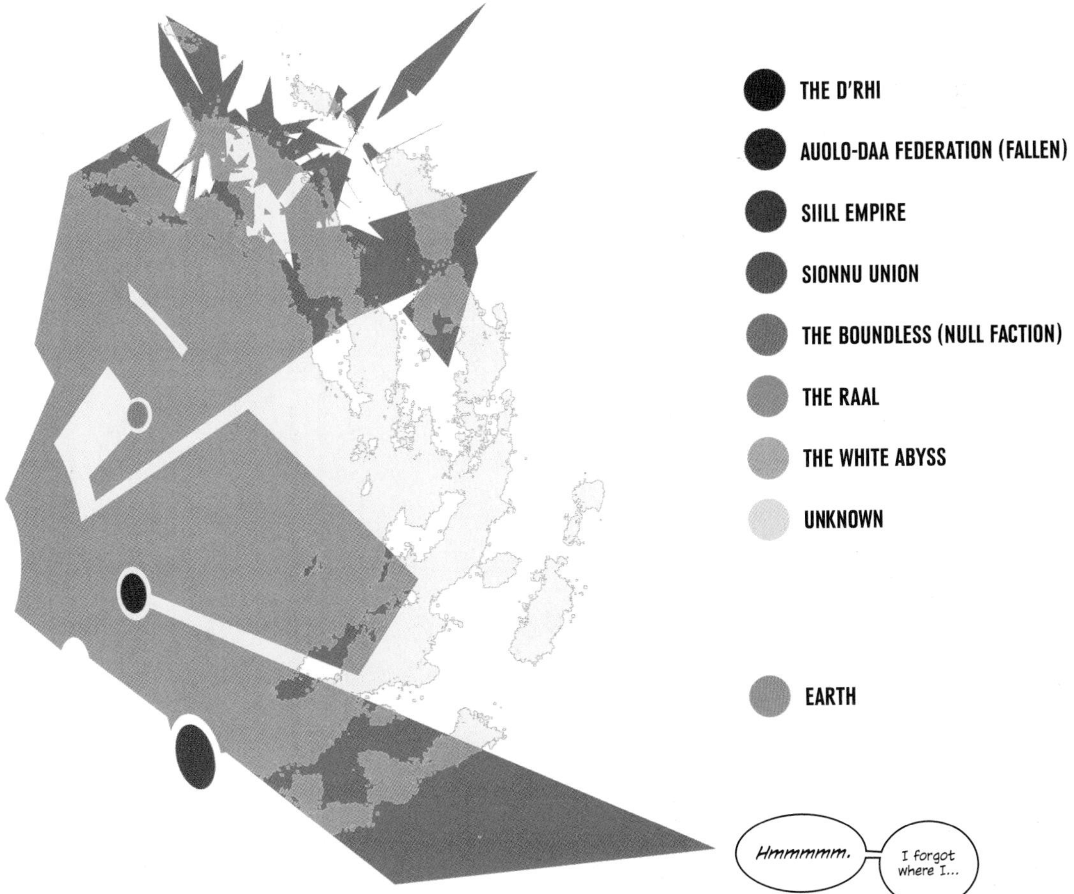
THE D'RHI
AUOLO-DAA FEDERATION (FALLEN)
SIILL EMPIRE
SIONNU UNION
THE BOUNDLESS (NULL FACTION)
THE RAAL
THE WHITE ABYSS
UNKNOWN
EARTH

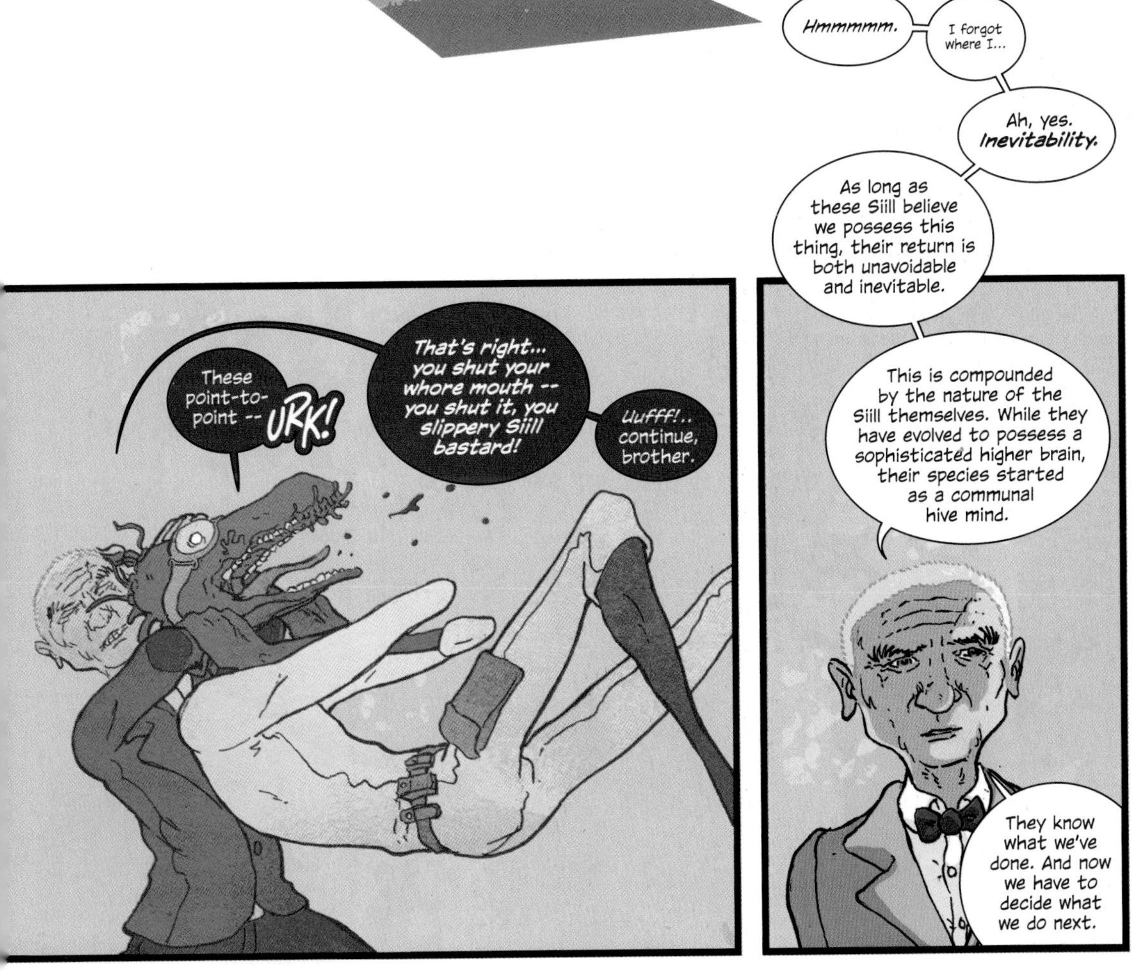
Hmmmmm.
I forgot where I...
Ah, yes. *Inevitability.*
These point-to-point -- URK!
That's right... you shut your whore mouth -- you shut it, you slippery Siill bastard!
Uufff!.. continue, brother.
As long as these Siill believe we possess this thing, their return is both unavoidable and inevitable.
This is compounded by the nature of the Siill themselves. While they have evolved to possess a sophisticated higher brain, their species started as a communal hive mind.
They know what we've done. And now we have to decide what we do next.

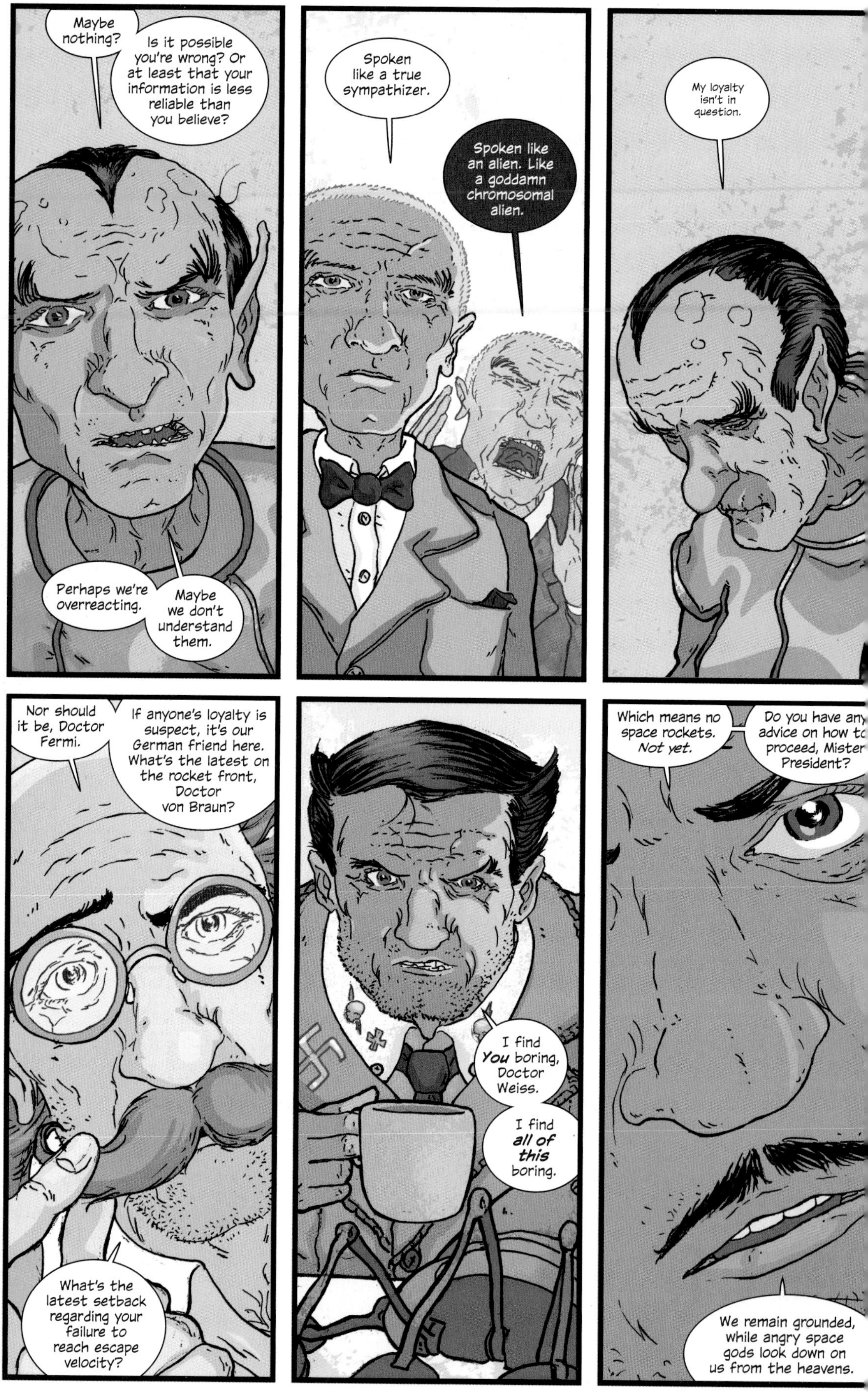

Maybe nothing?
Is it possible you're wrong? Or at least that your information is less reliable than you believe?
Perhaps we're overreacting.
Maybe we don't understand them.
Spoken like a true sympathizer.
Spoken like an alien. Like a goddamn chromosomal alien.
My loyalty isn't in question.
Nor should it be, Doctor Fermi.
If anyone's loyalty is suspect, it's our German friend here. What's the latest on the rocket front, Doctor von Braun?
What's the latest setback regarding your failure to reach escape velocity?
I find *You* boring, Doctor Weiss.
I find ***all of this*** boring.
Which means no space rockets. *Not yet.*
Do you have an advice on how t proceed, Mister President?
We remain grounded, while angry space gods look down on us from the heavens.

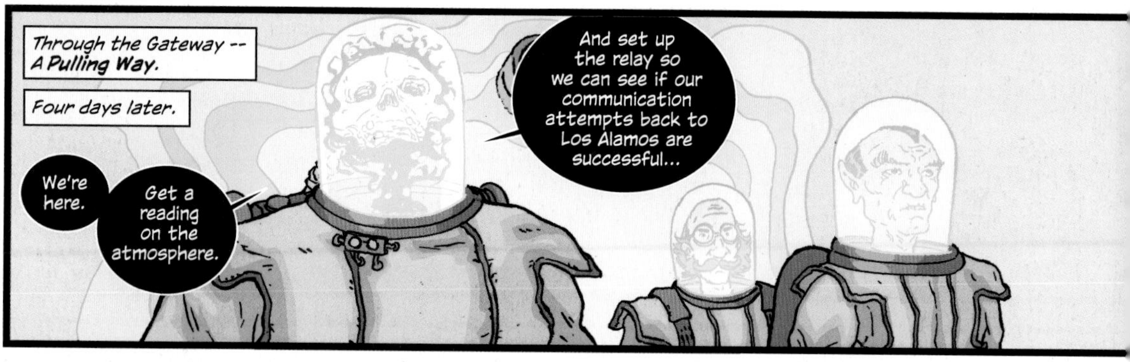
Through the Gateway --
A Pulling Way.
Four days later.
We're here.
Get a reading on the atmosphere.
And set up the relay so we can see if our communication attempts back to Los Alamos are successful...

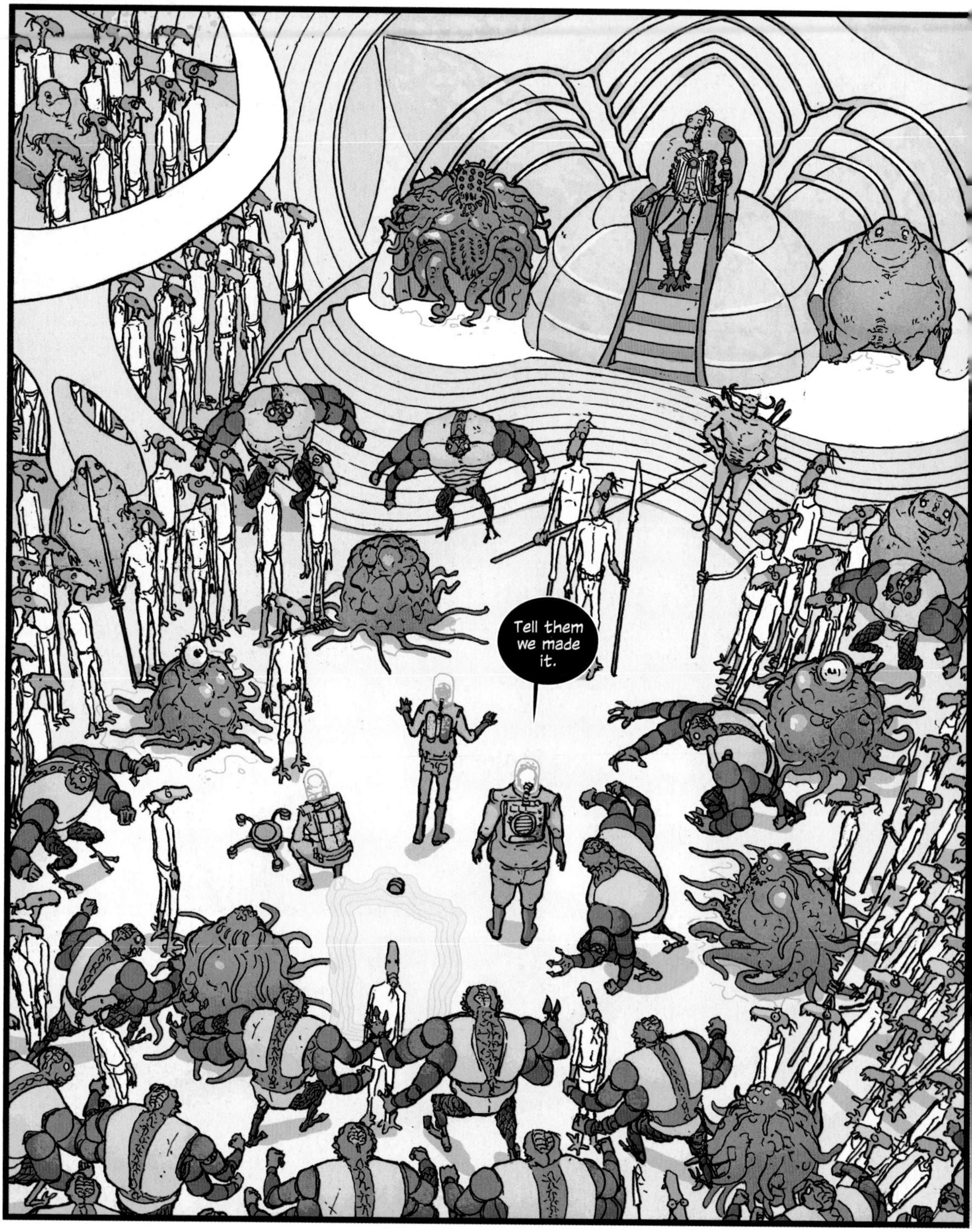
Tell them we made it.

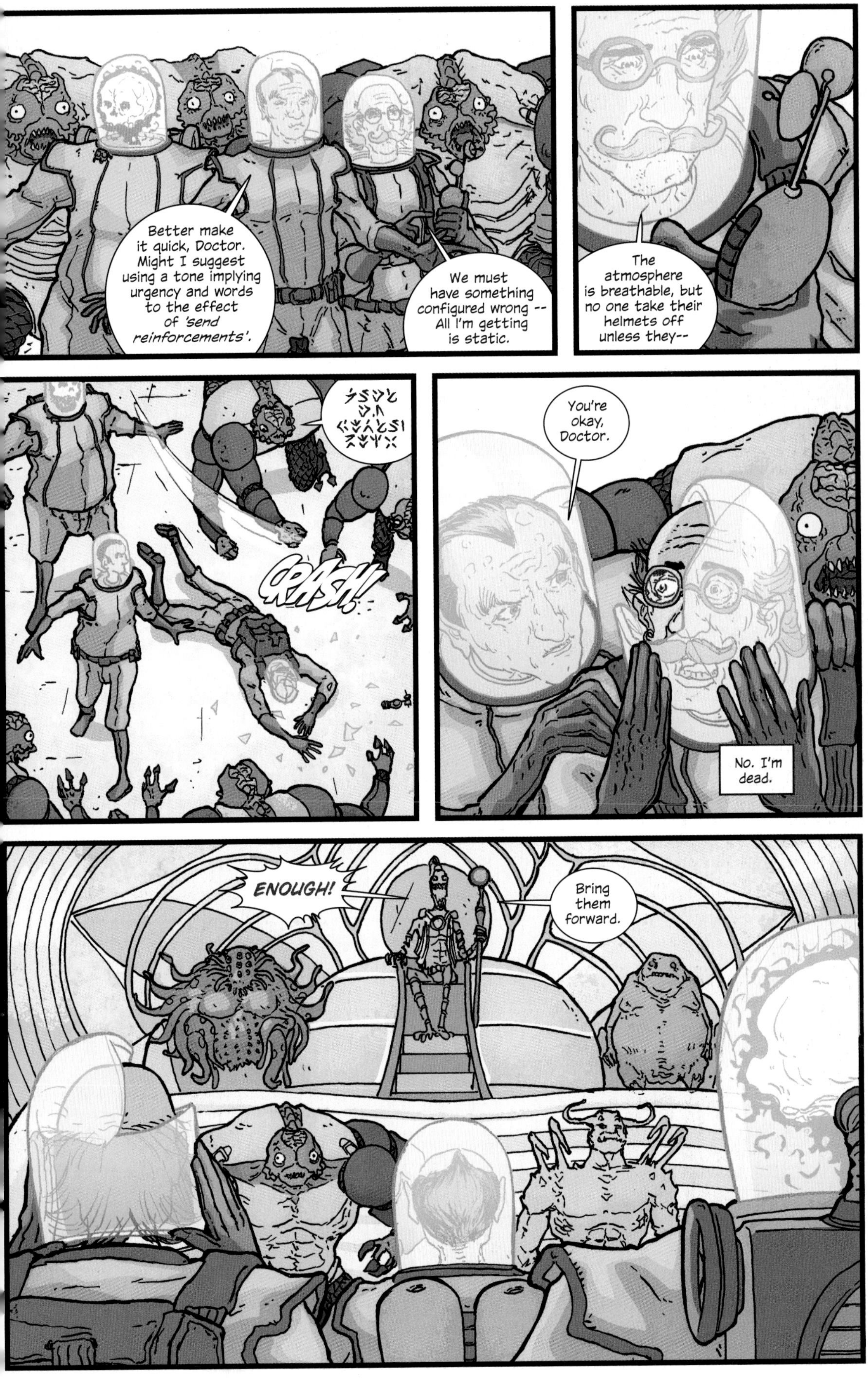
Better make it quick, Doctor. Might I suggest using a tone implying urgency and words to the effect of 'send reinforcements'.
We must have something configured wrong -- All I'm getting is static.
The atmosphere is breathable, but no one take their helmets off unless they--
CRASH!
You're okay, Doctor.
No. I'm dead.
ENOUGH!
Bring them forward.

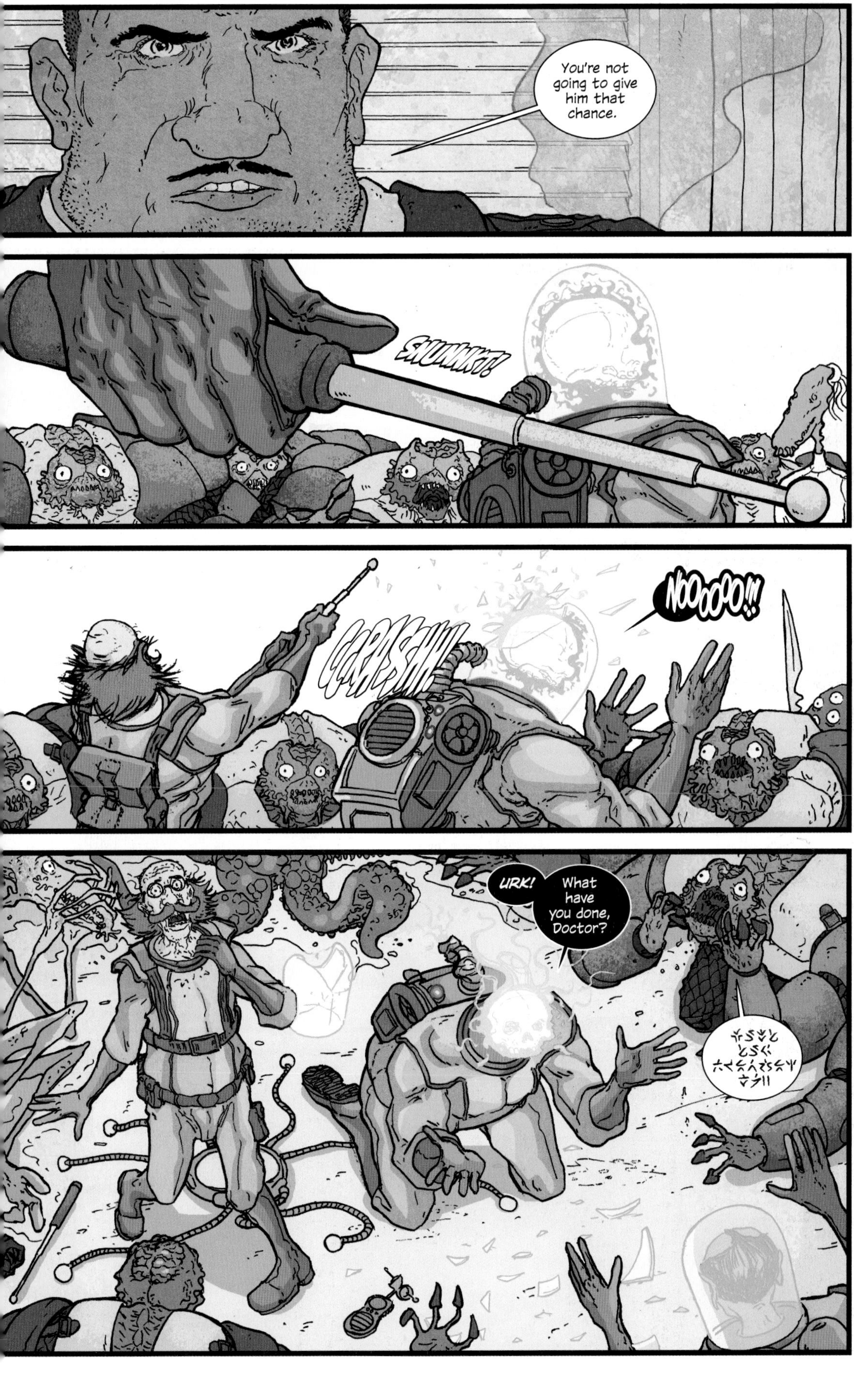
You're not going to give him that chance.
SNUNKKT!
CCRASSHH!
NOOOOO!!!
URK!
What have you done, Doctor?

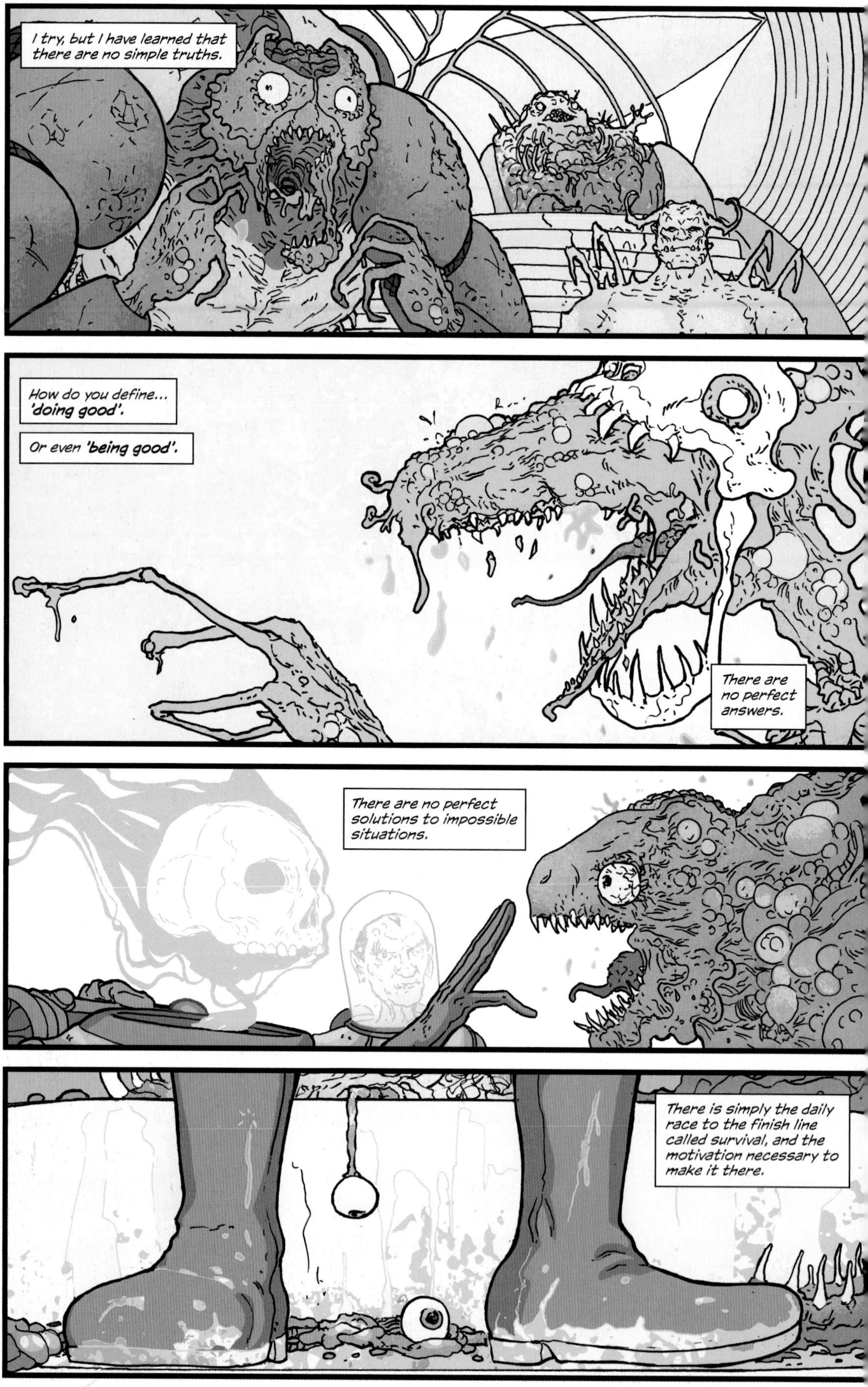
I try, but I have learned that there are no simple truths.
How do you define... **'doing good'.**
Or even **'being good'.**
There are no perfect answers.
There are no perfect solutions to impossible situations.
There is simply the daily race to the finish line called survival, and the motivation necessary to make it there.

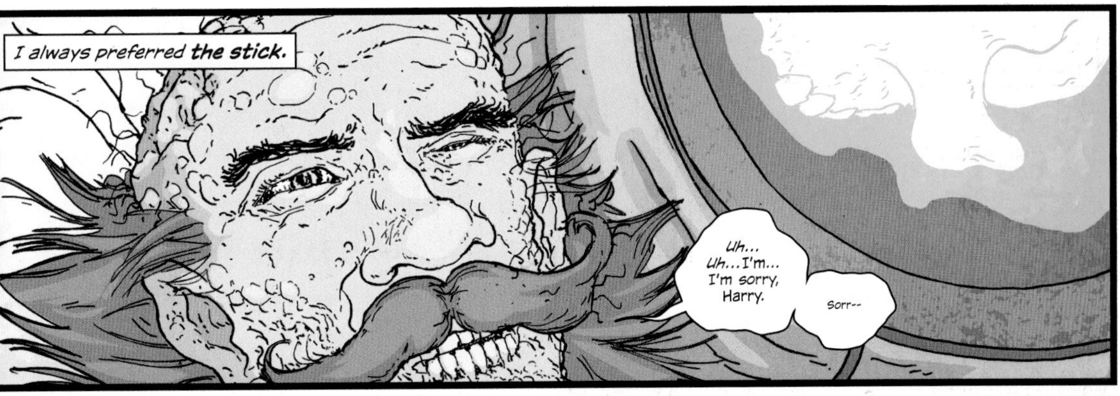
I always preferred **the stick.**
Uh...
Uh...I'm...
I'm sorry,
Harry.
Sorr--

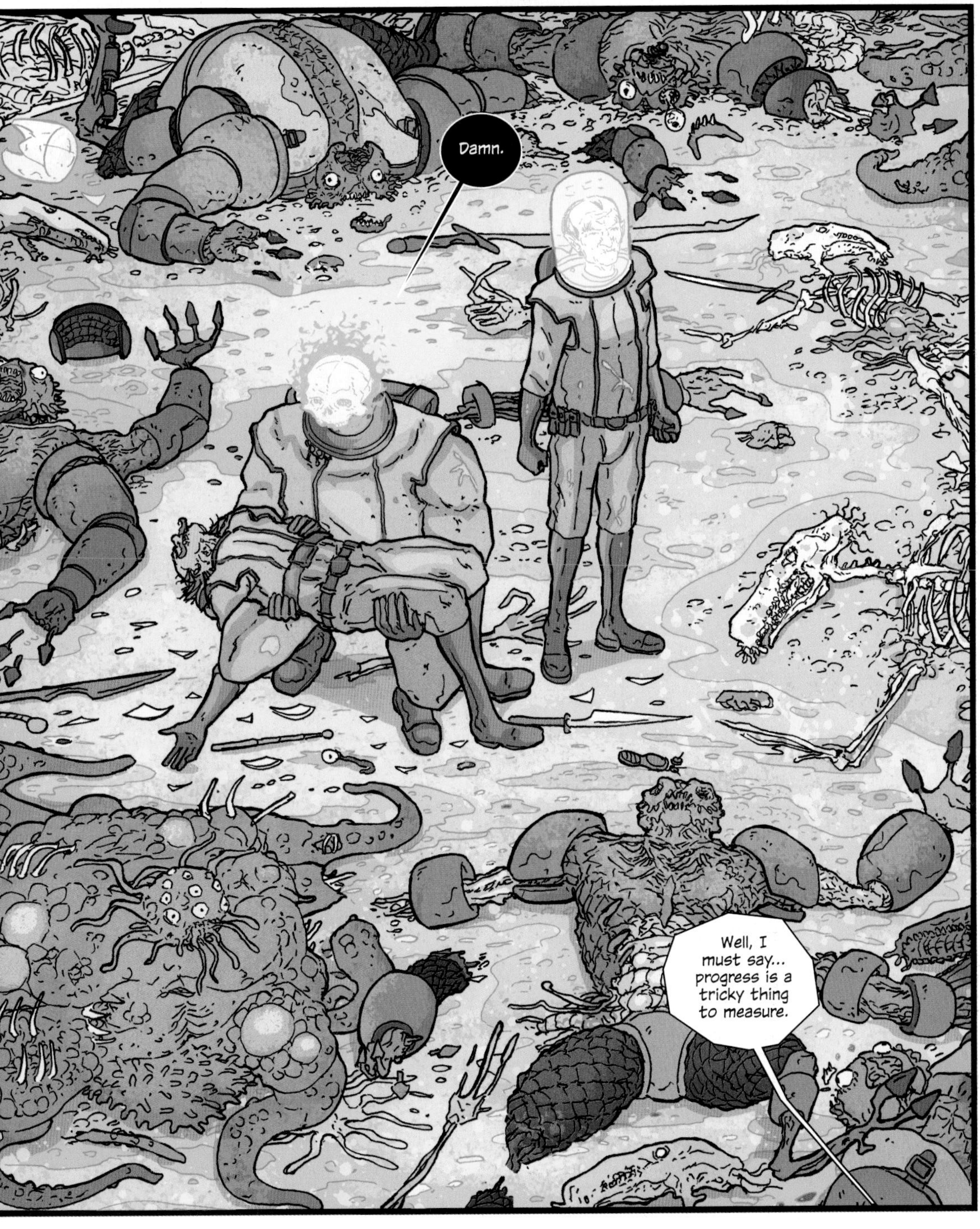
Damn.
Well, I
must say...
progress is a
tricky thing
to measure.

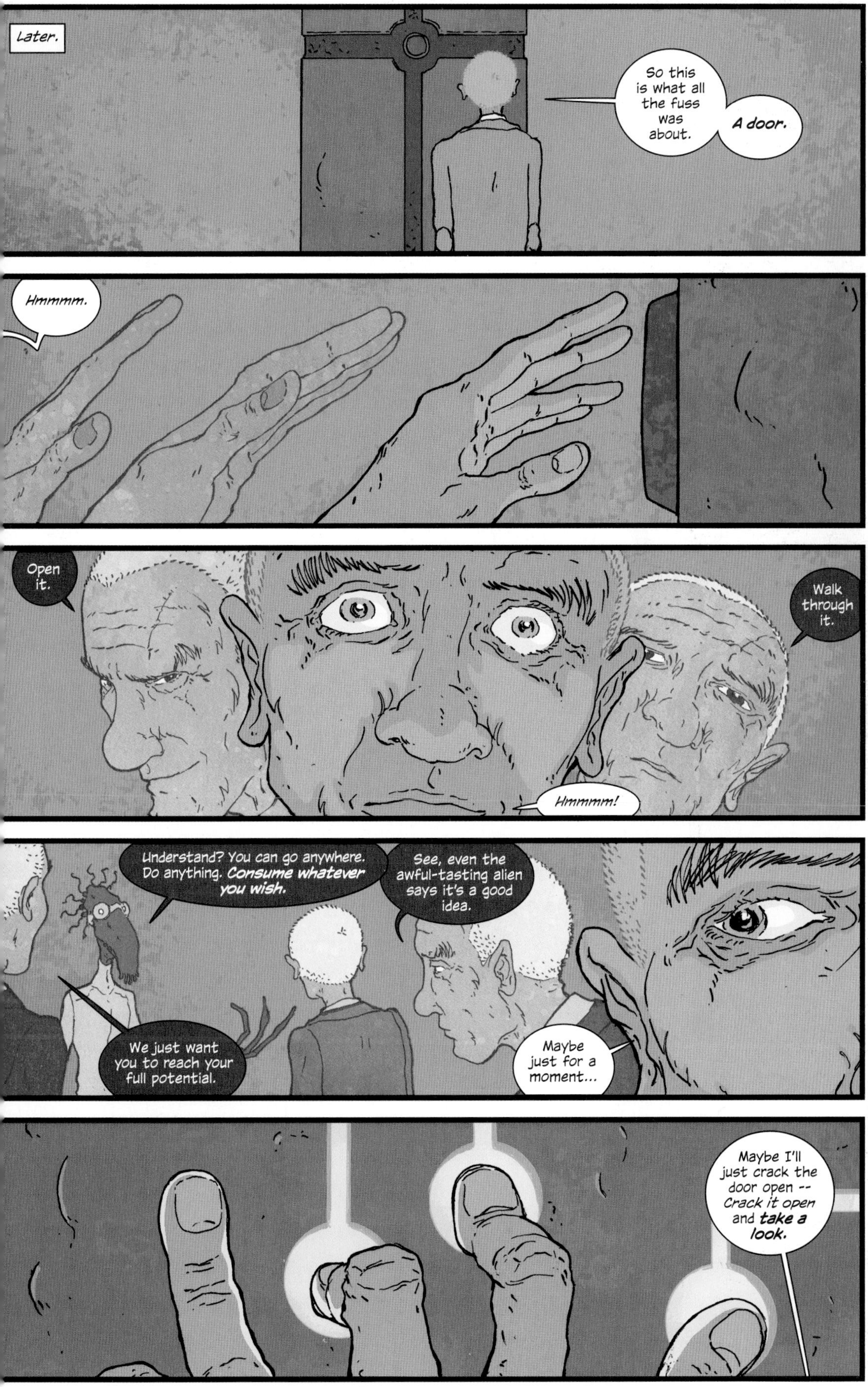
Later.
So this is what all the fuss was about.
A door.
Hmmmm.
Open it.
Walk through it.
Hmmmm!
Understand? You can go anywhere. Do anything. Consume whatever you wish.
See, even the awful-tasting alien says it's a good idea.
We just want you to reach your full potential.
Maybe just for a moment...
Maybe I'll just crack the door open -- Crack it open and take a look.

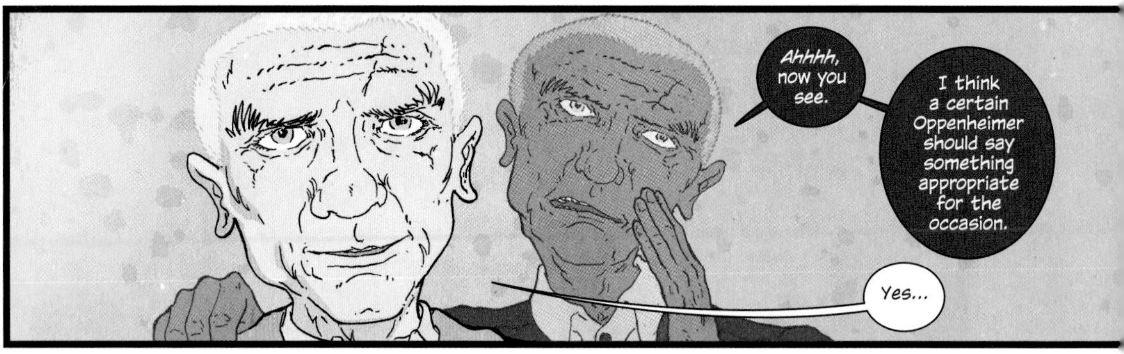
Ahhhh, now you see.
I think a certain Oppenheimer should say something appropriate for the occasion.
Yes...

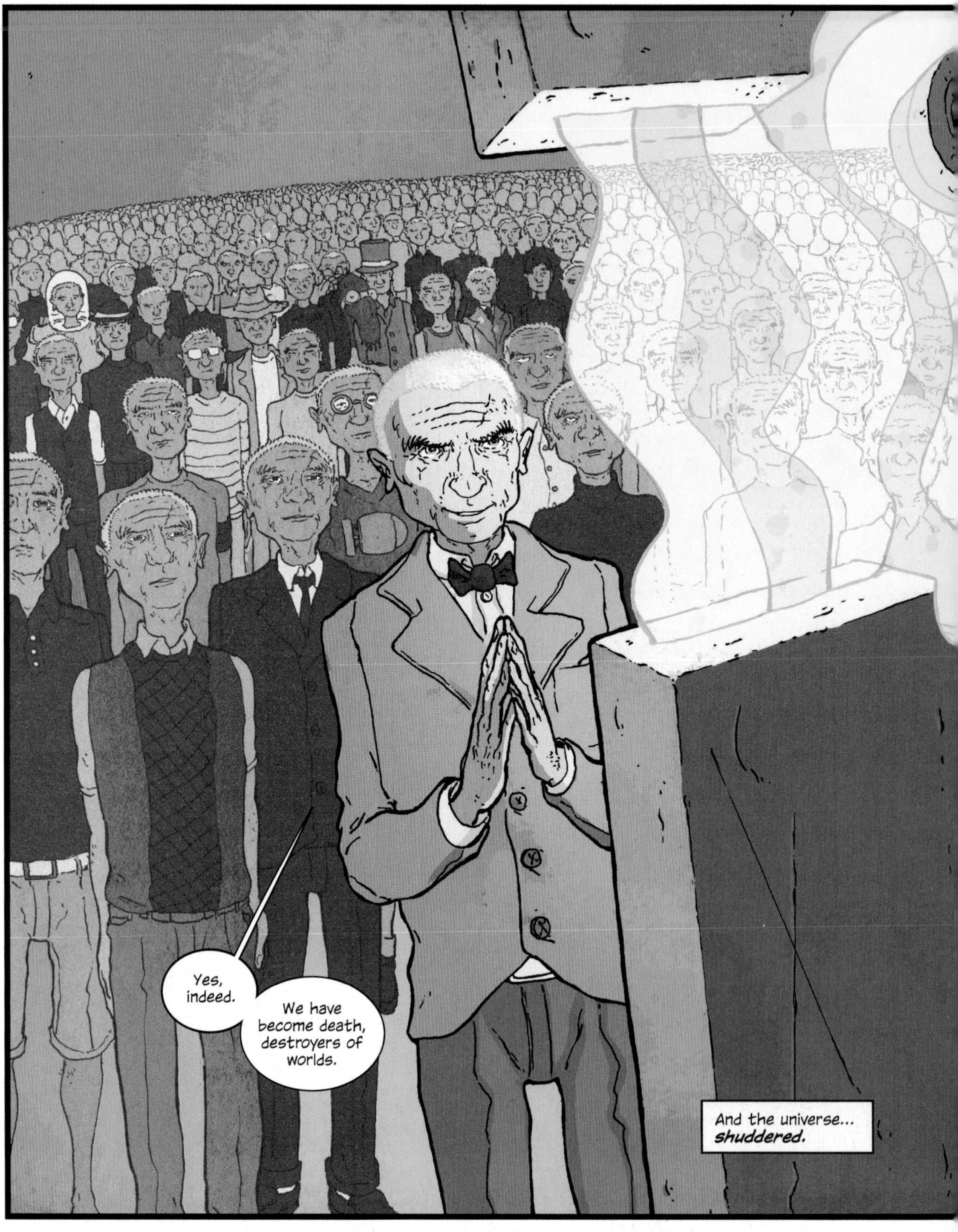
Yes, indeed.
We have become death, destroyers of worlds.
And the universe... *shuddered.*

"HMMMM!"

- OPPENHEIMER

CLAVIS AUREA
THE RECORDED FEYNMAN

VOL. 3

THE CAST

JOSEPH OPPENHEIMER
**Super genius.
American. Physicist.
Multiple personalities.**

ALBRECHT EINSTEIN
**Highly intelligent.
German. Physicist.
Drinks.**

RICHARD FEYNMAN
**Super genius.
American. Physicist.
Wormholer.**

ENRICO FERMI
**Super genius.
Italian. Physicist.
Not human.**

HARRY DAGHLIAN
**Super genius.
American. Physicist.
Irradiated.**

WERNHER VON BRAUN
**Super genius.
German. Rocket scientist.
Robot arm.**

LESLIE GROVES
**Not a genius.
American. General.
Smokes. Bombs.**

FDR: A.I.
**Computational super genius.
American. President.
Dead.**

HARRY S. TRUMAN
**Not a genius.
American. President.
Freemason.**

l

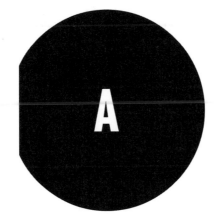

Jonathan Hickman is the visionary talent behind such works as the Eisner-nominated **NIGHTLY NEWS**, **TRANSHUMAN** and **PAX ROMANA**. He also plies his trade at MARVEL working on books like **FANTASTIC FOUR** and **THE AVENGERS**.

His twin brother, Marc, won the Gold in Fencing at the 2012 Olympics.

Jonathan lives in South Carolina surrounded by immediate family and in-laws, which he plans on leaving unless they start showering him with the love and affection he deserves.

This includes his wife.

You can visit his website:*www.pronea.com*, or email him at:*jonathan@pronea.com*.

·

Nick Pitarra is a native Texan and all around nice guy. As a senior in high school he was kicked out of honors English, and subsequently fell in love with comic illustration while doodling with a friend in his new class.

Sometimes it pays not to do your homework.